Driving toward Modernity

Driving toward Modernity

Cars and the Lives of the Middle Class in Contemporary China

Jun Zhang

Cornell University Press

Ithaca and London

First published 2019 by Cornell University Press

Library of Congress Cataloging-in-Publication Data

Names: Zhang, Jun, 1977– author.
Title: Driving toward modernity : cars and the lives of the middle class in contemporary China / Jun Zhang.
Description: Ithaca [New York] : Cornell University Press, 2019. | Includes bibliographical references and index.
Identifiers: LCCN 2018044262 (print) | LCCN 2018048271 (ebook) | ISBN 9781501738418 (pdf) | ISBN 9781501738425 (epub/mobi) | ISBN 9781501738395 (cloth) | ISBN 9781501738401 (pbk.)
Subjects: LCSH: Middle class—China—Guangdong Sheng. | Automobile ownership—China—Guangdong Sheng. | Automobiles—Social aspects—China—Guangdong Sheng. | China—Economic conditions—2000– | Economic development—China—History—21st century.
Classification: LCC HT690.C55 (ebook) | LCC HT690.C55 Z424 2019 (print) | DDC 305.5/509512/7—dc23
LC record available at https://lccn.loc.gov/2018044262

CONTENTS

Figures and Tables

Figures

Tables

ACKNOWLEDGMENTS

I am greatly indebted to the people who have talked to me for this research over the years. They have shared with me the aspirations, desires, frustrations, and perplexities in their lives. They have accommodated my curiosities and ignorance. My special thanks go to my cohorts from high school and college. One managed to get me the opportunity to intern in the dealership. Others introduced to me their friends, schoolmates, and colleagues who became my interlocutors and sometimes friends for this research. They further introduced me to their friends and colleagues. It is in this snowballing process that I realize how powerful alumni networks are among the middle-class social circles.

This book has taken a long time to complete. I am indebted to my advisers and teachers. I would like to thank Helen F. Siu, who has opened the door for me in anthropology and whose continuous "whipping" (*biance*) of me has kept me focusing on the manuscript whenever my diverse interests may have drawn me away. I cannot express enough my gratitude to Bill Kelly and Deborah Davis, not just because of their guidance in my research but also because of their support at critical moments in my academic career. My profound sense of gratitude goes to my late adviser, Cai Yanmin, at Sun Yat-sen University in China. She has been the role model for me to pursue my own interests and career despite social pressure. Even when I stumbled along the academic path and lost confidence in myself, she never lost faith in me. It is my pleasure to thank Linda-Ann Rehbun, Kathryn Dudley, Karen Nakamura, Thomas Hansen, and Erik Harms for their advising. My appreciation also goes to Ann Anagnost, Francesca Bray, Maris Gillette, Erik Mueggler, Tim Oakes, Biao Xiang, Robert Weller, and Li Zhang, who discussed my research with me when they visited my home institutions. My sincere thanks also go to Gordon Mattews, who has been nothing but encouraging when I was finishing this manuscript.

I have been lucky to be surrounded by helpful colleagues and friends. They are great companions in my journey in academia. Minhua Ling knows all the challenges and agony I have had in finishing the manuscript. She has read more drafts of the book than anyone else. Without her intellectual and emotional support, the journey would have been more difficult. I give tremendous thanks to Gary McDonough not only for the intellectual exchanges but also his and Cindy Wong's support in different aspects of my life during my time at Bryn Mawr College and beyond. I thank the colleagues who discussed with me my ideas, read and edited my writing, and provided great feedback at different stages of the manuscript: Allison Alexy, Durba Chattaraj, Isaac Gagne, Nana Gagne, Yi Kang, Gonçalo Santos, Radhika Govindrajan, Annie Harper, Josh Rubin, Oscar Sanchez-Sibony, Alethea Sargent, Ryan Sayre, Myra Jones-Taylor, and Angelica Torres.

During my field research in Guangzhou, I received help from many different people. The Center for Historical Anthropology in the Sun Yat-sen University provided me institutional support in my fieldwork over the course of my summer visits and one thirteen-month stay. I owe special thanks to Professors Zhiwei Liu and Maybo Ching and the center's staff, Ou Donghong, Chen Zhiling, and Pan Dong, for providing me with an engaging academic environment. Professor Wang Ning and his graduate students in the Sociology Department at the Sun Yat-sen University kindly provided me a chance to explain my project and shared with me their ideas on the topic. In particular, I enjoyed the open conversation with Lin Xiaoshan, whose doctoral dissertation topic overlapped with mine. I would also like to thank the staff at the Guangzhou Municipal Library, the Guangdong Provincial

Library, and the Sun Yat-sen University Library for their patience in helping me locate resources.

Different parts of this book have been presented in talks and conferences. My special thanks go to Beth Notar and Joshua Roth, who provided me the opportunity to present my research at the annual meetings of the American Anthropological Association and the Association for Asian Studies when I was a graduate student. Beth's invitation for me to give a talk in her class at Trinity College and her continuous encouragement meant a lot to me when I lacked confidence in my writing process. I appreciated the feedback from the audiences when I shared part of this research at Durba Chattaraj's writing class at the University of Pennsylvania, the Hong Kong Institute for the Humanities and Social Sciences at the University of Hong Kong, the Department of Anthropology at the Chinese University of Hong Kong, and the Hong Kong Anthropological Society.

I am very grateful to Roger Haydon from Cornell University Press, who has guided me through the publication process. The anonymous reviewers' highly constructive comments are very helpful in fine-tuning my arguments and analysis. Gershom Tse has been incredibly patient in fixing my writing in all my publications as I tend to make the same grammar mistakes again and again. The remaining mistakes are my own.

The MacMillan Center and the Council on East Asian Studies at Yale University have generously funded my field research. The Hong Kong Institute for the Humanities and Social Sciences hosted me during my archival research in the University Service Center at the Chinese University of Hong Kong, and its Hang Seng Bank Golden Jubilee Education Fund for Research provided financial support for part of the follow-up research. The Seeding Funding from the University of Hong Kong and the Staff Development Fund from City University of Hong Kong generously supported the writing and editing of the manuscript. Chapter 2 was first published in *Modern China* 43, no. 1: 36–65 and has been adapted for this book.

I always doubt I can express, efficiently and sufficiently, my appreciation for my parents and my brother. Although they do not always understand my work, and sometimes they disagree with my choices in life, they are always there for me. Without their love, patience, and tolerance, none of the accomplishments in my life would have been possible.

ABBREVIATIONS AND NOTE ON TRANSLATION

CCP   Chinese Communist Party
GEMAS   Guangzhou Enterprises Merges and Acquisitions Services
RMB   Renminbi
SAIC   Shanghai Automobile Industry Company
SOE   State-owned enterprise
USD   U.S. dollar
WTO   World Trade Organization

The pinyin system for Romanizing Chinese characters is used throughout the text. Statements made in Cantonese are transcribed in Mandarin pinyin spelling. For scholars who publish in Chinese in China, I spell their names in the Chinese manner, that is, surname first and then given name. For scholars who publish in English, I spell their names in the English manner with surname at the end.

DRIVING TOWARD MODERNITY

INTRODUCTION

A Mobile Lifestyle, A Middle Way of Living

In the summer of 2016 I visited Mingli in Foshan, an affluent city in the Pearl River delta in South China. Mingli and I had gotten to know each other through a mutual friend in the early 2000s; Mingli had just graduated from college and was an entry-level civil servant at the time. In the years that followed, she rose through the ranks to a middle-level position to be in charge of a department in a government bureau. She also upgraded her car from a Xiali, a Chinese brand of cheap, small cars, to a red Mini Cooper. In the mid-2000s, Mingli married her husband, who ran a design studio in the metropolis of Guangzhou. She gave birth to their son in the late 2000s. A few years after, Mingli's family moved from a large gated complex in the suburbs of Guangzhou to another at the center of Foshan so that her son could attend a good public school in the neighborhood. Her husband commuted by car every weekday between Foshan and Guangzhou.

As Mingli drove me back to my hotel, we talked about changes in her work routine since the current president came into office and finding a balance between work and life. We were caught in serious traffic in the middle of an elevated expressway, and as Mingli moaned about the traffic she said, "We can afford a car now. Cars used to be for bragging rights. You used to dream about owning a car, thinking, 'Then I could go anywhere.' Now everybody owns a car. Here we are, in the middle of the road, stuck—life is like this too."

Mingli's words reminded me of a similar comment from an acquaintance: "Above us are the elderly; below us are the young [*shang you lao, xia you xiao*]. We are the true *middle* class [*zhenzheng de zhongchan*]—trapped in the middle [*jia zai zhongjian*]!" This sense of "in-betweenness"/"middleness" (*zhongjian*) surfaced from time to time in my conversations with my interlocutors about their work and life.[1]

Three decades of market-oriented reforms, integration with the global production chain, and state pursuit of socialist modernization have brought many people out of the mire of poverty and given rise to a middle class.[2] In the past, people's social life had been limited by the availability of buses and subways, but now with burgeoning private car ownership, they drive to socialize with friends, to commute to work, and to explore remote areas. What have these people's experiences been like? How did their upward social mobility come about? In what ways does physical mobility interact with social mobility and inform people's perceptions about social mobility?

This book dissects the lives of these self-identified middle-class individuals, like Mingli, in the new material and infrastructural world of China of which the car is the epitome. It explores the entanglement between the rise of the automotive regime and emergence of the middle class and documents how identities, sociality, and material culture are challenged, negotiated, and produced. I show the ways cars and the automotive regime have shaped everyday middle-class sociality, solidarity, and subjectivity and the ways the automotive regime is made meaningful during the making of the middle class.

Car-oriented mobility is one of various forms of mobility that decades of reform have produced. Automobility, or the automotive regime (as I prefer to call it), is both a social and technical assemblage that comprises "humans, machines, roads and other spaces, representations, regulatory institutions and a host of related businesses and infrastructural features" (Edensor 2004, 102; see also Featherstone 2004; Sheller and Urry 2000; Urry 2004).[3] An automotive regime has been familiar to U.S. and European families ever since automobiles became part of everyday life in the postwar era (Flink 1988; Lutz and

Fernandez 2010). Roland Barthes highlights the symbolic importance of the car in contemporary society by comparing it to the great Gothic cathedrals: both are "consumed in image if not in usage by a whole population which appropriates them as a purely magical object" (1972, 88). Attending to the individuals' experience with the car, John Urry argues that automobility is "a sign of adulthood, a marker of citizenship and the basis of sociability and networking" (2007, 116).

In contrast, private car ownership was forbidden in China during the Maoist years, and cars only became widely available in the early twenty-first century. Astonishingly, within a decade China has become the biggest auto market in the world. With the arrival of an automobile-oriented society, both national and local governments have had to spend billions to build an extensive road infrastructure and network (Campanella 2008; Zhang Ju. 2016). Traffic congestion has become synonymous with urban living. As in many other countries,[4] the automotive regime not only facilitates spatial and physical mobility—more for the elite and middle class than the lower classes—but also creates spatial segregation and reproduces an imbalance in the structure of work opportunities. The automotive regime has reconfigured the urban landscape and the rhythm of the people's daily lives.

In talking about the relationship between cars and African Americans, Paul Gilroy remarks that their "distinctive history of propertylessness and material deprivation has inclined them towards a disproportionate investment in particular forms of property [cars] that are publicly visible and the status that corresponds to them" (2001, 84). In what ways, if at all, do many new or aspiring car owners in China resemble those African Americans? A lifestyle that involves cars encapsulates not only the promises and desires but also the constraints and frustrations brought forth by the new material world and the promise of the freedom to consume—something that the older generations have neither experienced nor imagined. A car brings more than bragging rights; it has become the material, visual, and metaphorical vehicle for the social and physical (im)mobility that people across the social spectrum have experienced over the past decades.

The inquiry into the automobile–middle-class entanglement thus provides a good entry point to illustrate the significance of everyday practices and encounters that naturalize the new social order, reproduce class relationships, and shape various governing strategies and images that reconfigure the state. By carefully analyzing how the intertwining of physical and social mobility takes place, this book paints a more nuanced picture comprising the continuity and rupture, as well as the structure and agency, of China's great transformations.

Let me clarify several event-time phrases for convenience of discussion: It is generally accepted that China's economic reforms started in the late 1970s after Chairman Mao Zedong passed away in 1976. I refer to the period before the late 1970s as the "Maoist years" and the period after the late 1970s as the "post-Mao" or "Reform era" (the latter is referred to by some literature as the "postsocialist era"). Reform policies in terms of priorities and focuses changed substantially in the mid- and late 1990s.[5] I refer to the time between the late 1970s and early 1990s as the "early Reform period" and the time from the mid-1990s to the time of writing as the "late Reform period."

In the rest of the introduction, I first explain how I collect data and whom I refer to as middle class. I then outline the rise of the automotive regime and the normalization of car ownership among the middle class and contextualize the emergence of middle-class sensibility in changed class politics; both of these will serve as important background for discussions in the chapters that follow. I then elaborate on how the unraveling of the automotive–middle-class entanglement can contribute to our understanding of China's great transformations.

From Cars to the Middle Class: Research Subjects and Methods

Over the course of more than a decade, changes in the field have reshaped my analytical focus. In 2003 and 2004, as my research was just beginning, car ownership in China was increasing dramatically, giving rise to an automotive regime, and my intention was to track it. After two summers of preliminary investigation, I conducted intensive fieldwork in Guangzhou and other urban areas in the Pearl River delta from July 2006 to August 2007. I lived in a gated complex in a residential area that is middle class by any standard.[6] I worked as an intern in a car dealership for more than four months. With the help of my alumni network, I used snowball sampling to conduct semistructured interviews on different individuals' perceptions of automotive ownership and life patterns related to cars. Some invited me to join their weekend excursions, sport activities, and dinners in restaurants. Our conversations would stray from cars to other aspects of life, but our interactions were always associable with cars. For a decade, I have been to the Pearl River delta almost every summer to follow up on my research and to pay regular visits to key interlocutors.

My field interlocutors ranged from government officials to car mechanics, the majority of whom I consider middle class. Defining "middle class" is notoriously difficult (Abercrombie and Urry 1983). In classical social theories, class has to do with production relationships and structured economic opportunities, and different classes have been imagined to form a gradation. In this spectrum, the middle class is "a series of shifting social layers" (Mangan 2005, 3) between the upper and lower classes, but the boundaries are unclear, presenting some difficulties when studying the middle class. There is an additional difficulty: "morally engaged" scholarship that portrays the middle class as exploiters of the lower classes and status-driven consumers that bear a semblance to foreign or colonial elites (Heiman, Freeman, and Liechty 2012, 5–6) may present further obstacles for studying them in depth. Nevertheless, despite these difficulties, a growing body of anthropological literature has been dedicated to studying the middle class, particularly in the less wealthy parts of the world.[7] Drawing upon insights from Max Weber, Pierre Bourdieu, and E. P. Thompson, ethnographers examine the middle class and their lifestyle to shed light on class politics shaped by globalization and neoliberalism.[8]

I follow a path that is lit by this scholarship: I see the making of the middle class as a multidimensional social project that entails ongoing negotiation and constant adaptation among different actors. The middle class is multidimensional because, like the concept of class, "middle class" can be an analytical concept used by scholars to capture structural inequality and power relations. It can be a census or statistical category that measures consumptive power and informs policymaking. It can also be an identity that is shaped by specific social, historical, and political conditions (Zunz, Schoppa, and Hiwatari 2002). The one thing that the middle-class identity does not have is stability; the process of "being" and "becoming" middle class requires a constant engagement and performance with the social and material world. To understand such a complex subject, an ethnographic approach composed of thick descriptions is an apt tool.

To begin with, most of my middle-class interlocutors were born between the late 1960s and early 1980s. More than half of them had come from other parts of China to settle in the urban parts of the Pearl River delta.[9] Most of them grew up in working-class or lower-rank cadre families, and a few came from the countryside during a time when families generally lived in poverty. They still remembered the food-rationing system and the limited choices of everyday necessities, if there were any choices to be had at all. Bicycles had been the major vehicles for everyday mobility in urban lives. In comparison to their parents' generation, they came of age when life was relatively stable and volatile political movements were scarce. Education did not cost much, and most of them went on to obtain college degrees before becoming civil servants (like Mingli), lawyers, engineers, doctors, university professors, schoolteachers, and small-time entrepreneurs (like Mingli's husband).

The demographics of my interlocutors share similarities with those in existing Chinese middle-class literature. However, unlike the entrepreneurs in Li Zhang's (2010) and John Osburg's (2013) accounts, individuals described here tend to have higher-education backgrounds, and the majority of them are "salaried professionals"—as Luigi Tomba calls them (2004, 2014). But the salaried professionals in Tomba's study work mostly in the public sector, while a higher proportion of my interlocutors work in the private sector.

When I started fieldwork, some had risen through the ranks to senior positions, but the majority of them were in the incipient stage of a career; they were highly mobile and were eager to prove themselves. By the time this book was in press, the majority of them, like Mingli and her husband, have now been married to spouses with similar education and family backgrounds, and with steady sources of income, they have started to raise children. Before real-estate prices skyrocketed over the past five years, almost all of them had already bought apartments, and the majority have by now finished paying off bank loans.

It is difficult to find accurate data on my interlocutors' household income or wealth, but based on our casual conversations between 2014 and 2016, I estimate that their annual income per capita ranges from RMB 120,000 to more than RMB 1 million (roughly $17,970 and $150,000), with more than half of them earning between RMB 200,000 and RMB 400,000. Their self-reported saving rate—including savings and investments—ranges from 30 to 50 percent, depending on house loans and costs for education. To put the numbers in perspective, the average annual disposable income per capita among urban residents in 2013 was RMB 45,792 ($6,858) in Guangzhou and RMB 26,955 ($4,021) nationwide.[10] Meanwhile, in a 2013 report, the consulting firm McKinsey defines middle-class households as those whose annual household (not per capita) disposable income falls between RMB 60,000 and RMB 229,000 ($9,000 to $34,000) (Barton, Chen, and Jin 2013). My interlocutors strongly disputed the lower boundary of the index in the McKinsey report, stating that the number was too low for the living standard in the Pearl River delta, one of the wealthiest regions in the country. According to them in 2014, a middle-class person should have an annual income of at least RMB 120,000 (RMB 240,000 for a double-income household) to afford all regular life expenses: management fees for living in a gated complex, a car, children's education, senior care, family vacations, social activities, and savings for the future and for emergencies. The number should go up if the person has not paid off his or her mortgage. As I will show in chapter 2, people typically will not buy a car before they have at least paid the down payment for an apartment.[11] Therefore, car ownership generally indicates that a family has solid economic standing.

The Rise of an Automotive Regime and Normalization of Car Ownership

Cars were introduced to China in the early twentieth century, and the processes by which cars enter the lives of ordinary people are very different than in Western Europe, the United States, the former Soviet Union, and some eastern European countries (Berdahl 2000; Flink 1988; Siegelbaum 2008, 2011). More details are provided in the prologue. Here I outline a brief summary to contextualize later discussions.

In China during the Maoist years, cars were only accessible to high-ranked officials in the state and party bureaucratic systems (Barmé 2002). The few passenger cars seen on the streets were vehicles of state power and bureaucratic privilege. In the early Reform era, the car industry was a space for the Chinese government to experiment the capitalist way of production. The total number of passenger cars produced domestically was low at that time. Throughout the 1990s, private car ownership remained under state control in most parts of the country; the majority of owners continued to be state authorities, government-affiliated organizations, and state-owned enterprises (SOEs). In southern China, where the economy moved a step ahead of the

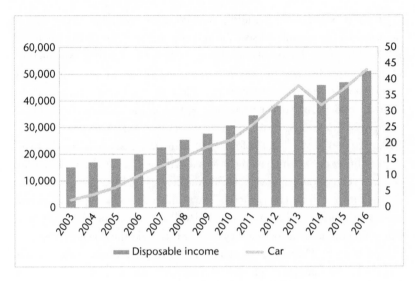

Figure 1. Number of passenger cars per hundred urban households against per capital annual disposable income (RMB) in Guangzhou, 2003–2016.

rest of the country (Vogel 1989), an informal economy of cars through smuggling emerged, at once sparking and sustaining demands for individual mobility and desires to demonstrate one's wealth.

   With China's entry into the World Trade Organization (WTO) in 2001, growth in both the production and the ownership of private cars started to gather tremendous momentum. For a case in point, between 2006 and 2007, when I did fieldwork in Guangzhou, police officers, traffic experts, taxi drivers, and car salesmen would proudly make known that more than five hundred new cars were registered daily with the municipal traffic department of the police. Between 2003 and 2016, the number of passenger cars owned per hundred urban households increased more than tenfold (figure 1). In less than two decades China has turned from a kingdom of bicycles into the biggest auto market in the world (Gerth 2010; Notar 2015). Multiple actors gravitate toward the rising regime of cars, from international carmakers and banks to the national and local governments and from migrant workers to the rising middle class.

   For the Chinese government and many Chinese, an automotive regime symbolizes modernity. By modernity I refer to the multiple projects, perceptions, and sentiments that different social actors not only associate with but also imagine as "being modern."[12] The rise of the auto industry and market both structures and embodies the national development agenda, technological advancement, and a capitalist labor market. Moreover, the automotive regime captures the imaginations of different actors as they feel the anxiety of falling behind and thus the need to quickly move ahead to catch up.

When I started my field research in the early 2000s, many of my field acquaintances were aspiring car owners. Some were college students who had obtained a driver's license just to add a skill to their resume. Meanwhile, I could recount almost all popular car models on the market and give a rough idea of their prices; after all, there were only a few of them. Since the 2010s, many of my acquaintances have entered the stage of life where they become car owners. They are the first generation of car owners in their family, and their first purchases have mostly been midlevel, midsize sedans. I have also seen a few of them upgrade from a low-end, compact car, such as a Chery QQ, to a midrange, midsize one, such as the Camry, or even to a high-end Audi. Some have even bought a second car. Many acquaintances from my interlocutors' social circles are car owners as well. Over the years, I have witnessed a rise in peer pressure to own a car. Now only very few people do not own cars, not because they cannot afford one but because they opt out of it.[13] As an observer of their lives, I can no longer remember most of the builds and models, as there are too many today.

Car ownership has become increasingly normalized among the middle class in the past few years. Granted, a car with a military license or a luxury car with a lot of horsepower, such as a Maserati or Rolls-Royce, are for those that have government power or are ultrarich. Luxury cars continue to be a symbol of power in a time of growing social inequality. This trend of normalization among the middle class takes place against the backdrop of the still low ratio of car ownership among the total population. According to the World Bank, in 2010 there were 517, 453, and 423 passenger cars per thousand people in Germany, Japan, and the United States but only 44 in China.[14] Timothy Cheek's observation of the relationship between cars and wealth in the early 2000s, which he calls "a battlefield of hierarchy" (2006, 90) in the streets, remains true to some extent.

But to Mingli and her counterparts, a car of an "ordinary brand" (*yiban pinpai*) nowadays is more about convenience and necessity and less about status (chapter 1). The perception about the changing status of cars is best captured in a conversation between me and Cecilia, a lawyer and mother who drove regularly in 2014. Cecilia made an analogy between cars and air conditioning. When air conditioning first appeared on the market ten years ago, it was a luxury item. But now in a city like Guangzhou, it is unimaginable to live without an air-conditioning unit in the summer. It was similar for cars. Cecilia said, "In the beginning, we all dreamed about owning cars. We thought, 'As soon as I have money, I'll buy a car.' Now it has become just 'an alternative to walking [*daibu gongju*].'" How the car is gradually perceived as an ordinary item that brings convenience to daily life is closely related to the larger transformations that have reshaped middle-class life-work relationship (chapter 1).

The normalization of private car ownership suggests that, while a car remains the sign and confirmation of one's accomplishment and upward mobility, the desire for car ownership should not be explained as simply "instrumental status intentions" (O'Dougherty 2002, 9). As cars transform from being a privilege item available only to officials to everyday items for the middle class, what has in fact changed is not just that their production costs have lowered but that, as Arjun Appadurai (1986) suggests, their significance has evolved with the social, cultural, and political networks they are embedded in.

Therefore, my attention also shifts from looking at cars to the overall automotive regime and one primary group of users, the middle class. In the rest of the book, I first provide the context in which normalization of car ownership took place by examining the formation and transformation of car production and the auto market (prologue). I then examine the role of cars in shaping and being shaped by middle-class social lives and family relationships (chapters 1 and 2). I zoom in on people in the car dealership where I conducted fieldwork, showing, through their stories, the transformations of car distribution channels and the workings of dealerships (chapters 3 and 4). Finally, I look into the issues of licensing and parking (chapters 5 and 6). By examining the different relationships enabled, embodied, or inhibited by the automotive regime (Featherstone, Thrift, and Urry 2005; Miller 2001; Seiler 2008; Siegelbaum 2008, 2011), I show how the rising automotive regime is shaped by and in turn reconfigures different forms of social interaction, hierarchy, authority, and political engagement. The way that the shaping and enactment of the automotive regime unfold thus provides a rich repertoire to delineate the making of the middle class, the primary group of car owners.

Changing Class Sensitivities, Emerging Middle-Class Subjectivities

The making of the middle class must be examined in the context of complex class politics in China throughout the twentieth century. Marxism, together with news of the revolution in Russia, came to China in the early twentieth century. To many intellectuals, Marxism seemed to have provided a script for staging a class-based revolution to save the war-ridden country. The language of class was gradually introduced to the larger population through intellectual debates, workers' protests in the cities, and wartime land reforms (Anagnost 1997, 2008; Li F. 2012). The Chinese Communist Party (CCP) employed class struggle as a strategy of political mobilization to solicit support from the masses even in the first two decades after it came to power in 1949. Official class labels were not tied to occupations but "were instead grounded in CCP interpretations of pre-1949 history and contemporary politics" (D. Davis 2000b, 254).

The act of classifying or naming creates possibilities of personhood. Yet for "a name to begin to do its creative work, it needs authority. One needs usage within institutions" (Hacking 2002, 8). In this class system, class labeling correlated with political punishment, as well as spatial and social entitlements. Vehement, volatile political movements spectacularly marked the significance of class identities. A class label could be a life determinant.[15] For Mao and his comrades, who built their power base originally in the poor regions of rural China, the bourgeoisie—intellectuals, professionals, and lower-level bureaucrats inherited from the old regime—were politically unreliable (Bian et al. 2005). They had to go through disciplining exercises, such as self-reflection, criticism from the masses, and reeducation in the countryside, and by doing so became part of the proletarian class. Any lifestyle that was considered bourgeoisie in taste, including life with a car, was publicly denounced.

Apart from its connection with political movements, the class system was coded with institutional entitlements and exclusion under the centrally planned economy from the 1950s until at least the early 1990s. This class system was correlated with the rural-urban divide that was institutionalized through the household registration system from the 1950s.[16] Under the household registration, peasants were rural residents who lived in the countryside, and workers were urban residents who lived in the cities. These identities were difficult to switch or obtain. Under the centrally planned economy, peasants were affiliated with the rural economy with a collective land ownership system and agriculture. Workers and cadres belonged to the urban economy that was mostly built around industries and work units (*danwei*).[17] This dual system, under a state redistributive economy, provided security and foreseeability—more for the urban than rural residents—at the expense of social and physical mobility (Walder 1986; Whyte and Parish 1984). Despite their low income, the urban workers had economic stability and social prestige that led the sociologist Li Qiang (2004) to call them the "quasi middle class" during the Maoist and early Reform years.

With the government's agenda starting to shift from political struggle to economic development in the late 1970s, this class system began to disintegrate. Rural economy experienced decollectivization in the 1980s. Tens of millions of rural residents left the villages to work in factories set up with foreign investment and operated under the capitalist mode of production (Pun 2005; Solinger 1999; Whyte 2010). The urban economy, formed under the centrally planned economy, faced serious challenges in the mid-1990s with waves of SOEs going bankrupt due to economic liberalization (Cheek 2006; Lu D. 2006). Workers who had once been promised lifetime employment were laid off or forced into early retirement (Cho 2013; Lee C. K. 2007). Most of them had tremendous difficulty finding jobs in the new economy because of their age and lack of proper education. The identity of being a worker became stigmatized (Hsu 2007).

A new occupational structure emerged, and work with prestige changed. Managerial staff, professionals, and entrepreneurs burgeoned with the expansion of higher education, industrialization, and professionalization of the tertiary sector. In the early 1990s, many government officials and intellectuals left stable jobs and "took a plunge into the sea" (*xiahai*) to do business. Meanwhile, the state apparatus went through bureaucratic reforms, with efforts to build governing stability and to reduce reliance on political mobilization. As a result, the state's bureaucratic system also grew substantially (Shambaugh 2000). Since the start of the 2000s, with fierce competition in the job market, as well as stability and welfare packages with state-affiliated workplaces, employment in government branches, courts, state-owned schools, and a few big SOEs, such as China Petroleum, have been highly coveted.

"Middle class" as a new term gradually came into being. Its first systematic appearance occurred in state-sponsored academic research and discussions, the most notable being the 2002 survey done by the Chinese Academy of Social Science and subsequent studies on social stratification.[18] These studies had clear objectives to provide empirical data for policymaking. Scholars, mostly sociologists, charted social stratification with quantitative data, using income and occupation as variables. Their conceptualization of social stratification, as Hai Ren argues, "underscores the construction of the middle class as a category of understanding for rendering social reality into a calculable form. . . . It also establishes a statistical form of knowledge that makes the middle class conceivable for the purpose of government" (2013, 37).

These scholars suggested that the Marxist class model was insufficient to encapsulate the society that was rapidly transforming and becoming diversified. They used "stratum" (*jieceng*) to replace "class" (*jieji*) because, as Ann Anagnost puts it, "unlike 'class' (*jieji*), the new language of 'social strata' (*shehui jieceng*) references social inequality in a way that does not assume social antagonism" (2008, 501). Scholars started to use such terms as *zhongchan jieceng* (midpropertied strata), *zhongchan jieji* (midpropertied class), and *zhongjian jieceng* (middle strata). These terms replaced *xiao zichan jieji* (petite bourgeois), the term used in the past. The change in terminology and the departure from a Marxist approach were intentional efforts to distinguish academic analysis and the present from the highly ideological use of class labels for political struggle and the Maoist years (Li P. 2004, 3).

Following these scholarly works, officials started to adopt these terms and the narrative that the middle classes would benefit society in the mid-2000s (Li C. 2010, 11). The central government then announced its vision to "enlarge the size of the middle-income group" in the country (Li C. 2010, 8). The middle class as a category finally had its political legitimacy in the first decade of the twenty-first century, the same time that the mass automotive market took shape.

In the second decade of the new millennium, middle class has become an increasingly self-aware identity. According to my observation, the self-identification as *zhongchan* (midpropertied), without the wording "class" (*jieji*) or "stratum" (*jieceng*), became noticeable after the global financial crisis of 2008. It is partly informed by a discourse on the Chinese middle class increasingly disseminated by international corporations and the media as they looked for new consumptive power in the Global South. The consciousness also stems from the middles class's increasing awareness of their life stages, material possessions, and distinctive life practices.

The emerging, distinctive middle-class lifestyle and identity are often examined within the analytical framework of studies on consumption (see, for example, Tsang 2014, Yu 2014). Li Zhang has pioneered the ethnographic study on the middle class through studying home ownership in gated complexes in the city of Kunming,[19] where homeowners are often "perceived as economically well-to-do but lacking symbolic capital" (2010, 9). To them, Zhang argues, consumption "becomes the main conduit to gain cultural and symbolic capital, and the key for claiming and authenticating social status" (9), and the middle class's self-worth, love, and conjugal relationships "are being revalorized with the increased importance of private property" (164). Meanwhile, predatory real-estate companies, complicit with the government, developed gated complexes that are tailored for the urban middle class, who desire a tranquil, safe life and status symbols. These gated complexes, as Zhang demonstrates, allow the middle class to "materialize itself through spatial exclusion, cultural differentiation, and lifestyle practices" (3).

Zhang skillfully threads together capitalist accumulation and postsocialist governance with how middle-class individuals articulate the notion of self. She convincingly shows how spatial segregation contributes to the consolidation of class boundaries. However, her success in highlighting the embeddedness of the real-estate industry in the new urban economy with the developmental state may have been achieved at the expense of an analysis of homemaking. The chain of events described in the ethnography gives the impression that the commodity value of an apartment—not family or other social relationship formed through homemaking—is at the core of an individual's middle-class identity. It is not clear how luxury housing, commonly seen as a sign of economic capital, could provide cultural capital to those middle-class residents.

While consumption is important in shaping their lifestyle, being middle-class, on most occasions, is not about brands, prices, or ownership, per se. For my interlocutors, middle class captures something they felt strongly about their lives: the sense of in-betweenness/middleness. I noticed that my interlocutors increasingly used the term "middle class" (*zhongchan*) to talk about themselves and certain lifestyles in the 2010s. They are middle-aged. They form the middle layer of the multigenerational family. They have reached the midpoint of their careers. In terms of their finances, they are comfortable, but they are careful with spending. They distinguish themselves from the new rich (chapter 5), and they do not consider themselves elites, unlike those in Osburg's account (2013), as they see themselves as merely "ordinary people" (*putongren*, or *yibanren*) who make a living through hard work and do not make much of an impact on society. If middleness means between the rich and the poor in India (Dickey 2012; Donner 2011) and "between the high and the low" in Nepal (Liechty 2003), the sociopolitical middleness in China is between the elite who have both political power and connections and the urban underclasses and peasants who are powerless and poor.

The middleness is at times positive, as it suggests upward social mobility, but it may also allude to immobility, as is evident from the choice of word "trapped" or "stuck" by Mingli and others. Their individual physical and work mobility is often subsumed to family needs. Given their family background and lack of connection to the politically powerful, they doubt whether they can continue to move up the social ladder. Many of my interlocutors are critical of the government and its officials on such issues as limiting freedom of speech, and many are afraid that rampant corruption and rising inequality may lead to chaos and destroy their lives. Yet they are reluctant to engage politically. Instead, some seek to migrate, leaving behind those "trapped" in the reality of China.

On some occasions, my acquaintances insisted that the label "middle class" did not mean much to them when they juxtaposed the new middle-class identity with old class identities. The old system was institutionalized with official documentation, privileges, and exclusion, and class identities were clearly defined and rigid. None of these applied to the middle class. One did not know, as they often told me, whether one was really middle class or not and why, one way or the other, the identity mattered.

This middleness without institutional recognition or clear vision for the future gives rise to high degrees of anxiety and vulnerability. Anxiety has been commonly found in middle-class individuals and families in other parts of the world. For those in countries like the United States, the anxiety often manifests itself in the fear of downward mobility (Ehrenreich 1989; Heiman 2015; Ortner 2003). In China, middle-class anxiety shares some commonalities with that in other rising economies, such as India: anxiety is experienced through upward social mobility, the uncertainty of a middle-class identity that is new to the society, and the precariousness of the rapidly changing environment (more in chapter 4).

Such complex feelings of ambiguity and anxiety are both shaped by and are shaping everyday encounters and interactions with the material and social world. Most of their daily practices and engagement with the material world are not geared toward a conscious pursuit of the middle-class identity. Rather, they are often a matter of pragmatic concern, which is not only influenced by but also contributes to their sociality (chapter 1), family making (chapter 2), their sense of self and their making distinction from other social groups (chapters 3, 4, and 5), and their sense of entitlement and disempowerment (chapter 6). These are lived experiences and processes that can be found in the ways the middle class interacts with the automotive regime.

Thus, I build my research upon Zhang's insight on housing and the political economy that structures the making of the middle class but focus less on the political economy of cars and more on demonstrating the ways in which middle-class individuals' life trajectories, social interactions, and solidarity are manifested in and are configured by the automotive regime. By showing how the middle class "feel[s] the car," "feel[s] through the car and with the car" (Sheller 2004, 228), I demonstrate that the making of the middle class, as a social project, invokes various kinds of emotional, rational, and ethical considerations that are beyond the notion of achieving a certain social status.

Automobility, Middle Class, and Politics of Transformation

In organizing materials to present the entangled rise of both the middle class and the automotive regime, I use the different aspects of the automotive regime as the organizing frame to depict different aspects of middle-class lives. The automotive regime is sometimes at the center of the account (prologue) and sometimes retreats to the background as I recount the life trajectories of the middle class and class encounters in a car dealership (chapters 3 and 4). Granted, the middle class is not the most important actor in the automotive regime. I have chosen not to get into some important issues, such as the environmental and gender aspects in this automotive–middle-class framework.[20] The analytical advantage of exploring the automotive–middle-class entanglement lies not in comprehensiveness but in illustrating the intricate correlations among individuals, things, institutions, and ideas, which shed lights on the complicated dynamics between the past and the present and between material culture, individual endeavors, and political legitimacy in changed contexts. Such analysis thus provides a nuanced depiction that challenges the one-sided, if not stereotypical, narratives about the automotive regime or the Chinese middle class. In doing so, it provides a critical lens to understand the complexity of China's transformation.

First, the rise of the automotive regime is often hailed as a poster child of the market force and globalization. Yet while it is about China's integration to the globalization of car manufacturing and consumption, it is also a process of reestablishing political legitimacy and strengthening government control. The auto industry has always been a part of the state's development agenda (prologue). During the Maoist and early Reform eras, state control over car production and distribution was exercised through national industrial plans, pricing, and official distribution channels. With the introduction of market mechanisms and foreign capital to auto production in the mid-1980s, local governments had more liberty in advancing local development, including manipulating the informal economy of car smuggling. Yet the legitimization of private car ownership remained to be established through government-backed public debates, as the "consumer revolution," as Deborah Davis (2000a) puts it, was already underway. While China's entry into the WTO may be seen as the triumph of global capitalism and neoliberalism, it also legitimized the central government's means of strengthening its power at the expense of local governments and was a sign of the consolidation of political legitimacy that had shifted from class struggle to development, progress, and consumption (for the latter, see Wang J. 2001; Wang N. 2007).

Furthermore, the grand narrative of the reform, conventionally understood as deregulation and letting the market be the mechanism for distribution, becomes destabilized from the experience and perspective of people who have lived through the process, such as the owner, managers, and mechanics in the car dealership where I interned (prologue and chapters 3 and 4). For many of these people, the time between the late 1990s and early 2000s was the "wild" and "free" period when the local government's experimental attitude gave rise to the niche space for their entrepreneurship (chapter 3). But this "free" period was also marked by a transitional system in which the government still had a lot of "allocative power" (Verdery 1991) to control substantively the circulation of cars through national economic planning and restrictive foreign trade. Yet in the supposedly "freer" era in the late 2000s and 2010s, for the dealership owner and its managers, the space for their entrepreneurial pursuits has been shrinking, and they have been increasingly subjected to the power of, and fighting a difficult battle against, big carmakers and corporations through which the state has sought to control market order.

From a bottom-up perspective, the central government did not have any coherent economic strategies. Instead, it has constantly readjusted its control and reasserted its authority whenever it was confronted with the presence of capital, foreign or domestic, seeking profit amid the rising demand for cars. Just as in Germany between the two world wars (Koshar 2004) and in Soviet Russia (Siegelbaum 2008), the state-backed rise of the auto market is part and a major force of the process of regime making in post-Mao China.

Second, the rise of the Chinese middle class is often seen as the result of the reforms in which a series of neoliberal policies have led to the new occupational structure and privatization of properties. The new occupational structure, which I have outlined earlier, indeed provides structural opportunities for those with social and cultural capital. Privatization of properties amplifies and reinforces this pattern in the labor market. The government's agenda concerning social stratification and stability legitimizes the label "middle class," a term deemed politically suspicious in Maoist times.

As I show with the life trajectories of the owner and managers in a car dealership (chapter 3), however, the socialist welfare system and work system also played a critical role for those who came of age between the late 1960s and early 1990s to achieve upward social mobility. The socialist welfare system and work system, which continued to function in the early Reform period, had provided relative equality at the beginning and kept educational costs low during their school years. These systems also shaped work connections, skills, and other resources for them to accumulate social, economic, and cultural capital to take advantage of the structural opening for mobility.

In the same dealership, the life trajectories of the owner and managers stand in contrast to those of the young salespeople and mechanics, who were born in the late 1980s and early 1990s (chapter 4). With the enlarging social gap, the elimination of social welfare, and the double-edge effects of higher education expansion, younger generations encounter many more difficulties in achieving the same kind of mobility as their predecessors in the new millennium. As the middle class are anxious about mobility for themselves and their children, their everyday practices in the workplace and their investment in their children have contributed to the hardening boundaries of the social hierarchy and their awareness of class differences.

Third, the red-hot car market, fueled by the middle class's purchasing power, may be another piece of evidence for a stereotype that has been circulating in global media (for example, Elegant 2007)—that the Chinese middle class has insatiable consumptive desires and is eager to chase a Western lifestyle but reluctant to become politically engaged. Existing literature tends to emphasize self-development and self-governing as the core values of middle-class individuals, values that echo the government's strategies to govern from afar (for example, Ren 2013; Zhang and Ong 2008). This focus on the self, to some degree, resonates with another observation about the political apathy among the middle class (Chen J. 2013; Tsang 2014). This overt apathy to liberal politics has a lot to do with the fact that the state has the capacity and determination to control speech and social organizations, significantly inhibiting the middle class's emergence as a critical voice for policies and other social issues. In addition, a great number of middle-class individuals are unwilling to engage in active political participation because their own work interest is closely tied to the government and the public sector (Chen J. 2013). If there is any awareness at all among the middle class as a collective, this awareness is not built upon the middle class's perceived independence in relationship to the state.

The Chinese middle class is not the only example to use in contesting the conventional idea that the middle classes are the backbone of civil society and modern democracy. Brian Owensby's (1999) study of the Brazilian middle class in the mid-twentieth century offers another good example. Owensby argues that "structure cannot be denied, but there are other reasons not to think of the middle class in terms of whether it was democratic or corporatist, liberal or conservative, populist or anti populist—or even whether it was political in any straightforward way" (242). Yet as the Brazilian middle class was an important force that supported the military government, it would be misleading to dismiss the middle class as an unimportant political actor in China. Literature in political anthropology suggests that political engagement can take various forms and is not always intentional. The authority and legitimacy of the state are reproduced as ordinary citizens dealt with government officials on ordinary matters (for example, Berdahl 1999; Gupta 2012) or made cynical jokes and comments about the state (for example, Navaro-Yashin 2002; Siu 1989).

In line with this scholarship, my ethnographic exploration of the entangled rises of the middle class and the automotive regime shows various indirect ways the middle class becomes politically engaged. Chapter 1 presents a form of nonstraightforward engagement, looking at how middle-class professionals have sought to establish accountability and to hang out with friends in ways that involve driving their cars. Political engagement also occurred in the dynamics between the car and multigenerational family practices (chapter 2). It occurred as managers drew and justified boundaries between them and the salespeople and mechanics in the dealership (chapter 4). It was in the conversations in which the middle class commented on auctions of license plates (chapter 5) and in the negotiations where middle-class homeowners sought to defend their rights to parking spaces at the buildings where they lived (chapter 6).

In these rather apolitical, mundane encounters and expressions, the middle class reappropriated official discourses on consumption, *suzhi* (quality), *hexie shehui* (harmonious society) and traditional family values, and status symbols of officials (a black car with a big trunk) and the state's parade culture to negotiate various kinds of social relationships in their lives that are facilitated and constrained by the car and by driving. They drove their parents and children around as filial children and responsible parents. Their commitment to family values resonates with but does not directly respond to the state's agenda that seeks to reassert traditional values not only to deal with an aging population but also to establish its soft power on the global stage. They staged car parades during weddings and group outings without thinking that it was a mimicry of official parade culture. Yet by tying their aesthetic taste to that of the state consciously and unconsciously, the middle class in turn sustains the power of state symbols and rituals through driving practices. They use the official discourse of *suzhi* and harmonious society to justify their class positions and to defend their rights against real-estate developers, only to perpetuate the authority of the state.

On most occasions, the middle class reappropriated these elements to grapple with their lives, to carve out their space in society, and to try to make sense of their newly obtained class identity but without any clear intention to engage politically. Yet over time the middle class's decisions, perceptions, and practices converge into trajectories and patterns. Their engagement provides legitimacy to and thus coproduces various state projects and strategies that have reconfigured institutional arrangements, social stratification, and the logic of governance in the Reform era. In these processes, the state reformulates itself in a way that allows it to be seen as if it governs at a distance. It is in this sense that the Chinese middle class is doing exactly what their Western counterparts have been doing all along—producing and reproducing the authority of the state—except that the Chinese state has a distinctive social-political configuration that does not always empower those that helped create it.

To conclude, the unraveling of the automobile–middle-class entanglement illustrates new class politics in a country where class struggle has gained notoriety and provides a nuanced account of what are conventionally called "reforms." The socialist past was never really left behind, as the structures and relationships that it shaped have continued to have an impact in the contemporary context. It has always been there as a reference for the middle class to see where they now stand and from which they, often unconsciously, look for symbols to formulate their performance and practices to handle the new material world that came into being all too quickly. This book is not just about the emerging middle class and automotive regime; it is also a story about the complexity, continuity, and ruptures in the negotiation of relationship between state, society, and individuals.

PROLOGUE

From Official Privileges to Consumer Goods

The first two decades of the twenty-first century have seen a spectacular rise in private car ownership in China. Prior to it, however, was the official denial of ordinary citizens' right to own cars for as much as half of the twentieth century. This tight control on cars for private use has not only differentiated China from such capitalist societies as the United States but also put China in stark contrast with socialist counterparts, including the Soviet Union (1922–1991) and the German Democratic Republic (East Germany, 1949–1990), before the collapse of the planned economy.

How automobiles changed from being a privilege for officials to consumer goods is the focus here: the objective is to provide a critical context for the issues discussed in the chapters to come. To do so, I outline the paradigmatic shifts of auto production and consumption on the national and local levels from the Maoist years till the first decade of the twenty-first century. Instead of giving a comprehensive history, I focus on the ambiguities, hesitations, debates, and conflicts embedded in the process of transformation. The core issues that have shaped the transformation are why the country and the local government need the auto industry, what kinds of vehicles are desired, and whom the cars serve. Without knowing the long process of transformation, it would be difficult to understand how, for ordinary citizens, decades of restricted access to cars during the Maoist years and early Reform days could give way to a real sense of individual freedom when that long-desired access was finally granted.

Auto Industry: From Trucks to Cars

Cars and the initiative of establishing a car industry emerged in mainland China in the early twentieth century. In 1901 a Hungarian brought two U.S.-made Oldsmobiles to Shanghai via Hong Kong (Zhang Ji. 1994). Municipal governments of cities like Guangzhou and Shanghai fully embraced the vision of using automobility to modernize the urban economy in the early twentieth century (Zhang Ju. 2015, 2017). Cars quickly became highly visible in major Chinese cities in the decades that followed. Cars traveled alongside buses and rickshaws. Taxi companies advertised in local newspapers, which also published second-hand car transactions.[1] Garages and factories for spare parts were set up. In 1931, a factory was established in northeastern China in an attempt to produce heavy-duty trucks (Chen H. 1949). In 1936, the China Auto Manufacturing Company (Zhongguo Qiche Zhizao Gongsi) was founded in Nanjing, and by 1937, the company had assembled its first bus—with import parts and powered by vegetable oils—in Shanghai (Xu 2007).[2] These visions and efforts to modernize China via automobility, however, were interrupted by the constant wars between the late 1930s and 1940s. Contemporary official narratives dismissed the significance of the developments of the auto industry and consumption in the early twentieth century, even though new setups after 1949, when the Chinese Communist Party (CCP) took over the country, would not have been possible without these early efforts and visions.

The CCP-led government and political leaders saw automobiles as an icon of the technological advancement of the modern age and the ability to make automobiles as an indicator of the nation's industrial power. Thus, establishing an auto industry not only had pragmatic but also symbolic significance for the state to modernize the country's agriculture, industry, science, culture, and military. In this regard, Maoist China was similar to such socialist counterparts as the Soviet Union (Siegelbaum 2008, 2011). The year 1953 was

regarded as *the* historical moment in the official history of China's auto industry.[3] On July 15 of that year, the construction of the First Auto Works (FAW)
took place in Beijing (Li Y. 2003b). Several other auto manufacturers had
been set up to experiment with the production of heavy-duty vehicles and passenger cars. Dongfeng, Hongqi, and Fenghuang were brands that produced
passenger cars in Tianjin and Shanghai.

At roughly the same time, the construction of highways, suburbanization,
and the rise of middle-class consumers turned the United States and Europe
into countries on wheels.[4] In the socialist bloc in Eastern Europe and the
Soviet Union, individuals could obtain cars for private use in the state-
controlled economy—whether the auto industry had the ability to deliver the
cars was a separate matter (Berdahl 2000; Siegelbaum 2008). China was different. Despite the political significance of the auto industry, passenger cars
were not received positively during the socialist era. The government denounced consumption as corruption and regarded the bourgeois as the class
enemy in a country led by proletarians and peasants. The government thus
censured privately owned passenger cars, equating them to the stamp of a
bourgeois lifestyle (Barmé 2002; Zheng 1996). Taxi companies were forced
to shut down. In big cities, such as Shanghai, Beijing, and Guangzhou, the
number of privately owned cars dropped dramatically after 1949. Only high-
end government officials had regular access to passenger cars.

More importantly, however, despite the vision, the mass production of automobiles never materialized in the country, because an auto industry would
place a heavy demand on not only technologies, engineers, and skilled workers but also capital, raw materials, and energy, which were resources that the
new government could not afford. Eventually, the auto industry went straight
into stagnancy during the Cultural Revolution from the mid-1960s to the
mid-1970s. After Mao, the central government refocused on the auto industry
as the state's agenda gradually shifted from political struggle to economic
growth. Starting with the 7th Five-Year Plan (1986–1990) and following up
with a number of important policy guidelines in 1994 and 2004, the central
government mandated the auto industry to become a pillar industry (*zhizhu
hangye*), providing impetus to national economic growth,[5] and deployed the
plan with careful control throughout the 1980s and most of the 1990s. Specific
factories were chosen as bases of production,[6] and the supply of raw materials
necessary for car production was controlled. Elaborate government guidelines
on the desired number and sizes of auto manufacturers were also given.[7]

This development plan initially focused on heavy-duty vehicles that served agriculture, different industries, and the military.[8] There was, however, another camp within the government that pondered the possibility of giving more emphasis to the production of passenger cars than trucks.[9] This idea was tested with the establishment of three automotive joint ventures: the Beijing Jeep Corporation (Beijing-Jeep) in 1984, Shanghai Volkswagen Automotive Co. Ltd. (Shanghai-Volkswagen) in 1985, and the Guangzhou Peugeot Automobile Company (Guangzhou-Peugeot) in 1985.[10] All three joint ventures focused on passenger cars and other non-heavy-duty vehicles. Eventually in 1991, the government officially announced in a national auto industry conference convened in Shanghai that production should focus more on passenger cars than on heavy-duty trucks. The significance of these government decisions was immediately reflected by the three leaps of passenger car production (see the highlighted numbers in table 1, figure 2).

The gradual shift in priorities from heavy-duty vehicle production to passenger car production, however, did not change the government's attitude that auto production should serve the general good of the country and the economy and not satisfy individuals' desires for private cars. One observer stated, "As recently as 1993, 96% of all vehicle sales in China were to government departments or state-owned enterprises" (*Economist* 1997).

A change in attitude surfaced in the mid-1990s after a heated debate between 1993 and 1995 on whether to encourage private car consumption. It started as a topic for a debate competition among universities. Soon, well-known scholars and writers—including the sociologist Zheng Yefu, economist Mao Yushi, and children's books author Zheng Yuanjie—joined the debate.[11] Both sides agreed that the auto industry was considered essential in providing jobs and generating revenue for the national economy. Those in favor of private car ownership pointed out that passenger cars could bring convenience that public transportation could not. For example, a car would make it easier to go shopping and come home with lots of purchases or to go to the beach. More importantly, some argued that private consumption embodied the principle of equality, as car ownership would no longer be limited to the rich and powerful. Their opponents argued that the limited resources of the economy would not be able to support the general desire for cars. Moreover, private car consumption would degrade the environment and, given the limited road capacity, cause traffic congestion.

Table 1. Production of passenger cars, 1978–2012

Year	Numbers of Passenger Cars Produced	Year	Numbers of Passenger Cars Produced
1978	**2,640**	1996	391,099
1979	**4,152**	1997	487,695
1980	5,418	1998	507,103
1981	3,428	1999	566,105
1982	4,030	2000	608,445
1983	6,046	**2001**	**703,525**
1984	6,010	**2002**	**1,092,762**
1985	**5,207**	2003	2,037,865
1986	**12,297**	2004	2,312,561
1987	20,865	2005	2,767,722
1988	36,798	2006	3,869,494
1989	28,820	2007	4,797,688
1990	42,409	2008	5,037,334
1991	**81,055**	2009	7,471,194
1992	**162,725**	2010	9,575,890
1993	229,697	2011	10,137,517
1994	250,333	2012	10,767,380
1995	325,461		

Source: China Automotive Industry Yearbook *2013.* Boldface numbers indicate the substantial increase in car production immediately after policy change.

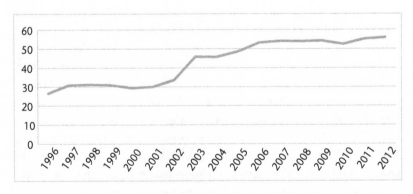

Figure 2. Percentage of passenger cars in total auto production, 1996–2012.
Source: China Automotive Industry Yearbook *2013*

This debate was carried out in major official newspapers, such as *Guang-ming Ribao* (Bright Daily, directed by the Central Propaganda Ministry), *Keji Ribao* (Science and Technology Daily, the central government's newspaper to promote science and technology), and *Zhongguo Qingnian Bao* (Chinese Youth Daily, official newspaper of the Chinese Youth League). The fact that government mouthpieces carried the debating pieces suggested that the government was at least open to the possibility.

This debate took place at a time when consumption gradually became depoliticized and was no longer seen as morally decadent (D. Davis 2000a). As I will show later, individuals' desire for car ownership was looking for a way out, particularly in the informal economy of cars. Yet there was still hesitation in the government's attitude toward making cars more widely available. It was not until the year 2000 that the line "letting passenger cars into the family is encouraged" (*guli jiaoche jinru jiating*) was formally written into the 10th Five-Year Plan of national development. That said, "most car sales still went to fleets, such as taxi firms and governments" by 2002 (*Economist* 2003; see also Goldman Sachs 2003, 13).

As the debate on private car consumption continued, China began negotiations to join the WTO in 1995. From the perspective of the governments of the United States and countries with strong car industries, negotiations took years mainly because of the Chinese government's protectionism. Concerns expressed in China were real. For one, the domestic auto industry had been suffering from a lack of capital, obsolete technologies, and inefficient management and had long been relying on protection through restrictions on foreign investment, import quotas, and tariffs (table 2). If the market were to open to the world, it would face severe challenges from big foreign car companies. This anxiety can be seen in official newspaper articles and such captions as "here comes the wolf" (*lang lai le*) and "dances with wolves" (*yu lang gong wu*). By describing foreign carmakers as predators, these articles alerted their readers that China's auto industry would struggle to survive any competitions from such auto giants as Volkswagen, Toyota, and General Motors. For ordinary people, the concern was of a different kind. As part of the reform, a great number of SOEs collapsed. Workers who had been promised "iron rice bowls" (*tie fanwan*) faced unexpected layoffs and consequently struggled to find any job (Hsu 2007; Lee C. K. 2007). The possibility of existing auto factories undergoing bankruptcy cast a shadow over the lives of tens of thousands of people who worked auto-related SOEs.

Table 2. Whole-passenger-car tariffs before and after China joined the WTO (with petroleum engines)

Year	Tariff (%)	
	Less than or equal to 3L	Larger than 3L
1986	180.0	180.0
1994	110.0	220.0
1996	100.0	120.0
1997	80.0	100.0
2000	63.5	77.5
2001	51.9	61.7
2002	43.8	50.7
2003	38.2	43.0
2004	34.2	37.6
2005	30.0	30.0
2006	28.0	28.0
2006/7/1	25.0	25.0

Sources: For numbers from 1986, 1994, 1996, and 1997, see Zhang B. 1998; from 2000 to 2007, see People's Daily 2002; Xie and Xu 1998.

Note: For tariff purposes, the 3-liter distinction was for cars with petroleum engines, and the 2.5-liter one was for cars with diesel engines at least until 1997. But the tariff for each category was the same. Importation quota was also eliminated in 2005 (Noble 2006).

Nevertheless, China was determined to become a member of the WTO. For the Chinese government, this move was an important one under the strategy generally described as "market share for technologies" (*shichang huan jishu*). The entry brought dramatic transformation to the auto landscape. The annual sales of cars immediately jumped by 62 percent and 75 percent in 2002 and 2003, respectively (Goldman Sachs 2003), which the Chinese media described as *jingpen* (blowout) (figure 3). Unlike in the mid-1980s and 1990s, when two or three joint ventures had dominated the auto market, now almost all major carmakers had found their Chinese partners and were engaged in producing cars under their own brands in China. New cars continued to roll off production lines, and prices continued to drop. By 2010, China had surpassed the United States in auto production. A decade after China's entry into the WTO, the *China Automotive Industry Yearbook*, published in 2011, wrote, "China began to step into an auto society" (3).

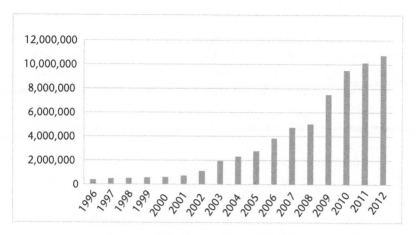

Figure 3. Sales of passenger cars, 1996–2012.
Source: China Automotive Industry Yearbook *2013*

One Step ahead of the Nation: Car Smuggling in South China

Before car consumption was officially encouraged in the new millennium, car ownership was controlled by the government through production and two main mechanisms of distribution during the Reform era. One of the mechanisms was a centralized distribution system through a quota scheme (more in chapter 3). The car quota system resembled the food-rationing system during the Maoist era and the early Reform days. In the case of cars, quotas were not given to individuals but to work units, such as government agencies, SOEs, and other government-affiliated organizations (e.g., hospitals). The government would decide which units were entitled to purchase cars. Since the mid-1980s, the government allowed work units to trade their car quotas for goods that were supposed to help improve the work units' productivity, but such bartering had to be conducted via state-owned commodities companies.[12]

The other mechanism was price control. From the beginning of the Reform era in the late 1970s until the end of the twentieth century, China's economy operated on a dual-track system. To put it simply, a dual-track system is one where the production and distribution of some commodities and resources are subjected to central planning, while the market mechanism regulates the production and distribution of other commodities and resources.

Automobiles belonged to the former. Throughout the 1980s, the central government repeatedly stated its authority to dictate auto prices.[13] The introduction of "state instructed prices" (*guojia zhidao jia*) into the pricing scheme under the dual-track system in 1994 gradually made room for carmakers to adjust prices.[14] To be specific, the central government would decide the base wholesale prices with a certain percentage of flexibility within which carmakers could determine the actual sales price. This state control on car prices was only abolished in 2001.[15]

As scholars have shown (Berdahl 1999, 2000; Borneman 1992; Dunn 2004; Fehérváry 2013; Humphrey 1998; Verdery 2003), the Soviet-style, centrally planned economy was essentially an "economy of shortages," which entailed "a second economy in which social relations and access to goods and services were based upon connections, barter, and bribes" (Berdahl 2000, 132). In China, with car production and consumption being put under such strict state control, a second economy of cars emerged in the South in the 1980s and 1990s.

Guangdong province borders the South China Sea and is adjacent to Hong Kong and Macau. The region has extensive networks with Chinese overseas, which were an important source of investment during the early Reform days (Smart and Smart 1999). In 1979, the central government designated four cities and Hainan Island to be special economic zones. Three (Shenzhen, Zhuhai, and Shantou) out of the four cities were in Guangdong (the fourth being Xiamen, in neighboring Fujian Province), and Hainan had been under the jurisdiction of the Guangdong government until it became a province in 1988. Guangdong was the frontier of market-oriented economic reforms. Wealth rapidly accumulated in its coastal areas, particularly in the Pearl River delta (Ikels 1996; Vogel 1989).

With new wealth came the desire for cars. A consumer culture and images of cars were already spreading to Guangdong as car magazines, TV dramas, movies, and popular novels from Hong Kong trickled into China, legally and illegally, in the early Reform era. Yet cars in the planned economy were not for private consumption. Smuggling arose and became a major channel for individuals with newfound wealth.

The first wave of car smuggling took place in the mid-1980s, and the base was Hainan. A place of exile during imperial times, the multiethnic Hainan Island remained remote and underdeveloped under the CCP-led regime. Its mountainous areas hosted thousands of "sent-down youths"—urban youths sent by the state to the countryside for reeducation—during the 1960s and 1970s. In 1983 the central government allowed Hainan, as a special economic zone, to import cars and other goods, such as televisions, with preferential tariffs, on condition that those goods should be used for production and consumption within the island.

Between January 1984 and early March 1985, Hainan's local government approved the importation of more than 89,000 vehicles, over 90 percent of which were passenger cars and minivans. According to the official report of an investigation conducted by the provincial and central governments, more than 79,000 of them had landed in Hainan, and more than 10,000 were sold to more than twenty inland provinces.[16] Local officials saw this informal car economy as a way to improve the local economy (Vogel 1989). Many companies and state-owned organizations, including kindergartens and schools, were involved in the car trafficking business.[17] According to my conversations with some people from Hainan, many local residents thought that the local government and officials did a good job in providing them with opportunities to improve their livelihoods. But for the central government, this was nothing but smuggling, so Hainan's trade privileges were withdrawn, and local officials were punished.

Car smuggling made a comeback in the 1990s, with Guangdong being the key node of operation, only this time it was on a larger scale, with more stakeholders and stronger consumption desires and capacity (table 3).[18]

According to customs officials in Guangdong whom I spoke with in 2007, car smuggling took various forms. Some forms were conducted under legal cover. Bartering was one of the forms; another way was to take advantage of tariff privileges given to joint ventures and foreign-invested companies. In order to attract foreign investments, the government offered tariff reductions or exemptions on passenger cars if the joint ventures or foreign investors imported them as company assets. Some of the qualified companies used their tariff-free quotas to import cars and then sold them for profit.

The most common way of smuggling was overtly illegal: cars were shipped to Guangdong from other countries without importation quotas, permits, or customs clearance before they were sold. The smuggled cars included top models of Audi, BMW, and Mercedes-Benz and mostly midrange Japanese passenger cars. According to customs officials, Japan and Hong Kong were the two main places of origin. Guangdong's curvy coastline was convenient

Table 3. Total numbers of legally imported and smuggled passenger cars, 1990–1999

| Year | Total Number of Imported Passenger Cars | Among them | | Sales of Domestically Produced Cars |
		Normal Importation	Smuggling	
1990	47,769	15,923	31,846	42,409
1991	43,215	14,405	28,810	81,055
1992	82,581	27,527	55,054	162,725
1993	208,989	69,663	139,326	229,697
1994	103,239	34,413	68,826	250,333
1995	73,092	24,364	48,728	325,461
1996	173,826	57,942	115,884	389,000
1997	96,057	32,019	64,038	474,203
1998	54,138	18,046	36,092	506,846
1999	42,501	14,167	28,334	518,622

Source: Sun, Jin, and Su 2000.
Note: Most of the normal importation numbers in this table are similar to those in customs and auto yearbooks. It seems that Yuchun Sun, Lin Jin, and Dongshui Su use the ratio 1:2 between normal importation and smuggling to produce the numbers of smuggled cars each year. Their estimates sometimes are lower than the more official estimate. For example, the *Auto Trade Yearbook* estimates 100,000 smuggled vehicles in 1997 *(Auto Trade Yearbook* 1998, 16). Despite the discrepancy, the message regarding the prevalence of car smuggling is clear.

for smugglers, because round-the-clock surveillance was challenging for customs agents. One version of the car smuggling story goes like this: A middleman notified buyers where and when the boat would come. The buyers prepared cash and waited at a designated, privately built pier. As soon as the boat arrived, these people rushed on board, picked their cars, bargained, paid in cash, and drove the cars away. The boat would then leave, and the pier would return to looking like nothing had happened. The interval between the boat's arrival and departure would only amount to one or two hours. "They could not stay long," one customs officer said. "If they stayed any longer, customs would catch them."

The informal economy built upon car smuggling in South China was different from that of other popular smuggled goods that could easily go into private consumption unnoticeably, such as cigarettes and alcohol. It also differed significantly from the informal circulation of car parts outside the formal economy structure in East Germany as described by Daphne Berdahl (1999, 2000). As a cross-border business, smuggling cars required large-scale mobilization and the connection of authorities, capitals, and actors. More importantly, while it was difficult to tell whether a spare part was obtained through official or informal channels, it was relatively easy, particularly for the police, to tell a smuggled car from a car obtained through legal means. Thus, smuggling would not have been possible without the complicity of a series of private businesses, the local government, and other state authorities.

Smuggling gave rise to many auto workshops in the Pearl River delta. A smuggled car could be new or second-hand or could have been written off. Some cars were smuggled whole; some were cut up before they were loaded into containers and reassembled upon arrival. Some of the smuggled cars needed only a new coat of paint, some needed touch-ups, and some required substantial remodeling. Some cars had their steering wheels moved to the left-hand side before they were taken out on the road.

During my fieldwork in 2006 and 2007, I met a senior mechanic called Master Dai who used to work in one of these auto workshops in Dongguan, an industrial town that later became a city. Master Dai, then in his fifties, had grown up in Sichuan Province. There he worked in a state-run auto factory. During the 1980s and early 1990s, China's economy took off in the South, but the reform had yet to make a major impact on inland cities like the ones in Sichuan. Dai left his hometown and went to the Pearl River delta in the early 1990s. According to him, Dongguan at that time was full of garages that specialized in remodeling cars. Dai's work might be reassembling a car from its parts, moving the steering wheel to the left, or other remodeling work. To me, the work sounded very difficult, and the reassembled or remodeled cars seemed unsafe to drive. Master Dai said, "Sure. You think the buyers did not know that? But who cared? Otherwise, how would you get a car?" Dai was paid by the number of cars he fixed. In his heyday, he could work on more than thirty cars and earn over RMB 10,000 a month. At that time, the average income per capita was less than RMB 500 per month in Guangzhou, the capital of Guangdong Province.[19]

As driving a car is always under the state's disciplinary control through taxation, registration, annual examination, and other regulations, state authorities were inevitably involved in the informal economy of car smuggling. It was no secret that in the mid-1990s (1993–1996), some smuggling boats were escorted by the navy. Customs did not have its own policing forces at that time. But even if they did have the force, it would not have been enough to tussle with the military. Local governments were also deeply implicated in what can be considered a "car laundering" business. Local authorities, particularly the police department, imposed fines on these cars. Once the fine was paid, a certificate was issued to officially confiscate a car and acknowledge payment. The car was thus "cleansed" and would become a legal car. These certificates became commoditized, and what ensued was their circulation on the black market. In addition, the local governments set up auctions to sell the smuggled cars that they confiscated. Some bidders were government officials.

That said, the audacious involvement of the local government was not meant to challenge the central government's authority. Such involvement shall be considered a part of the larger social, political experiments that need to be contextualized in the highly contingent reform process. It is convenient to think of China's economic reforms as a socioeconomic engineering project carefully planned, staged, and maneuvered by the state. But careful examination of the laws, policies, and practices shows that the so-called reforms have been marked by a series of local initiatives that were sometimes in line with but sometimes worked against national laws and regulations. What happened on the ground was much more complicated and uncertain than what official narratives about the reforms may suggest. There were no textbooks or readily available experiences that officials and other decision makers could draw upon to model the reforms after. Two famous phrases coined by the late chairman Deng Xiaoping best captured the spirit and guidelines of the reforms. One of the phrases was "feel the stones to cross the river" (*mozhe shitou guohe*), which described the experimental dimension of the reform endeavors; and the other was the "white cat, black cat" theory, which described the pragmatic attitude in which the ends justified the means in the process.

Guangdong in particular was a test bed for reform. It was two thousand kilometers away from the political center of Beijing, and it contributed little to the fiscal income of the central government before the reforms. Even if an experiment failed, it would not cause severe consequences to the political center. Meanwhile, Guangdong had the overseas connections that could bring in capitals, knowledge, and practices to kick-start the reform. The central government asked the originally impoverished local government to fund its own reform initiatives. In turn, the central government granted the province the privilege of not having to submit its entire fiscal and tax revenue and a certain autonomy to experiment with new practices.

The nature of the reform, the central-regional structure, and the fiscal arrangement, to a good extent shaped the rationale of the local government's practices in car smuggling. After all, the local customs were under direct control of the central government. Income from tariffs belonged to the central government, and none of the local governments would get a share. A local government should fight smuggling, but to destroy all the smuggled cars seemed a waste of valuable resources. Pecuniary punishments, therefore, allowed the local governments to fight illegal practices and to simultaneously extract revenue at the expense of the central government's income.

From shipping to landing, from reassembly and remodeling to licensing, the informal economy of car smuggling would be impossible without networks among entrepreneurship-inclined individuals who possessed connections and capital, skilled workers from different parts of the country like Master Dai, and local governments and other state authorities. This created opportunities for windfall, jobs, and power. The car smuggling story compliments Xiaohua Yang's observation after studying the development of the auto industry in China from the early 1980s to early 1990s. He commented, "Competition is not based on market but on the needs and ambitions of regions" (1995, 176). "Thus, regional boundaries are getting stronger through decentralization while national boundaries are becoming porous" (177).

The central government did strive to control the rampant car smuggling. In 1998, it convened several national meetings to discipline local governments. Meanwhile, it allowed customs to establish its armed forces in 1999. Preferential tariff policies for joint ventures or foreign investing companies were amended or abolished to stop the previous practices of circumvention. Together with the opening up of private car ownership and China's entry into the WTO, these endeavors finally ended large-scale car smuggling.[20] The elimination of the informal economy of car smuggling and the establishment of a "free" auto market according to the WTO framework, in many ways, confirms Karl Polanyi's argument that "laissez-faire itself was enforced by the state" (2001, 145), and "the introduction of free markets, far from doing away with the need for control, regulation, and intervention, enormously increased their range" (147).

Legality aside, the informal economy of car smuggling had, to a good extent, shaped regional perceptions and practices of cars and driving. In the early and mid-1990s, in the villages along the coastline of Guangdong Province, smuggled cars, with or without license plates, were parked or running on muddy, poorly built roads. Cars with steering wheels on the right—legally steering wheels should be on the left—seemed normal in the eyes of the local residents in the cities in Guangdong. Unlike in many parts of China dominated by Shanghai-Volkswagen cars, cars of many brands could be seen in the streets of Guangdong. When the national debate on private car consumption took place in the mid-1990s, it did not seem to have invoked many responses in the cities in Guangdong. To put this in a larger context, in Shanghai there were fewer than 10,000 registered privately owned vehicles in 1996, and the number remained the same in 1998. In contrast, Guangdong Province had more than 392,000 privately owned vehicles in 1996 and 594,000 in 1998, most of which were in the coastal cities and industrial towns of the province.[21] While passenger cars remained mostly for government, SOE, and other state-affiliated organizations in the rest of the country, passenger cars were also associated with wealth and private consumption in the Pearl River delta area.

Local Development: The Emerging Landscape of an Automotive Society in Guangzhou

Located at the heart of the Pearl River delta, Guangzhou (previously known as Canton) has been the political center and transportation hub in South China for centuries. As one of the wealthiest cities in China, Guangzhou has more than ten million people living and working there. The auto industry is one of its major industries that have stimulated local economic growth and secured the city's central position both in the region and in the country.[22]

The ambition of having an auto industry can be traced back to the early twentieth century when the city went through a major transformation politically and infrastructurally (Zhang Ju. 2015, 2017). But it was not until 1985 that Guangzhou had its first factory that assembled cars—the Guangzhou Peugeot Automobile Corporation (Guangzhou-Peugeot), six months after Shanghai-Volkswagen and two years after Beijing Jeep.[23] Cars started to roll off the assembly line late in the summer of 1986. Guangzhou-Peugeot's annual production of passenger cars ranged between 1,500 and 2,500, except in 1995 when the production surpassed 6,000.[24] Together with Shanghai-Volkswagen, Guangzhou-Peugeot provided the majority of domestically produced passenger cars in China until the mid-1990s.

Yet, while Shanghai-Volkswagen had taken up more than 50 percent share of the market by the 1990s, Peugeot in France decided to withdraw from the joint venture, and Guangzhou-Peugeot came to an end in the mid-1990s. The reasons for Guangzhou-Peugeot's failure were complicated. Some reports pointed fingers at the Chinese side of the joint venture's lack of proper management and entrepreneurship skills and suggested that the French managers were selfish and exploitative. The latter would bring into China models that had already become obsolete in France (Hao 2004; Lei 1998, Li and Huang 2004; Wang W. 1998; Wang X. 2005).

Another main reason had to do with the supply of spare parts (see table 4 for the influence of the importation of spare parts on car prices in the case of Shanghai-Volkswagen's Santana). Manager Wang (more in chapter 3), who had worked in Guangzhou-Peugeot from beginning to end, offered me some insider's perspective on the problem with spare parts.[25] First, Guangzhou-Peugeot had to rely on importing certain key parts, such as engines, because local suppliers had neither the technology nor capacity to produce them. While Guangzhou-Peugeot was still in existence, tariffs for car parts varied from 50 percent to 80 percent, causing import parts to become very expensive (see also Zhang B. 1998). Second, parts that were produced locally had poor quality, leading to many problems, such as overheating.[26] However, due to the localization (*guochanhua*) requirements for joint ventures, Guangzhou-Peugeot was bound to use parts produced locally up to a certain percentage.[27] The third reason was corruption: Guangzhou-Peugeot's managers accepted bribes from certain suppliers. While they became rich, the company "paid much more than necessary," to use Manager Wang's words, for the locally produced parts.

These issues were exacerbated by the sudden depreciation of the Chinese yuan. Between 1993 and 1994, the state adjusted the nominal foreign exchange rate for one U.S. dollar from RMB 5.80 to 8.75, so cars that had imported parts saw their costs go up suddenly. As all auto yearbooks and academic articles showed but failed to explain, Guangzhou-Peugeot had been well managed up until 1993, but deficits appeared quickly in 1994. In addition, Manager Wang also mentioned that the diplomatic relationship between

Table 4. Prices of Shanghai-VW's Santana, 1991–1999

Time of Tariff Adjustment	Price of Santana (standard) (RMB/USD)
1991/1	215,000/53,750
1992/12	193,500/48,375
1993/12	185,000/46,250
1994	174,500/43,625
1995/3	168,000/20,000
1995/7	160,000/19,048
1996/4	158,000/18,810
1997/1	143,000/17,024
1998	114,000/13,571
1999	113,000/13,452

Source: Wu and Fei 2002. Tariffs for parts were between 50 and 80 percent from 1985 to 1996 and then adjusted to 35 to 60 percent in 1997. Passenger car production relied heavily on imported spare parts in the early years of the joint ventures. The prices of passenger cars assembled in joint ventures were therefore determined according to the prices of their imported counterparts (Xie and Xu 1998). While the example here is about Shanghai-Volkswagen's Santana, Guangzhou-Peugeot had the same issue.

China and France had worsened since the late 1980s, mainly because the French sold a warship to Taiwan and because of the French government's attitude to the June Fourth movement (see also Yao and Han 2008). Expensive parts, outdated models, and dubious production quality produced second-rate but expensive Peugeot cars. These cars were inefficient, and their maintenance costs were high.

The local government attempted to save the company in the mid-1990s. It asked all state-owned taxi companies to buy Peugeot cars, but many taxi drivers were reluctant to drive these high-maintenance and expensive cars. Peugeot left China in 1996. For some older residents in Guangzhou, their impression of Peugeot cars remained negative when Peugeot came back to the China market in the new millennium (more in chapter 3).

In the same year, a new joint venture, Guangzhou-Honda, came into being.[28] The Japanese company Honda built its assembly lines using the facilities left behind by Guangzhou-Peugeot. It produced only one model, the Honda Accord, in the first few years. According to official reports, Guangzhou-Honda achieved an annual output of 30,000 cars and began to turn a profit by the second year of operation.[29] The Accord was widely popular among consumers in the late 1990s. Even in the first several years of the twenty-first century, when car prices began to drop substantially after China's entry into the WTO, the Accord series was one of few domestically produced cars that had high selling prices. Guangzhou-Honda was depicted as "rewriting the history of auto production in Guangzhou," and the establishment of Guangzhou-Honda was often considered the real beginning of Guangzhou's auto industry (Yao and Han 2008). With then vice mayor Zhang Guangning, who was the president of the board of Guangzhou-Honda, becoming mayor, Guangzhou-Honda also became a major achievement in the political annals of high-end officials.

In the 2010s, Guangzhou-Peugeot was a forgotten past for many local residents in the city. Drawing on years of experience and technological advancement from collaborating with foreign partners, Guangzhou Automobile Manufacturing has also transformed into a complex corporation, the Guangzhou Automobile Group Co. Ltd (GAC Group), which has produced cars under its own brand. Following Honda's success, other major Japanese carmakers came to Guangzhou. Toyota, Nissan, Mitsubishi—all of which collaborated with Chinese automakers—and their suppliers have formed an industrial cluster with Japanese genealogy along with Honda by the 2010s. No other Chinese cities have had as many Japanese carmakers as Guangzhou.

For many local car owners, particularly those who grew up in the city, they became familiar with Japanese brands much earlier than the emergence of the joint ventures with Japanese carmakers. Many joint ventures established by Hong Kong and Taiwan businessmen in the early Reform era imported Japanese cars as company assets. The informal economy of smuggling cars also contributed to the local experience with Japanese cars. Well-functioning cars of the most updated models and bearing the logos of Lexus, Crown, and Camry were running side by side outdated models of Peugeot and Volkswagen on the roads of the Pearl River delta area. According to Guangzhou-Peugeot's Manager Wang, few local people would simply assume that European cars were superior to Japanese cars.

Japanese cars and their owners were targets of violence in different parts of China when relations between Japan and China became tense at times in recent years. I have heard car owners living in other cities—such as Wuhan, a city that is home to one of the largest auto groups, Dongfeng Motor Corporation—mention that they would never buy Japanese cars, simply for being Japanese.

In Guangzhou, however, rarely have I heard current or prospective car owners refuse to buy Japanese cars because of patriotism. Instead, many interlocutors told me that letting nationalistic sentiments (*minzu qingxu*) decide what car to buy was a sign of immaturity because one should focus on practical concerns. For those who preferred European to Japanese brands, they believed European cars were more robust and safer than their Japanese counterparts. For those who favored Japanese brands, Japanese cars were more fuel efficient and cheaper to maintain than European cars. The majority of my urban middle-class interlocutors distrusted Chinese automobile brands, thinking that domestic cars were poor in quality and unsafe.

The thriving of private car ownership has dramatically changed the landscape of Guangzhou. Dating back to the early twentieth century, the car had already reshaped the form of the city. Aiming at improving the commercial development by facilitating the flow of transportation, streets that accommodated automobile traffic were built on top of the relics of city walls, and old residential buildings were demolished to make room for them (Zhang Ju. 2015, 2017). In 1933, a bridge was built over the Pearl River (*zhujiang*) for the first time in the city's history, which helped to overcome the natural barrier for spatial extension and make mass transportation possible.

In comparison to the early twentieth century, the Maoist years were relatively unproductive in terms of road infrastructure building. Bicycles were the major means of daily commute (Gerth 2010; Notar 2015). But the coming of the automobile age has again reconfigured the urban landscape (Zhang Ju. 2016). The new favorite embellishments among urban planners are boulevards, often with more than ten lanes for cars. Street development has also moved upward—that is, vertically. Multiple layers of overhead passes, inner-city expressways, and intercity highways have colonized the vertical space of the city, manifesting the "depth" of modernity, of which the automotive regime is an epitome.

Conclusion

The structural transformation of car production and supply is a vital part of the transformation of China's political economy in the Reform era. It has embodied the uncertainties, ambiguities, and contradictions in the reform practices. It is not quite accurate to call these practices neoliberal, because they were often executed on a trial-and-error basis with a concern for pragmatics (such as the lack of kick-start funds or technologies) but lacked clear commitment to the logic or concerns associated with such neoliberal thinkers as Friedrich von Hayek and others.

Car smuggling became an informal economy that encapsulated these characteristics of reform practices. This informal economy was the product of the symbiotic relationships between the lingering planned economy, the experimental nature of the reforms, the local government's initiatives to look for revenue, profit-driven entrepreneurs, and individuals' rising consumptive desires. Curbing the smuggling led to the strengthening of the customs bureau with military power, and China's entry into the WTO in fact solidified the central government's control of the regional economies. The changing economic practices and individual desires are not only shaped by but are also an important force that reshapes political relationships and legitimacy. All of these are not planned results but are products of long-term interactions between visions, negotiations, and contingencies.

The connection between automobiles and politics is not unique to China. The auto industry, as a powerful symbol of industrial achievement, has been crucial to the Soviet Union and other former socialist countries (Siegelbaum 2008, 2011), but even in such societies as the United States, the auto industry is more than mere factories that produce cars. In 2008, the U.S. government refused to bail Lehmann Brothers out of bankruptcy, triggering the global financial crisis. Yet the same government granted a bailout to the "Big Three" U.S. carmakers: Ford, General Motors, and Chrysler. Meanwhile, such governments as Germany and South Korea also provided similar or other forms of financial support to their carmakers as a way of saving their national economies.

That said, the political signification of the auto industry may vary between countries. In the United States, the auto industry has long been intertwined with the history of labor and unions (Dudley 1994), and the popularization of passenger cars was a product of and a driving force for postwar state-orchestrated reconstruction projects, suburbanization, and racial politics (Heiman 2015; Jackson 1985). But in popular and everyday discourses, neither cars nor the auto industry has been particularly related to the state, even though many postwar government policies and projects, such as the construction of the interstate highway system, have facilitated the growth of private car consumption.

In contrast, for many Chinese citizens, the auto industry has been related to national development and pride. Cars themselves have long been associated with the government and privileges during the Maoist and early Reform years, and the strict state control of car production and distribution—supplemented by a regional, informal economy of cars—led to cars being identified as a symbol of the nouveau riche in the 1990s and early 2000s. Only in the 2010s were cars seen generally as a middle-class consumption item. Exclusive access to passenger cars has left a legacy in popular perceptions and tastes in cars and in driving practices in ways that are still discernible today, which will be explored in the chapters to follow.

Chapter 1

DRIVING ALONE TOGETHER

Sociality, Solidarity, and Status

For almost a decade I lived in the northeastern part of the United States. I bicycled to school, to the office, to the gym, and to run errands and buy groceries. Occasionally my friends and colleagues would give me a lift in their cars, but most of the time I would walk. I used public transportation to nearby cities to visit friends and for other excursions. I told this to my middle-class interlocutors in China. "Which part of the world did you actually live in?" a young engineer, Shao Jing, jokingly asked me when he drove me home after our lunch meeting. In the 2010s, the majority of my middle-class Chinese interlocutors have been car owners. Driving is becoming an everyday experience: they drive to work and to do sports, to meet clients in and outside the city, to try out restaurants in the periurban areas, to find entertainment in nearby cities, and for weekend and holiday travels.

In such societies as the United States where cars are an integral part of everyday mobility, there is a tendency to associate owning and driving a car as the materialization and enactment of freedom, autonomy, and mobility (Boehm et al. 2006; Flonneau 2010). This perceived relation is, to a great extent, ideological, not only because the rhetoric of automobility—liberating, individuating, revivifying, equalizing—is a product of the political ideology of being a free American and the apparatus of corporate capitalism in post–World War II America (Seiler 2008) but also because existing social inequalities have their imprint on the kinds and extent of freedom people obtain with cars, and the ways of mobility enabled by the car and driving have been shaped along the lines of racial, class, and other power relationships in U.S. society (Lutz 2014; Lutz and Fernandez 2010; Packer 2008).

Yet driving as a reification of autonomy and freedom is so deeply ingrained in people that having a car has been considered a means of fighting existing inequality. Women drivers are an outstanding example of this. Professional women and housewives drive their children to attend all kinds of extracurricular activities and for grocery shopping. A car enables them to juggle tasks between work and family without changing a woman's role in a gendered division of labor (Heiman 2015; Lutz 2014). Although they are often locked in a specific form of everyday-life rhythm made possible by that very vehicle, the car remains a quintessential vehicle for them to experience being free from the constraints of time and space (Jain 2002). This paradoxical experience is well captured in Gilroy's analysis of African Americans' desire of owning a car.

Not unlike the African Americans in Gilroy's description, ordinary Chinese citizens were denied car ownership during the Maoist and early Reform years. With China becoming a member of the WTO in the twenty-first century, car ownership has been rapidly normalized among middle-class families. Global carmakers and advertising companies seek to sell their cars by promoting a narrative about a new lifestyle that emphasizes technology, freedom, autonomy, and status. In this context it is understandable why middle-class people like Shao Jing would ask me, "Which part of the world did you actually live in?"

That said, they do not seem to have an inclination "towards a disproportionate investment"—to borrow Gilroy's words—in car ownership. It is outright puzzling for them to know that in the United States even someone living in a shelter may still own a car (Rowe 1999), or "in the years of deepest depression, the automobile remained a priority for many, including the unemployed" (Gudis 2010, 372).

Therefore, to what degree does the narrative of cars, autonomy, and mobility capture the Chinese middle class's imagination and practices involving cars, if at all? This chapter tries to present the nuances of those imaginations and practices by examining how the middle class use and speak about their cars in their *quotidian* lives and how they drive on *special* occasions—organized and semiorganized driving tours and wedding car parades. My findings suggest that middle-class professionals tend to describe the significance of their cars in everyday life in practical terms, such as, most notably, "convenience" (*fangbian*) rather than "freedom" (*ziyou*). And the significance of the car in their lives, as described by them, was intensely social.

My description here does not intend to suggest a stereotype that individuals from the Chinese middle-class are obsessed with status or are keen to become a part of a collective or that they lack individuality or autonomy. The way the urban middle class use and talk about cars contains a significant level of self-consciousness and employs first-person pronouns (e.g., *my* life, *my* work, *my* friends, *myself*). When I asked them whether having cars made them feel free and mobile, their answers were usually affirmative.

Nevertheless, the sketches presented in this chapter illustrate, first, how cars and driving have become integral in the new form of middle-class sociality; and second, the perceived "pragmatic" value and prestige attached to certain cars and driving practices are not merely perceived thus because they are expensive. I contextualize the middle-class narratives and practices of having and driving a car in decades of social transformation, showing the complex interactions between the past and the present and between the state and the individuals. I argue that the specific ways of understanding automobility among the middle class have not only been shaped by but have been shaping the changing temporal-spatial arrangements in handling work and close social circles. Furthermore, the far-reaching influence of political practices, which are fond of a parade culture and endow officials with material and symbolic privileges, may serve as a useful context for us to understand the aesthetics and spatiality of the middle-class sociality as embodied in specific car and driving preferences.

Everyday Life Convenience: For Credibility and Sociality

"Happiness is the smell of a new car . . . It's freedom from fear. It's a billboard on the side of the road that screams with reassurance that whatever you're doing is okay," said Don Draper, the talented and egotistical protagonist in the popular TV drama series *Mad Men* that depicts the advertising industry in 1960s America. Don Draper's romantic depiction of the smell of a car and the road is also what carmakers try to sell to their twenty-first-century Chinese consumers. However, my middle-class interlocutors' remarks on Don Draper's words were often cynical: phrases such as "What you're doing is okay" and "freedom from fear" are idealistic, and "the smell of a new car" is, as several of them joked, "just too much formaldehyde in the car's upholstery."[1] When I asked them whether they thought a car would bring freedom, they all answered yes. But if I let them describe what a car meant for them, they would tell me that they had or wanted to have a car because of practicality (*shiji*). In their descriptions, the term that was most frequently used was "convenience."[2]

For some China observers, this reference to convenience as a reason for having a car sounds ironic. Traffic congestion has been a serious problem in major Chinese cities (Zhang Ju. 2016). In Guangzhou and nearby places, for example, the rapid construction of public transportation systems makes the subway a more reliable means than a car to move from place to place in terms of punctuality and time-cost efficiency.

Many middle-class drivers know it is illusive to think that a car can get a person around in a timely manner. While lawyers and entrepreneurs tend to drive regularly to work and for social life, many professionals, such as doctors, engineers, and corporate managers, have told me that they regularly rode the subway, took the taxi, or took a bus to go to work or meet with their friends. In fact, some of my interlocutors confessed that they had once, as they were aspiring to become car owners, fantasized about the fun of driving, but once they became car owners, they felt that driving was actually an exhausting form of labor, especially when they were stuck in traffic after a long day of work. The car was usually used when the family went out together or when they hung out with friends. This pattern is also more visible among those who worked and lived in or near the city center than those who lived in periurban areas and worked near the city center or vice versa.

It would be, however, a mistake to disregard my interlocutors' frequent referral to "convenience" when they talked about their cars and driving experience. As Elizabeth Shove—writing about everyday normality and technologies—points out, "convenience-related consumption is not simply about saving or shifting time as such, but is instead about re-designing and re-negotiating temporal demands associated with the proper accomplishment of specific social practices" (2012, 300). What I would add to Shove's point is that "convenience" in the Chinese middle class's driving practices is more than managing temporal demands. Here I present scenarios about four individuals that are illustrative of the ways in which the majority of my interlocutors think and talk about the car and convenience. I then contextualize their stories in their changing social lives—temporal-spatial management and work-leisure relationship—to illustrate the significance of "convenience."

Dong Mei was a college lecturer in her late twenties in 2007. Both Dong Mei and her husband had been faculty members in a university in Guangzhou since they finished graduate school. They lived in a subsidized apartment near the university. During one of our conversations, Dong Mei expressed her desire to have a car:

> The weather is so hot, so people sweat easily. Public transportation takes so much time. Sometimes when my friends call me to have dinner together or to play badminton, I simply do not want to go through all the trouble to be there. You know we live near the campus. It is a long walk to the bus stop or to find a taxi. With a car it would be different. Many of our friends have cars now. It is convenient for them to go out. They are willing to give us a ride, but I do not feel I should bother them all the time. It would be much more convenient if we have our own car.

Dong's words echoed Lawyer Qin's, who described to me in 2008 his experience as a car owner:

> After [my wife and I] bought our car, whenever our friends gave us a call to play cards or go sing karaoke, we would immediately drive out and join them. We would often leave home at 9:00 or 10:00 p.m. and come back past midnight. Before we bought our car, we seldom went out that late. It was so difficult to get a taxi home so late at night. But ever since we had a car, it was much more convenient to meet friends at night.

Qin and his wife were both lawyers but in separate firms. I first met the couple when I had dinner with Lawyer Lu and his wife. Lu and Qin went to the same university, came together to southern China to advance their careers, and married around the same time in the mid-2000s. Their wives also had similar trajectories. The Lus and the Qins became good friends. They lived in separate cities but with only a thirty-minute drive between them. When I met Lawyer Qin—again with the Lus—in 2011, the Qin couple was in their late thirties and had a baby girl. After they had the child, Lawyer Qin and his wife no longer drove out at night to socialize with friends or colleagues. Instead, they spent more time with friends who had children, such as the Lus. These two families would drive to visit each other and hang out regularly during daytime on the weekends.

Lawyer Lu came from a small town in inland China. Among four children, he was the only one who received higher education. After graduating with a law degree from a small college away from his hometown, he came to Guangdong in the late 1990s. He worked in a district-level—the lowest level—court before he joined a local law firm that handled contracts and legal disputes for factory owners in the Pearl River delta. After years of hard work, he made partner in the late 2000s. Lu lived with his wife and his parents in a four-bedroom apartment in a gated complex. His apartment building was well situated, and the location guaranteed his child a spot in a well-reputed primary school nearby. His first car was a dark blue, midsized Ford sedan. In 2010, Lu and his wife were looking for a second car, and I visited car dealerships with them. I suggested a Volvo S60, as Volvo was ranked one of the safest cars and was considered a low-profile, middle-class car in Western countries. Lu rejected it, saying, "No one would know the brand." As we wandered into an Audi dealership, he explained to me,

> The more competent the lawyer is, the more money he makes. Competence is not necessarily how well he knows the law. It has a lot to do with his networking and social skills. The more cases he wins, the more he earns, and the better the car he drives. Some clients decide on their lawyers based on what they drive. It's stupid, but how else can they tell if you are a good lawyer? . . . An apartment doesn't make a good basis, because no one knows where you live or whether you have bought it or are renting it. But nouveau riche factory owners know about cars. Cars are the most convenient thing for them to judge whether you are a good lawyer or not.

Lawyer Lu's words echoed those from Xiaowang, a younger lawyer who also came from a small inland city. After graduating from college, Xiaowang worked in a small law firm in Guangzhou, while his parents still lived in his hometown in northern China. When I interviewed him in his office in 2007, Xiaowang began by saying, "A car is a production tool [*shengchan gongju*] for a lawyer, because it makes it easier to meet with clients." The term "production tool" struck me, for it reminded me of the Marxist terminologies in China's high school textbooks. I tried to interpret it on my own terms: "Do you mean easier in terms of transportation?" "No," he corrected me:

> Arriving in a car to meet your clients makes the meeting easier: The clients would trust a lawyer more if they see the lawyer coming in a car . . . A business suit? Nowadays people think you are selling insurance if you wear a suit and a tie. That is what people thought what I was before [when I wore a suit]. They thought I was there to sell them insurance plans. If you have a car, no one would question you that way.

Xiaowang was a junior lawyer who had practiced law for less than two years when I interviewed him. Nowadays, lawyers, particularly junior lawyers working in small law firms, such as the one Xiaowang worked in, have different work experiences from those working in big law firms. Big law firms often adopt a corporate structure with internal labor division and hierarchy. The names of these big law firms, to a great extent, are an indicator of the capacity of their lawyers and a source of confidence for the clients. Small law firms, which make up the majority of the legal service market, operate under a loose management structure. These firms are composed of contractual lawyers who pay a certain percentage of their fees to the firm to share the costs of running the office, utilities, paying the secretaries, and for other general management. Lawyers who can have their own cases instead of working on other lawyers' cases are considered "independent" in a law firm. They sometimes handle their cases by themselves or often hire junior lawyers to work for them. The income of a small law firm depends on the cases these "independent" lawyers can bring in. For these lawyers, personal reputation, social networking, and legal knowledge are all crucial for securing clients and settling cases, and it is important for them to prove their competence to their potential clients.

In 2007 Xiaowang did not have his own clients yet and worked on cases that his supervisor gave him. Lawyer Lu, a more experienced lawyer from another small law firm, had passed the stage that Xiaowang was in and gradually moved up the ladder. I had similar conversations when I spoke to young and middle-aged lawyers between 2006 and 2015. The emphasis was that clients and other lawyers judged the ability of a lawyer by the car he or she drove. A car was a symbol of a lawyer's ability and reputation. It showed others how successful he or she was. Having a car, therefore, was a "convenient" sign of credibility (*xindeguo*).

To understand the weight of the convenience the car is thought to have brought to the middle class, we need to contextualize these scenarios amid the larger transformation in urban life—work, leisure, and social life—during the late Reform period. Our discussion of the transformation begins with the older generation's life experiences, which my interlocutors would often use as a reference to measure their own lives against.

For older urban residents (typically from the generation of my interlocutors' parents), a work unit (*danwei*) was the node of their social life (Bray 2005; Lu D. 2006; Tomba 2014). Prestige was less attached to the individual than to the individual's work unit. As housing was a major work benefit, one's workplace and home were often located close to each other, and often colleagues were also neighbors (Bray 2005; Lu D. 2006). Bikes were the main mode of transportation for many (see also Gerth 2010; Jankowiak 1993; Notar 2015), which was partly facilitated by the fact that urban residents typically did not have to travel far to work (Gaubatz 1995). In addition, people's mobility was highly limited during the Maoist years and early Reform era. There were not that many strangers in one's immediate life.

For middle-class professionals who were born between the late 1960s and early 1980s, life differed significantly. The work-unit system as the central mechanism that used to organize individuals' social and political lives was collapsing or had collapsed when they started working in cities. Except for very few cases, their workplaces no longer had institutional affiliation with their residence.[3] Their housing choices increasingly depended on real-estate prices, transport facilities, school resources, and proximity to their parents' home rather than on work location. Living patterns have become more diverse than those in the previous eras.

Leisure as a structural space separated from work and home has arisen in an individual's life (Oakes forthcoming; Rolandsen 2011; Wang S. 1995; Yu 2014). Dong Mei and Lawyer Qin's stories are examples of these changes. Friends, particularly schoolmates from high school and college, constitute an important part of the middle class's social circles in contemporary urban China.[4] They are networking resources to handle life and work, but they are also companions in leisure times. These professionals spent a good amount of time with their friends outside the workplace or home. (This sociality provided great convenience for my snowball-sampling research.) They go out with friends for weekday dining, weekend card games, sport activities, sightseeing excursions, or food explorations. With cars, physical distance would no longer limit their options.

The middle class's everyday life—work, home, and leisure—covers a much larger area than that in the work-home commute pattern their parents were used to, and this everyday life pattern requires different ways of compartmentalizing their time compared to their parents'. The car is deemed a convenient means that facilitates the imaginations and practices of such time-space management configured by this new form of middle-class sociality.

Meanwhile, encounters and interactions with strangers have become mundane experiences. Lawyer Lu once gave me an illustrative example: His father was a primary school teacher who knew most of the people that lived in the small town where he came from. "That is a society of acquaintances. Everyone knows everyone else, and there is no need to prove your worth," Lu told me. For him and Xiaowang, moving out of their hometown is undoubtedly a sign of upward mobility. But it also means that they have moved to a society of strangers where they have to work hard to establish a reputation and social network. Among professionals, the brand and alumni network of one's alma mater often open some doors. The more reputable the school or university one has graduated from, the larger the alumni network one finds himself or herself in. For people like Lu and Xiaowang who did not graduate from an elite university and were new to the city, the sense of having to prove oneself seemed particularly strong. A car, on such occasions, is thus perceived as a convenient proof of one's ability at work. In my interviews, this link was articulated more by professionals from smaller cities and less reputable universities and small-time entrepreneurs than professionals from big cities and elite universities.[5]

Interestingly, in all four scenarios, the convenience of having a car was often talked about in relation to other people, be it strangers or acquaintances, in their social lives. In my other interviews and conversations with my interlocutors, the experience of driving with families and friends was particularly prominent. In fact, during my fieldwork, I spent a good amount of time riding in my interlocutors' cars, along with their friends, to look for good food in different parts of the city or nearby towns, to go to sport venues, and to go on weekend excursions. Rarely did my interlocutors talk about individual freedom in the strict sense of the term. The car is now *conveniently* integrated into and facilitates this middle-class everyday sociality.

Driving Alone with Friends and Acquaintances

As driving out with friends has become increasingly common in the leisure part of the middle class's lives (see also Notar 2012), some collective forms of driving practices—organized and semiorganized driving tours and wedding car fleets—have also become visible.

Driving tours have become increasingly popular among the Chinese middle class when they travel on the weekend and during holidays inside China and abroad. While the number of driving tours tailored to the individual grows, organized and semiorganized tours are also on the rise. Organized driving tours are often used by businesses, such as automakers, dealerships, and sports clubs, to promote business and foster customer loyalty. Auto-Fan, the dealership where I interned for fieldwork, for example, organized a self-driving tour in the early 2000s. However, according to my conversations with Auto-Fan's managers and a couple of employees who participated in such organized driving tours, the effects in terms of marketing were dubious at best.

Nevertheless, for the participants, the experience of driving as and in a collective was more impressive and vivid than the sightseeing in these tours. Several years after the abovementioned organized tour, Manager Lu, Auto-Fan's sales manager, remained excited when he told me about this event and showed me some photos: "You know, in that trip we even had police cars at the front to clear a path for us. Fifteen cars followed! Didn't it look great?"

Yuan Yi participated in a driving tour organized by an automaker through its dealerships. Working in the marketing industry, Yuan considered himself a person of character (*you gexing*). Yuan Yi bought his first car, a QQ, in 2003. Despite having a reputation of being cheap and unsafe, the car made Yuan one of the earliest car owners among his schoolmates and friends. When I met Yuan in 2007, the year when he turned thirty, he had just sold the QQ and bought a compact hatchback, a new, American model that was intended to attract young consumers. Yuan liked to travel by car, usually with his girlfriend, who later became his wife. He described his tours as adventurous: "You never know what awaits."

In 2007, Yuan received an invitation from his dealership informing him that he was one of dozens of "lucky" car owners in a members-only, organized driving tour to a city in neighboring Guangxi Province. The "lucky" car owners were allowed to bring friends and family and would be responsible for their own expenses. The automaker and its dealerships planned the route, accommodations, places to eat, and other logistics. The organizational challenge was to keep all participating cars together in single file on the road. The organizers gave each car a number and a walkie-talkie. The cars formed a line according to their numbers. The organizers put experienced drivers in the front and at the back. With the walkie-talkies, the organizers reminded the cars at the front to slow down whenever someone began to fall behind and informed drivers that would become stuck in traffic or be halted by traffic lights how to catch up with the rest of the convoy. All cars in the fleet turned on their emergency lights the whole way, signaling to other vehicles that they were a group.

An organized driving tour is a paradoxical concept: it puts control and discipline back into a supposedly liberating experience. Yuan Yi admitted that he was not particularly fond of the organized self-driving tours because "they restrain you, keeping you from going wherever you want." Nevertheless, when relating his organized tour to me, Yuan's eyes beamed: "It looked grand when dozens of cars drove in one line on the highway, with all their emergency lights flashing. It was spectacular!"

An organized driving tour put great pressure on the organizers because of its logistics. There is a more popular variation of this collective driving, which I call semiorganized driving tours: Typically, a group of friends and family go out for an excursion somewhere away from their home cities. There is no single central organizer, such as the dealerships mentioned above. Instead, several members—usually the most enthusiastic of the group—collaborate to plan the itinerary, course, or route and program. They meet somewhere in the city that is near a highway entrance. They try to drive together as a group, with their emergency lights flashing, particularly in areas where there is a lot of traffic. They use walkie-talkies and, increasingly, smartphone apps, such as WeChat, to stay in touch with the group while driving. Communication is frequent, not just for keeping all the cars together but also to plan lunch breaks, make fun of each other, and comment on other drivers and cars on the road.

A semiorganized driving tour shares many similarities with a wedding car parade, another form of collective driving. While the former is more visible on highways or in the countryside, the latter is more regular and more eye-catching in the city. A wedding car fleet is usually small, composed of four to six cars. In traditional wedding rituals, despite local variations, there would usually be a parade of a sedan chair (*jiaozi*) that carried the bride and laborers that carried the dowry to celebrate the union of two families and demonstrate their wealth.[6] The wealthier and more powerful the families, the bigger the parade would be. Today, cars have taken the place of the sedan chairs and horses in wedding parades. In the fleet, the main car carries the new couple, the maid of honor, and the best man. The remaining cars are for bridesmaids, groomsmen, and sometimes relatives of the new couple, such as cousins, nieces, and nephews. As in other family rituals, wedding practices exemplify and reproduce kinships and social networks. Senior generations do not participate in wedding car parades. Bridesmaids and groomsmen are close friends and, sometimes, younger siblings and cousins.

Cars in a wedding car fleet are called "flower cars" (*huache*), which resonates with "flower sedan chairs" (*huajiao*), the name for sedan chairs used in weddings in the past. The main car with the new couple is the most expensive one in the fleet; it leads the parade. It is also the most decorated one. Often on top of the hood, close to the car brand logo, there will be roses arranged in the shape of a heart or a couple of plush teddy bears or other lovely cartoon figures that represent the new couple. For the rest of the "flower cars," colorful ribbons and flowers are attached to their bodies. They are so formulaically decorated that anyone can easily identify them. The order of cars is arranged according to how expensive they are, and sedans go before seven-seat minivans. Increasingly the new couple will hire a cameraman to film the whole course of the wedding. The car for the cameraman will either be a hatchback or one with a sunroof for the convenience of filming. Most of the time, the cameraman's car travels in front of the fleet to capture the whole fleet. From time to time, the car drives to the side or the back to film from other angles.

Distance between homes is not the reason for having a wedding car parade. Even if the bride's and groom's families live close to each other, a car fleet is still a must in a formal wedding. On the day of the wedding, the groom or his friends drive the cars early in the morning to the florist where the cars will be decorated. At the auspicious hour, the groom and his friends bring the fleet of cars to pick up the bride and her bridesmaids from the bride's natal home and travel back to the groom's home.[7] The way back to the groom's home involves a detour: the cars will travel through streets with auspicious names, such as *jixiang lu* (lucky road), *duobao lu* (great fortune street), *baizi lu* (a hundred sons street), and *taikang lu* (safe and healthy street) for good luck.[8]

Between 2006 and 2007, I noticed a common practice in many wedding car fleets: the license plates were usually covered by a piece of red paper. On the paper there would be written some phrases of blessings, such as "A hundred years of harmony" (*bainianhaohe*) and "Forever in love" (*yongjietongxin*) (figure 4). Stacy, a young marketing manager, joked about the similarities of the wedding car decoration, the cover-up of the license plate, and cruising in a similar route. She once received five invitations to weddings all on the same day in 2008. She said, "I was so worried that the *huache* I sat in would follow the wrong fleet on that day." My interlocutors said that such practice was "normal." Yuan Yi had been a groomsman and wedding driver several times. I asked him, "Can you do that [cover the license plate]? You would get yourself into trouble with the police, wouldn't you?" With a big grin, he explained to me: "No, those are *huache*. . . . Getting married is a big deal in one's life. The police do not want to make things difficult for people on their big days." The practice of covering the license plate continued for a while and gradually disappeared in the 2010s. Blessings written on red paper are still stuck onto the cars but now either above or below the license plates.

Wedding car fleets first appeared in Guangzhou in the late 1980s, if not earlier. At that time, car ownership was extremely rare, and few people had a driver's license. Most people rented taxis and vans driven by chauffeurs. Some high-end hotels offered to let newlyweds use the hotels' cars—without any "taxi" signs attached—to lead their wedding parade if the couple would hold their wedding banquet in the hotels' restaurants and the total bill exceeded a certain amount. According to some local interlocutors, in those days, having a Rolls-Royce from the White Swan Hotel in one's wedding car fleet was a spectacle. There were only two Rolls-Royces in the city. The White Swan Hotel—owned by a Hong Kong tycoon—had bought them in 1986

Figure 4. A wedding car with its license plate covered with greeting words, 2007.
Photo by the author

for Britain's Queen Elizabeth to visit Guangzhou. The purchase of the Rolls-Royces received a lot of special TV and newspaper coverage. As a result, in an era when most people knew little about most car brands, Rolls-Royce and its Spirit of Ecstasy figurine became familiar to many local residents.

In the new millennium, taxis are no longer used in wedding car parades in Guangzhou. I have seen parades consisting of only the BMW 7 series or Mini Coopers. Vans have been mostly replaced by seven-seater minivans, such as the Buick GL8 and Honda Odyssey; they usually serve as the caboose. The most frequently used wedding cars are midrange sedans, such as the Passat, Camry, and Reiz. Usually none of the cars belongs to the wedding couple or their families. Even if they have one, the couple would still have to borrow cars from relatives, friends, or colleagues to form a fleet. They try to borrow as luxurious a car as they can to be the main car of the fleet. Close friends not only offer their cars but also become drivers on the wedding day.

Like in the organized driving tours, all cars in a wedding fleet travel in single file and try to stay together even when traffic in the city is heavy. While on the road, the wedding cars flash their emergency lights, signaling that they form a group. Other vehicles usually will not jump the queue of a wedding fleet. Some interlocutors have told me that sometimes the wedding cars may even jump a red light in order to keep up with the fleet. Although wedding cars break many laws—having their license plates covered, jumping red lights, and not having the cameraman fasten his seat belt—I have been constantly reassured that the traffic police are generally more tolerant of wedding cars than of regular ones.

Over years of fieldwork, I have participated in a couple of weddings and a few semiorganized driving tours. I have noticed one thing that is very important for participants in these collective driving practices: to keep the formation of a fleet (*baochi duixing*). Participants try their best to drive as a group, and they expect other cars in the street to respect that. If other cars cut into their fleet, they get upset. I have witnessed on different occasions drivers who are usually gentle and polite begin to shout: "Can't they see that my lights are flashing? Can't they see there is a fleet? Everybody knows that!"[9] Sometimes they would become so impatient that they started to honk continuously to drive others out of their lane, even though honking was forbidden in the city. While I have not witnessed clashes between drivers who are and are not part of a fleet, newspapers have reported escalated confrontations when nonparticipatory drivers do not respect a fleet and its desire to maintain formation integrity.[10]

Collective driving practices exist in other countries. From Harley-Davidson fleets in the United States to kamikaze bikers in Japan (Sato 1991), images of those motorbike fleet riders are associated with working-class or youth subcultures and identity. They are seen as an expression of defiance toward middle-class values. In contrast, collective driving practices are very middle-class in urban China. Almost all of my interlocutors who are car owners have taken part in wedding car parades and semiorganized driving tours. Nonetheless, middle-class collective driving has something in common with a Harley-Davidson fleet: it is about group solidarity. On those collective driving occasions, the middle class feel a sense of togetherness: being with their own kind. This is an alone-together experience—driving in one's own car yet being connected to their peers. By driving together, they create a shared social space that is partitioned by their cars. Participants demand respect for the visible boundaries of this social space; cutting into the fleet of cars or interrupting the parade trespasses upon this shared space.

Parade with Cars: From the State to Status

Nevertheless, there is something more than group solidarity and command-ing respect at work when these middle-class drivers form part of a fleet and emphasize the need to "keep its formation intact." They expect respect for the physical formation but cannot tell why that is important for them, other than "we are together." Why did they insert themselves into our fleet? they wonder. Their concern about the disruption of the fleet is not about com-munication, because walkie-talkies, mobile phones, and the Internet allow them to drive separately yet stay in touch easily.

The captivation has to do with aesthetic experience. My interlocutors have often described these collective driving practices as "spectacular," "looking great," and "feeling special." The aesthetic aspect is also embedded in the above-mentioned discourse of convenience. The car's ability to enhance credibility and bring convenience to its middle-class drivers is not merely determined by the brands; to perform this function, the car should also have a certain look. This aesthetic experience is historical, which, to a good extent, has been con-figured by a series of state practices that are reinforced by global automakers.

Automobiles have been seen as the material embodiment of Western mo-dernity and technology ever since they began to appear in big Chinese cities in the early twentieth century (Dikötter 2006; Lee L. O. 1999; Lu H. 1999). During the Maoist years, passenger cars were in an intricate position in the highly politicized environment. While the state purposefully developed the auto industry, passenger cars were associated with the exploitative, corrupt-ing urban elites during the Republican era. Unlike in some other socialist countries where cars were supposedly accessible (but often unavailable) to or-dinary people (Siegelbaum 2008, 2011), cars in Maoist China were seen as part of the bourgeois lifestyle and were thus not suitable for private use. Until 1994, government agencies and state-owned enterprises owned approximately 80 percent of all passenger cars in the country.[11] Even in 2006, less than 30 percent of the 600,000 passenger cars produced domestically were sold to individual citizens.[12] Passenger cars were primarily used by party and gov-ernment officials for official purposes. Geremier R. Barmé vividly describes the Maoist-era car scene in China this way:

> Only the highest-level cadres in the party, army and state bureaucracy could travel by the new Chinese-made limousine, the Red Flag, for example. The

Soviet 'Gim' was reserved for ministers and provincial leaders, the 'Volga' was assigned to bureau chiefs and divisional commanders, and the Polish 'War-saw' was left for the common riff-raff, known derisively as 'cigarette, oil, sugar and bean' cadres. (2002, 180)

Up to the early 1990s, the main types of car on the road besides government cars were not for private use but taxis. Taxis had disappeared in other cities during the socialist period. Thanks to the Canton Fair, the state council granted Guangzhou the right to have taxis in 1956. The fleet served political leaders and foreign participants for the fair and later overseas Chinese in the early Reform period. Taxis were not as prestigious as cars that belonged to the government or SOEs. However, taking a taxi remained a rather expensive means of public transportation (Zhang Ju. 2016). For some senior Guangzhou residents who were born and raised during the Maoist years, "dik si," the Cantonese phonetic transliteration of "taxi," became the general term used to refer to any nongovernment passenger cars.

Government cars have maintained a similar appearance throughout the years: they are midsize to large, black sedans with plenty of legroom and a big trunk. The image of the official car has been exploited and reinforced by international carmakers that are eager to attract the up-and-coming middle class. In the mid- to late 2000s, when most major international car companies began to produce cars in China, some tailored the designs of certain models to the Chinese market. For compact cars, such as the Peugeot 206, the two-door European version was converted to a four-door model in China. Some models, such as the Honda Fit (Jazz in Europe) and Peugeot 307, added a trunk. Luxury brands, such as Audi, BMW, and Infinity, have adopted another strategy. They produce stretched (long-wheelbase) versions, adding ten to fifteen centimeters to the total length. The Audi A6, for example, was stretched to produce the Audi A6L.

Audi seems to have worked out the Chinese market particularly well, understanding that many people look toward the image of a stately government car as the standard of a "proper" car. A lot of customers in Auto-Fan and my middle-aged, middle-class interlocutors considered dark, midsize sedans to be more composed (*wenzhong*) and trustworthy (*zhide xinren*). Several of them have said that these features make a car look "proper." Audi seems to have successfully forged an image of being "officials' cars" (*guanche*); many local governments have used Audi as official cars, and the black, midrange Audi sedan has won the favor of many professionals, such as Lawyer Lu, Lawyer Qin, and Xiaowang. Such a preference is most visible among generations who grew up during the Maoist and early Reform years. It is also observable among younger people, particularly men, lawyers, and state employees.

In contrast, a compact car—according to many of my interlocutors—is suitable only as a second car in the family (more on this in chapter 2). Since 2010, the number of compact cars has increased noticeably, suggesting that the car market is perhaps becoming diversified.[13] Younger car owners, particularly young women, and people like Yuan Yi consider a black, four-door sedan "boring" and "lacking personality." Instead, they emphasize *gexinghua* (personalization) in their choices. Nevertheless, for seniors and middle-aged professionals, "a passenger car looks ugly without a butt [the trunk]." A certain stigma is often attached to small cars: if the compact car is a low-end brand, it means that the owner cannot afford a bigger car. If the compact car is a VW Beetle or a Mini Cooper, it may be perceived as a toy of the wealthy, a gift for a mistress, or the stamp of a self-indulgent woman.

Some interlocutors explained their preference as a concern of, again, practicality. They told me that the fact that the government liked to use this brand was an endorsement for its quality. Lawyer Lu's comment on his choice of Audi serves as a good example:

> Who would dare mess with the government? So for Audi to be the choice brand it has to live up to a certain standard. It will not dare to reduce any labor and material input [*tougongjianliao*]. Government officials are demanding; their cars must be safe and comfortable. The fact that the government is using it is the best advertisement and testament you can have in China.

Lu's comment hints at an uneasy, ambivalent relationship between the government, the market, and the individual that the middle class often experience. While the middle class embrace the market-oriented economy for work opportunities and the consequent abundance and availability of goods, they are skeptical of the morality of the market force.[14] They see the government as the necessary force to curb any immoral practices in the market, but they are often cynical about any claims that the government is the protector of the people.

This ambivalence is shown in many car-related practices. As such scholars as Agnieszka Joniak-Lüthi (2016, 139), Beth E. Notar (2017), and Osburg (2013, 124) have noted and documented, while the middle class do not like the transgressive driving practices of government officials or whoever drives a car with a government license plate, they also emulate, instead of resist, such practices by obtaining government license plates and breaking traffic rules or participating in drag racing or drifting. From this ambivalence, one may even make sense of why the middle class emphasize the need to "keep the formation of the fleet" in their collective driving practices. Among the Chinese, watching the military parade in front of Tiananmen Square on National Day has been a memory and experience shared since childhood. The format and formation of the parade are at the center of the public gaze, and they are difficult to ignore or forget: neatly organized troops marching with extreme discipline, every leg always raised to a precise height. Local governments and other authorities, such as schools and state-owned enterprises, mimic the national military parade and create their own parades in their events and celebrations. Participating in a parade is an integral part of one's experience from the time of one's schooling. Such an experience is refreshed and often reinforced by the heavy media coverage of the National Day military parade or of special occasions, such as the opening ceremony of the Beijing Olympics. Growing up with a parade culture contributes to the development of an appreciation of a particular form of beauty, an aesthetics that is built on the familiar image of the parade.

Along with the large-scale military or sport parades, official car fleets served as spectacles at a time when private car ownership was highly restricted, if not forbidden. Passengers in an official car fleet were likely to be important political leaders or foreign visitors. Police cars and motorcycles escorted the official car fleet through the main streets in big cities, making sure that all other vehicles would make way for the fleet. While ordinary citizens could only be spectators of these car fleets, either in the streets or through television or newspaper, they were familiar with the image of those authoritative car fleets.

I do not wish to suggest that the middle class's fascination with collective driving and the fleet's formation has originated from their experience with the military parade or official car fleets. After all, in the eyes of my interlocutors, they were just following "customary practices" in weddings or semiorganized tours. Nonetheless, they never gave a second thought to what entitled them to claim the space amid busy traffic. They just took it for granted. Moreover, they talked about organized driving tours or wedding car parades in a similar way as they talked about the military parade or the Beijing Olympics opening ceremony (particularly in contrast to the London one): it was not about the power manifested but the spectacular and thrilling formation and representation of the collective. In line with a political culture that puts emphasis on the collective over the individual, such aesthetic experience imbues middle-class sociality with a spatial dimension—claiming space as a collective. On another level, by using the forms and practices legitimized by a political culture, middle-class drivers in both organized tours and parades can do something that they would not or cannot do in their daily settings: they transgress legal boundaries, carve their own space, and demand respect without being punished. To a great extent, such collective driving practices provide a liminal stage of time and space, in which the drivers transcend their daily identities and obtain a sense of empowerment, and the very source of such a sense of empowerment lies in the familiar political performance of the state.

The emerging middle class provides momentum for the ever-rising car sales in contemporary China. Nonetheless, the middle class's desire to have a car should not be reduced to false consciousness induced by consumerism; nor should their discourse of convenience be seen as mere rhetorical camouflage for vanity. What having and driving a car means in everyday life is a historical experience. The car as an ultimate symbol of freedom and autonomy across class, gender, and racial boundaries in the United States is deeply embedded in the American hegemonic culture that glorifies mobility and individual achievements (Lutz 2014; Ortner 2003, 2006). Yet, as Notar (2012, 2017) argues, there is no inherent link between the car and freedom. In China, different social and political processes have shaped interlocking layers of meanings and practices of having and driving a car, through which not car prices, per se, but the car itself is made a class status symbol.

The car is a symbol of upward social mobility, a value that the middle class strongly identify themselves with. Growing up in a society in which individual car ownership was forbidden, having one's own car is a sign of success. The middle class read people's cars to determine how well-off other people are, and they know that they are under the same gaze. Although my interlocutors claimed that they did not participate in status competition, all of them considered it important that the brand names of their cars should be "recognizable."

Yet the car as a desirable object of class status is not determined merely by its economic affordability. On the one hand, the middle class acknowledged the effect of car brand names on status, but their attitude toward the luxury brands was ambiguous. They often joked about different kinds of high-end cars and their owners and blamed the nouveau riche for tainting the brands: Mercedes-Benz and BMW were both for affluent people, but the latter was often coupled with the arrogant, brutal, and irresponsible nouveau rich; and Mini Coopers and Beetles were for mistresses.[15] But many middle-class professionals admitted that BMW was their dream brand and Audi was evidence of engineering accomplishment. In distinguishing themselves from the nouveau riche who liked to flaunt wealth through their luxury cars, such as Maseratis or sports cars, the middle-class professionals emphasized that they bought or liked the reputed brands, such as Audi, because of work necessities or technologies. When sitting together and talking about which car to buy, these middle-class professionals (usually men) often had intense, if not competitive, discussion on engineering, economics, safety features, and aesthetic designs of various car models (of recognizable brands).

On the other hand, the status effect of the car is interwoven with the complex relationship between the past and the present. The middle class's desire for automobility is related to their earlier memory of physical immobility due to work-home spatial patterns, the lack of infrastructural facilities, and their understanding of social immobility due to institutional constraints under the political economy in the socialist and early Reform period. The status effect of the car is also embedded in the specific form of sensibility shaped by official practices. Passenger cars used to be prestigious items for high-end officials and car fleets associated with important political events. Various forms of parade have been and remain a means of demonstrating authority and a structure that configures individuals' aesthetic experience.

With such sensibility, the car has become the material medium for shared practices and imagination through which sociality and solidarity among the middle class are built. Those who drive around with friends for leisure and fun may not intend to flaunt their success in front of their friends, but many of those who sit in the car feel that peer pressure. Over lunch, dinner, or weekend outings with friends, the car owners may ask those who do not own cars when they will get a car or why they have not bought a car. People like Dong Mei were very aware which of their friends or colleagues had purchased a car and what models they were. What they feel is not just anxiety but also desire, a desire to live the same way as their friends and peers. The car is thus the vehicle to identify people of their own kind, people who share a lifestyle with distinctive patterns of work-home relationship, quotidian rhythm, and sociality.

This newly obtained mobility through and represented by the car undeniably has brought a sense of freedom to the middle class. However, this sense of freedom has little to do with freedom and autonomy as democratic values. Instead, the sense of liberation resembles that brought by refrigerators and washing machines: these technological inventions allow them to juggle different needs and priorities of work, family, and other social activities without intentionally challenging the existing hierarchy and political constraints in society (Boyer and Boswell-Penc 2010; Cockburn and Ormrod 1993; Cowan 1976).

The car connects space, time, and people. The old days were gone, yet previous life experiences, the lingering images, and the continuous grand political rituals have lasting influence in contemporary practices. As the middle class enjoys the sense of control and mobility enabled by cars, they are working to reconstitute the sociality that is deeply entrenched in the changing built environment, social norms, and political culture. Yet, as they continue to use the political symbols and performances in their leisure activities, their susceptibility to the authority of the state and the power of the political rituals has been continuously reproduced.

Chapter 2

FAMILY CARS, FILIAL CONSUMER-CITIZENS

Becoming Properly Middle Class

On a late Friday afternoon in the spring of 2007, I went from the city of Guangzhou to neighboring Foshan, roughly an hour's drive away, for dinner with Xiaofen and Mingli (see her story in the introduction), both of whom were midlevel civil servants. Mingli arrived more than an hour late, completely exhausted. As she apologized for having been held up by heavy traffic, she joked, "We should have met in Guangzhou for dinner tonight!" In fact, she had just driven back from Guangzhou. Her aunt, who lived in Guangzhou, had seen an advertisement for a medicine in the newspaper and asked Mingli, who lived and worked in Foshan, to get the medicine for her, so Mingli took half a day off work, drove from Foshan to Guangzhou, found the pharmacy, delivered the medicine to her aunt in Guangzhou, and drove back to meet me for dinner in Foshan. For all that, she spent four hours on the road in total. When I asked, "Why couldn't she buy it herself? She lives in Guangzhou. It's close and convenient," Mingli answered, "No, she said she didn't know how to get to the pharmacy." I said, "Well, she could have taken a taxi, given the address of the pharmacy to the driver, and the taxi driver would have taken her there. You're not a local person, and you don't know the streets in Guangzhou." Mingli replied, "She expected me to do it. I just had to do it."

Continuing from the previous chapter on the car and middle-class sociality, this chapter continues to problematize the relationship between the car and individual mobility by looking into the relationship between individual subject, family, and the making of the middle class. The rise of China's middle class has intrigued many scholars. As they endeavor to map its social configuration, their empirical frameworks are often oriented toward an individual-centered approach. For those who use quantitative methods, an individual-centered approach allows researchers to quantify and rank an individual's social standing and, furthermore, to measure the size of the middle-class population (see the introduction). For those who provide ethnographic studies, although ethnographic accounts mention the family and multigenerational cohabitation (for example, Tomba 2004), the focus is less on family relationships and more on the reverberations of the privatization of housing on self-making (Zhang L. 2010) and community building (Tomba 2014). This orientation echoes the widely circulated diagnosis, proposed by the anthropologist Yunxiang Yan, that the Chinese society is becoming individualistic, given the expressivity of emotions and desires and increasingly self-centered morality, at the expense of traditional family values (2003, 2009, 2011, 2013; also see Wang and Nehring 2014). To some degree, Yan's view resonates with a popular sentiment that laments the loss of filial piety in society when, as some census-based studies show, the nuclear family is now the main form of family in urban China (Ma et al. 2011; Wang Y. 2006).

Thus China seems to be moving along a path depicted by Anthony Giddens (1992) and William Josiah Goode (1963) in their classic theorization of modernization. Their conceptualization of individualization, romantic love and pure relationships, and the nuclear family as products of industrialization and urbanization, however, has been critically reexamined by scholars from different disciplines. On the one hand, the growth of the nuclear family may have historical roots in Western contexts. Historians point out that family size was relatively small, and multiple-generation cohabitation was not the norm in preindustrial France and England (Thornton 2001). On the other hand, using China as an example, scholars provide a complicated picture of family practices. Both quantitative studies and case studies have indicated and demonstrated the resilience of family values and multigenerational family structures during rapid industrialization and urbanization (Evans 2010; Hu and Scott 2014; Huang P. C. 2011; Kipnis 2016; Ma et al. 2011; Whyte 2003; Zhang W. 2009; Zhang and Sun 2014). Such periods are characterized not by a breakdown of family and community but by a reconfiguration of intimate life through the nexus of forces that have shaped postsocialist China's own project of modernity (Donner and Santos 2016; Santos 2016, forthcoming; Santos and Harrell 2017). Current studies tend to focus on rural areas, periurban spaces, and secondary cities with socially and economically disadvantaged populations. I join this scholarship to investigate a rarely explored sector: the middle class in a metropolis.

I see the family as a critical institution, an emotional realm, and a field of practices that shape middle-class subjectivities and lifestyles. Scholars have shown the salient role of the family as part of the sociocultural field for class production and reproduction in European contexts.[1] Historians have demonstrated that it was in the bourgeois domestic sphere that gender relationships and morality were contested, negotiated, and reproduced, a process that allowed class distinction to be articulated in industrial Europe (see, for example, Frevert 1990; Hausen 1981; Hull 1996; Kuper 2009). Pierre Bourdieu's (1984) seminal work on class distinction in French society highlights the family as a major institution through which cultural, social, and economic capitals are fostered, converted, and reproduced.

What distinguishes China from the Western contexts is that the family in China is multigenerational. China's birth control policies have greatly contributed to the prevalent family form of two sets of grandparents, parents, and, in most cases until very recently, a single child. This form is more common in urban areas than in the countryside (Fong 2004; Santos 2016) and more among the salaried middle class than elite men, who may have mistresses, multiple households, and multiple children (Osburg 2013).[2]

The focus on the family is not to deny the phenomenon of individualization but rather to emphasize that it is merely a part of the complex processes in China's transformation. "Being middle class" is often an individual's identity in daily life, yet this is an individual "as part of a field of relations and of being open to paths and modes for the constitution of the self" (N. Z. Davis 1986, 63). This chapter provides only one, but nonetheless important, piece of this emergent sociocultural mosaic by exploring a mutually constructive process of a middle-class lifestyle and the making of the extended family, through the lens of an increasingly auto-oriented way of living.

To do so, I will first outline how the investment of multiple generations makes a car-oriented lifestyle possible. Yet the family is more than a corporate unit that provides financial resources. In the next part, I will elaborate on the life experiences of different generations and intergenerational relationships in middle-class families as configured by the changing political environment, birth control policies, and parenting practices. The significance of the family as an emotional and ethical space is built into middle-class professionals' car purchases and driving practices, which will be examined next. I do not see filial piety as an abstract Confucian value; nor do I see it as a mere tradition or part of the "Chinese" culture. Instead, I emphasize the translation of a moral principle into ethical practices in mundane decisions by demonstrating how urban professionals juggled individual preferences with family needs. Meanwhile, by referring to urban professionals as filial consumer-citizens, I highlight, instead of the rights and duties associated with citizenship, the complex relationship, mediated through material goods, that they have with the government. As the car and related forms of mobility enable the middle class to imagine, redefine, and practice domestic life in a manner they deem proper, their conduct resonates with the government's agenda that seeks to reassert traditional values, not only to deal with an aging population but also to establish its soft power on the global stage. The relationship between the government, the urban middle class, and the automotive regime is multilayered, dynamic, and sometimes unintentional but nonetheless symbiotic.

The Car, Life Stages, and Family Economy

Having a family car is quite a new concept in China. In Guangzhou there were less than three private cars per hundred urban households in 2003, when private car consumption had just taken off. The number increased tenfold within a decade, reaching thirty-two in 2012, and has since continued to grow.[3] The Chinese auto market favors bigger cars, typically the so-called three-box (*san xiang*) sedans. While ultracompact cars, such as the Smart and Mini Cooper, have begun to catch people's attention in recent years, they are considered conspicuous consumption items in the eyes of middle-class car owners (see also chapter 1). Such compact cars as the Volkswagen Polo are not popular. Some compact car models, including Honda's Fit and Peugeot's

307, were redesigned into three-box sedans so that they would look bigger than the original two-box versions. The remark of a customer in the dealership Auto-Fan about the Peugeot 206, a compact hatchback, was representative of many others among my interlocutors: "A small hatchback can only be a second car. It's practical to drive such a car when I go out only with my wife and daughter. For more people, one needs a bigger car." He settled on a Peugeot 307 because "the rear seat has more room for [his] parents."

This comment alludes to the prominence of the family in the car-related lifestyle. Such a lifestyle involves not just the car but also a set of values and practices that make up a "proper" life trajectory marked by various material acquisitions. An apartment is considered a necessity, whereas a car remains an add-on that improves the quality of life. Over the years of my fieldwork in Guangzhou, some young interlocutors, mostly college students, told me they would consider getting a car and living in a rented apartment. But rarely do people buy a car but still live in a rented apartment.[4]

For many urban families and individuals, regardless of their class status, the preferred sequence of events begins with first getting married and buying an apartment as newlyweds.[5] If they cannot afford a car upon marriage, the next best time to get a car is with the arrival of a child. The general priority placed on apartment ownership and the cash economy impose great financial pressure on middle-class professionals who seek a lifestyle with a car. For middle-class young people whose parents live in the same city, marriage is the time when they move out of their parents' apartments and form their own families. For those coming from other parts of the country, the decision to get married often entails a transition from renting to owning an apartment.

Due to the marketization of housing that started in the late 1990s and the skyrocketing of real-estate prices since the mid-2000s, many young couples need their parents' financial support to purchase an apartment and then a car. Frequently, the parents give or lend the young couple money for the down payment, and the couple then takes care of the mortgage payments on their own.[6] In some cases, parents lease out their own apartment they had obtained through the socialist housing system and move in with their children in the often better-equipped, new apartment, usually in a gated community. The rent from the old apartment often goes toward the daily expenses of the multigenerational family in the new apartment. On several occasions, young couples mentioned that they paid for the apartment themselves, and the parents gave them a car as a wedding gift. In several interviewees' stories about their marriage, the groom's family contributed to the down payment on the apartment, and the bride's family purchased the car. But I found more often that the young couple would buy the car out of their own funds with the arrival of their child. Although bank loans were available, most people still paid cash for their cars. This indicates that many couples would save up for some time for a car or borrow money from their parents.

Despite China's rapid economic growth, a car remains an expensive item for many urban families. In Guangzhou, one of the wealthiest cities in the country, the per capita monthly disposable income was RMB 1,872 (roughly $242), which translates to RMB 22,464 ($2,904) annually, in 2007. In the same year, popular passenger cars ranged between RMB 80,000 and RMB 200,000, four to ten times the per capita annual disposable income. Admittedly, the price range of popular car models has been relatively stable, while the official average income has been consistently on the rise in recently years. But even when the per capita annual disposable income reached RMB 42,049 (roughly $6,570) in 2013, car prices remained several times an individual's average annual income.

Moreover, maintaining a car is costly. The monthly expenses for any midsize sedan have been above the average disposable income. A local TV car show, which targeted aspiring car owners, once provided a calculation of the routine expenses for select car models (see table 5), and the numbers matched those from my interviews.

Dong Fang and his wife, both midlevel managers in state-owned banks in their midthirties in 2007, had a household income substantially above the city's average. With easy access to bank loans, they purchased an apartment, without their parents' involvement, in a gated community a bit away from the old city center. Dong got his driver's license when he was in college. He ordered a Camry, his second car, when the first batch of Toyota cars rolled off the assembly line in Guangzhou in 2006. It cost more than RMB 200,000, and he had to wait four months to see his car after he had paid for it. He used inner-city highways to travel to work every day. When asked the monthly cost of his car in 2006, Dong smiled and said, "Roughly RMB 1,600 altogether, including gas, insurance, and annual fees. I have my own parking space and got a discount for insurance because I'm an experienced driver. But that doesn't include tickets from the police. You know how easy it is to get a ticket nowadays. Fines are a big revenue for the police. If my parents knew about the number, they wouldn't let me keep the car."

Table 5. Routine expenses of operating a car in Guangzhou in 2007

	VW Polo	GM Lecheng	Peugeot 206	VW Passat	GM Junyue	Ford Mondeo	Honda Accord
Insurance	2,800	2,100	2,200	4,430	4,500	4,360	4,220
Annual fees for streets and bridges	2,400	2,400	2,400	3,000	3,000	3,000	3,000
Parking fees	2,400	2,400	2,400	2,400	2,400	2,400	2,400
Gas	4,800	4,800	6,000	14,500	17,000	16,000	15,500
Car maintenance	2,000	1,000	6,000	6,400	7,600	8,100	7,800
Other expenses	2,000	800	750	1,600	1,600	1,600	1,600
Total annual expenses	16,400	13,500	19,750	32,330	36,100	35,460	34,520
Monthly cost	1,366.7	1,125.0	1,645.8	2,694.2	3,008.3	2,955.0	2,876.7

Source: "Auto Power" *(che dongli)* on the Guangdong Sports Channel, April 24, 2007. Units: RMB, roughly $1.00 to RMB 7.75.

In recent years, gasoline prices and, particularly, parking have pushed the expense of keeping a car to a new high. Due to the limited space available for parking in a densely populated city, the price of a parking space rapidly increased with the feverish consumption of cars (more on parking in chapter 6). Many car owners have to rent parking spaces in public parking lots or from private owners. Some informants reported that, in 2013, the monthly rent plus management fees for a parking space summed to more than RMB 1,000, and the total monthly costs for a car rose to RMB 5,000 (roughly $800) in 2013. For many families, it was the daily cost of automobile ownership that made them hesitate to buy a car. As they often told me, "a car is easy to buy but difficult to keep" *(maiche rongyi yangche nan)*.

Undeniably, using average income as a reference misses the income disparities and the yawning social gap in urban areas, but undoubtedly there was an uneasiness among the salaried middle class who lead a car-related life. The small survey of my interlocutors indicates that, in 2013, civil servants, judges, and schoolteachers and university faculty in their thirties typically made RMB 5,000 to RMB 10,000 (after tax, but not including benefits or bonus) per month. Professionals working for private companies or law firms often earn even more. Nevertheless, it still requires careful calculations to fit a car into a family's budget. For example, both Shao Jing and his wife are engineers in big corporations and live with Shao's parents in a gated community. Their apartment's loan payments are about RMB 9,000 a month, and their car costs another RMB 5,000. Together, these two items alone just about use up all of Shao's monthly income. Another interlocutor, Cecilia, a lawyer for the past ten years, told me, "Easily I spend RMB 10,000 every month, for the car, food, my daughter's kindergarten, her lessons, and daily necessities. I don't have a mortgage anymore. But the 10,000 covers just the basics—it doesn't include going out for a nice dinner once in a while and clothes."

A middle-class lifestyle with a car in fact typifies a middle-class family lifestyle. Pulling together resources from two generations has made possible the rapid growth of car consumption even when average per capita income remains relatively low in cities where housing and car-related expenses are high. Nonetheless, the family as a corporate entity that seeks to maximize its financial returns, as Myron Cohen (1992) argues, is just one aspect of the story. Emotions and ethical considerations are as important as the material base that holds the family together.

The Intergenerational Bond: Care and Emotions

In his influential ethnography on private life in northern China, Yunxiang Yan (2003) makes two related observations about the rise of the individual as a result of decollectivization in rural communities: first, emotional expressivity was increasingly seen in domestic life, and second, filial piety was in crisis. Yan further develops the second observation into an argument of individualization of society in his later work. He emphasizes the relentless sense of entitlement to their parents' wealth among the younger generation. Instead of "sacrific[ing] one's time, labor, wealth, and even life to make parents happy," the younger generation see that "their happiness in life makes their parents happy and thus their pursuit of pleasure and comfort in life should be viewed as their way of fulfilling the duty of filial piety" (2011, 37). He argues that the emerging new morality of individualization, which centers on the pursuit of personal interests, has led to the "new game of intergenerational reciprocity based on the new moral reckoning of balanced exchange rather than on the logic of filial piety" (2013, 279). Intriguingly, a decade of observation seems to have led Yan to suggest that "the family [is] primarily . . . an economic entity composed of rational, self-interested members" (2003, 3), which was the corporate model that he built upon and critiqued in his 2003 ethnography.

My analysis builds upon and critiques Yan's propositions. I elaborate on the less-developed emotional aspect in Yan's earlier writing, showing how family ethics are reconstituted through contestation and negotiation among middle-class professionals confronted with a new material world in which many consumer choices had previously been unavailable. The family is a multilayered entity that is rich in emotional and material exchanges, and the reconstitution of family ethics is essential in the making of middle-class subjectivities.

Luigi Tomba (2004) documents how state projects have given rise to middle-class professionals like Mingli and her peers or the so-called "fourth generation of those who got rich first." Born between the late 1960s and early 1980s, these middle-class professionals in my research tend to have experienced more upward social mobility than their parents' generation and the generations that follow theirs. The parents of the majority of my interlocutors had stable jobs and medical and child care through their work units during their adolescent and early adult lives.[7] Family income was low but was relatively equal across society. My interlocutors benefited from low-cost education up to the college level. Despite their working-class or lower-rank cadre family backgrounds, they were able to land professional jobs (more on middle-class life trajectories in chapters 3 and 4). Their spouses are usually professionals as well, with similar educational and family backgrounds (see also Li Y. 2008).

Cecilia, mentioned earlier, is an illustrative case. She came from a northern city where her parents had been state employees before retirement. Cecilia went to university in Guangzhou in the late 1990s and worked in a midsized law firm from graduation. She met her future husband at work and settled down in the city. They bought their first apartment when they planned to get married, with their parents' help for the down payment, which they paid back in a couple of years. Seeing the potential in the real-estate market, the couple invested in another apartment soon thereafter, again with the parents' support. When Cecilia's daughter was one year old, the couple bought their first car. Her parents left their familiar home city and came to Guangzhou to help Cecilia take care of the child. In terms of income, Cecilia may be better off than her college friends who have become civil servants, judges, and professors. Nevertheless, they have more or less followed the same path, securing an apartment when they got married and obtaining a car right before or soon after their children were born; and their parents typically helped with childcare and, often, their housing down payment.

The multigenerational feature of middle-class families not only builds upon economic ties but also care and emotion. Emotions are structured feelings (Lutz and Abu-Lughod 1990), and care is a dynamic movement that requires constant adjustment and engagement (Mol 2008). The family as a sentimental and ethical space is fostered by daily exchanges in the middle-class domestic sphere, which is shaped by and in turn is shaping an array of institutional and discursive practices in the changing larger environment.

In my research, the parents' generation grew up in a volatile political era that challenged patriarchy and so-called feudal thinking, including filial piety, and demanded each individual's loyalty to the nation-state. At high school age many were sent by the state to the countryside for "reeducation" during the Cultural Revolution and would only return to the city and get married in the late 1970s and early 1980s.[8] In view of the limited supply of housing combined with the possibility of people inheriting their parents' jobs, the work-unit system under the planned economy "created demographic and material conditions conducive to large, multi-generational households with extensive economic and social ties to nearby kin" (Davis and Harrell 1993, 1). Relationships between this generation and their parents were close but not as expressively emotional as their relationships with their own children.

These middle-class professionals came of age in an era when the state shifted its priority from class struggle to economic development. Their family lives were more routinized and less politically dramatic, thanks to the normalization of work and education. This was also the time when state reproduction policies were launched, revised, and solidified (Greenhalgh 2008). Many of my interlocutors have siblings, usually just one; and in general, they have fewer siblings than their parents. Until they reached college, they typically stayed home. Many of them were very close to their parents; mother-daughter relationships were often particularly strong.[9]

Yunxiang Yan (2003) considered parents' efforts to strengthen the emotional bond as a strategy to build a reciprocal relationship, with the long-term goal of having the children take care of their parents in their old age. This may be true, but it is only partial, because the subjective world and mundane life in the parent-child relationship are multifaceted (Zhang and Sun 2014). As family stories unfolded in our dialogues, I learned that many of my interlocutors' parents were in fact in a relatively independent financial situation. Many were healthy and were enjoying life after their children got married and moved out. These parents either retired at the usual age of retirement or were forced to retire at an earlier age because the SOEs they worked for had gone bankrupt or wanted senior employees to give their places to younger ones as part of the state's institutional reform (*jigou gaige*). But even when forced to retire, they were still entitled to a pension and medical care. Depending on their previous jobs, the pensions may have been below the local average (e.g., a retired SOE worker) or higher than the average (e.g., a former government employee); they also had partial or full medical coverage. Many of them had an apartment thanks to the socialist welfare system. Usually, the combined pensions allowed the parents to have a decent life in retirement. While they may have wanted to be close to their children, these parents may not have been keen on living in Guangzhou because of the unintelligible local language, food customs, climate, and lack of social network. But in the eyes of the urban professionals in my study, it would be best if the parents were to live with them since they could keep an eye on the parents' health and ensure that they had a materially comfortable life.

When these professionals got married and had children in the late 1990s and the 2000s, it had been more than twenty years since China's birth control policies that allowed only one child in urban areas were formalized (Greenhalgh 2008). If these birth control policies reduced the time women spent in reproduction labor, they did not quite empower women to decide whether and how to become mothers on their own terms. As several interlocutors and close friends told me, because they could only have one child, they felt that they had to have that only child, and they had to do everything "right" for the child. From pregnancy to child-rearing, every stage was carefully prepared, carried out, and monitored by these young middle-class couples who pored over popular books on eugenics and child education. Emotion is at the center of a disciplining discourse on parenting. An intense childbearing and child-rearing culture has developed among China's urban families (Fong 2004; Kuan 2015). This culture comes with a high level of anxiety, particularly among middle-class mothers.

The arrival of a grandchild is a time when the concerns of both generations converge. The senior generation felt they needed to offer help. As
some told me,

> Mothers love and care about [*xinteng*] their own daughters. Giving birth is so
> stressful. Who's going to take care of the new mother? The new mother barely
> knows how to take care of herself. Now she even has to take care of her own
> baby!

Young couples, particularly the mothers, felt they needed their parents
around. Day care is no longer as widely available nowadays as in their parents' times. Having a part-time helper is common.[10] But the young couples
trusted their own parents to watch over the apartment when they were at
work. Moreover, they could take care of their parents, who in turn would
take care of them and their children.[11] Money was often a minor concern.
Often, living with their parents was neither cheaper nor more convenient
than hiring a nanny. Care and emotional exchange are as important as
economic calculations in daily life in the multigenerational middle-class
families.

The size of the middle-class family thus goes through cycles. It splits into
nuclear families at the time of marriage and merges again with the coming
of the new generation. Among the urban professionals I studied, parents
moved in with their children, particularly when the parents were nonlocal
residents. For local families, the young couple might move back to their
parents' home, which, nowadays, increasingly more commonly refers to the
home that belongs to the wife's parents. If they could afford it, the young
couple might live in a separate apartment but in the same building or
gated community where the parents lived. If the young couple chose not to
move back formally, they would still spend a significant amount of time
in their parents' place, where their child could be taken care of during
the day. Cohabitation or not, family life for urban professionals is often
multigenerational.

The moment of middle-class family expansion was when the purchase of
a car became most feasible, even though the car might not be exclusively for
family use. Many interlocutors acknowledged that it would be cheaper to take
public transportation than to keep a car for daily life. But buying a car was
not so much the result of an economic calculation as a matter of care and

convenience (also see chapter 1). Public transportation seemed dangerous and inconvenient for pregnant women, young mothers holding a baby, and frail parents. The often stale air inside public transport was full of germs, which was considered particularly harmful to pregnant women and babies. Buses and subways were often overcrowded and were not designed with specific facilities for baby strollers or for seniors. Anecdotes circulated among middle-class couples telling of comminuted fractures and other injuries caused by an indifferent bus driver's abrupt braking and sudden acceleration.[12] Like car ideologies in Western contexts that associate cars with autonomy and masculinity (Lutz and Fernandez 2010), this discourse of safety is neither about the technical features, medical theories, or a statistical comparison of mortality rates between using public transportation and driving one's own car; nor does it exclude other considerations, such as status. Rather, the prominence of this particular discourse on safety reflects the anxiety and care that are embedded in the relationships within a close-knit family and in new parenting practices.

According to my observations in the dealership during my internship, these professionals were meticulous about the features of a car that catered to the family, particularly the parents. There had to be enough legroom in the back seat so that passengers would not have to curl up their legs, since the parents' joints would no longer be flexible. The seats should not be too low so that parents would not have difficulty getting in, sitting down, or getting out of the car. The young professionals would drive their children to kindergarten or school every day before they go to work. They would drive their parents to see the doctor and run errands for the parents. On weekends and holidays, they would drive the whole family to an outing at the park or to go dining or shopping.

Driving for the Family, Negotiating Filial Piety

China's rapidly growing economy has provided middle-class families with the kind of material life that they or their parents had not been exposed to in earlier decades. Middle-class professionals now have more authority than their parents used to on many familial issues, not just because they are the financial pillars in the households. The new middle-class lifestyles, including such things as having a family car, require skills and knowledge that the parents' generation lacked. This reshapes the intricate power play between the older generation and the younger. Filial piety no longer comes in the form of categorical authority from the elder and obedience from the younger half of the relationship. Yet the moral power of filial piety and family values remain so strong that few people would dare to defy it. To middle-class professionals, showing respect to their parents and taking care of and being responsible for the family are ethical essentials, but how to show that respect and care "involves the exercise of practical judgment about the 'best good' within the particularities of circumstances" (Mattingly 2012, 170; see also Das 2010; Lambek 2010). What complicates family ethical practices is the materiality of the new political economy.

This is another one of Mingli's stories: Once her paternal uncle from a small town in northern China came to Guangzhou for sightseeing and to visit family members. He proposed to meet Mingli and her mother in Shunde. Her uncle was not particularly fragile and could travel by himself. Mingli had to work that day. She first apologized to her uncle for not being able to pick him up and then provided detailed information on how to find his way on public transportation. Had Mingli's uncle followed her instructions, he would have arrived in about one hour at their meeting spot. On the day of his visit, when Mingli was busy with work, she suddenly got a call from her mother, asking her to look for her uncle in Guangzhou. He had tried to take a cheaper route that involved more bus transfers in order to save money. However, neither did he have much experience navigating in a giant city nor could he speak the local language, Cantonese. He got lost but managed to call Mingli's mother. Mingli's mother immediately called Mingli and asked her to deal with it. Angry and frustrated, Mingli left her office and drove to Guangzhou. After listening to the poor description of where he was, she asked her uncle to stay put, and she told him that she would come to pick him up. Four hours or so later, Mingli arrived home with her uncle, completely exhausted. After she told me the story, I asked her, "Why didn't you just ask him to take a taxi and you pay for it upon arrival?" Mingli shook her head and simply said, "No, I couldn't do that."

Later I related Mingli's story to our common friend Xiaofen. Xiaofen said, "No way. Had she told him so, her family would have reprimanded her. It's not about money or time. They just think that Mingli has an obligation to chauffeur her uncle. If not, she's not being filial [*buxiao*]." Putting herself out and spending time locating her uncle was an act for Mingli to demonstrate filial piety. Had she simply paid for his taxi, her behavior would be seen as having disrespected her uncle because it would appear that she looked at him as being poor and/or she wanted to buy her way out of a filial obligation. The same logic also led Mingli to drive to Guangzhou and buy medicine for her aunt who lived in Guangzhou, as mentioned in the beginning of this chapter.

When I told Mingli's story to Cecilia, the lawyer mentioned earlier, Cecilia's response was more nuanced:

> Everyone may have a different opinion about filial piety. [Mingli] thought she had to drive around as a member of her family had asked, and that was filial piety. But I don't necessarily think so. If I were in her shoes, I might have gone if I had nothing to do. But I was busy all the time. I had to work. Usually even when I'm off work, I have to take care of my family. I don't drive my parents around all the time. It's impossible. I have to go to court or to meet my clients. They have to wait if I'm not immediately available. It's much more convenient for all of us that they take the subway or a taxi. It's not about filial piety. It's just being practical.

The difference between Mingli and Cecilia actually lies not within their general attitude toward filial piety. In fact, Mingli and Cecilia are similar in many ways. Like other interlocutors, both Mingli and Cecilia considered filial piety to be an unquestionable moral principle. They both came from cities in northern China. Both were successful career women, both were married, and both had their only child around the same time. Neither they nor their family spoke Cantonese. Mingli had a sister and Cecilia had a brother, but the siblings lived in their hometowns. Mingli's parents liked to stay with Mingli more than with her sister. Cecilia's parents also preferred to stay with Cecilia. The reasons were also the same: their parents were pleased and proud of their daughters who had been taking good care of them. Thus, despite their different reactions, Cecilia was no less filial than Mingli. The intricate differences were found in the ways they translated a general moral principle into mundane ethical decisions. In the new material world, how to act so as to be a filial family member requires continuous, day-to-day, case-by-case consideration and negotiation.

As seen in Mingli's case, contestation and compromises abound when it comes to cars and daily driving. Car buyers are typically the middle generation of the extended, middle-class family. Although their decisions to buy a car tend to meet their own needs first, other family needs are often prioritized very high in their decision on what kind of car to purchase. When I interviewed him in 2009, Mr. Tian was planning to purchase a car for his family but was fighting with his wife over which car to get. She insisted on buying a seven-seat minivan because only a big car could carry everyone in the family, including the couple, their son, and all four grandparents at the same time. Mr. Tian had been a driver for many years. He did a careful calculation on how much more a minivan would cost over a sedan. He was strongly opposed to buying a minivan: "How often do we need to drive the whole family? Only during major holidays like Lunar New Year. Most of the time I drive alone." Tian's wife, however, disagreed, pointing out that if they had a big car, they would go out together more often, such as trying restaurants in the suburbs or going on road trips together. With the couple failing to agree, the plan to purchase a car was put on hold.

In another story, an engineer, Xiaohe, was looking around for a compact car at Auto-Fan in 2006. Xiaohe had once studied in London for a year in his early thirties. His preference for a small car was partly due to his living and travel experiences in Europe, where small cars were ubiquitous. When I showed him different models at the dealership, he explained to me his preference: "I have several older sisters. All of them have cars, from family-sized cars to multipurpose vehicles, so I don't have to think about whether the car could fit my parents or not. I want a car for myself. I like a small hatchback." He preferred the compact Peugeot 206 but did not make up his mind. When I met him again in 2011, Xiaohe indeed had bought a hatchback, but a larger one that was spacious enough to hold his family, including his wife, a child on the way, and their parents. His preference for individual freedom eventually yielded to familial concerns after years of negotiations and debates. Xiaohe's case is not unique. When I interviewed young professionals who were still single back in 2007, many had said that they wanted a car for themselves and wanted to experience the feeling of freedom away from routines and constraints. Therefore, technical features in relation to the overall driving experience were important. When they settled down with their extended families after several years, interior space and comfort became major concerns. For Xiaohe, the car dream had come true but had entailed a compromise between personal desires and family needs.

Once a family owns a car, driving becomes an option for long-distance family trips. The Chinese Lunar New Year holiday is notorious for being a difficult time to get a train ticket, since trains are extremely overloaded, and now the difficulty has even extended to air travel. Thanks to the much improved highway system in recent years, some middle-class families have started to drive to their native place for this important family holiday. They say that buying gas is cheaper than buying train tickets, and they can avoid the stress of having to fight for a seat on the train or airplane. That said, in their stories, their car trips have been stressful, expensive, and often unpleasant. The families would be on the road early in the morning in order to beat the traffic. The high prices of gas aside, gas stations are sometimes few and far between, obliging the driver to carefully budget their fuel and monitor the tank. Service areas along the highway are usually poorly equipped, and conditions are worse as one travels inland: restaurants are expensive but offer suspicious-looking food, and toilet facilities are far from the standard these middle-class families are used to in their gated communities and high-rise offices. Because tolls were a good source of revenue for local governments, my informants often had to pass numerous tollbooths and paid a handsome amount before they arrived after a drive of six or seven hours. At their native home they continued to drive around, shopping, going out to eat, or sightseeing, because most of their relatives or friends did not have a car. After several days of intense socializing with families and old friends, they drove back to Guangzhou, where they had to return work the next day.

Undoubtedly, the rising urban middle class is at the front line of consciously accepting the idea of and actively practicing self-governance (Hoffman 2010; Zhang and Ong 2008). Yet the relationship between individual autonomy and family values is not all or nothing. As Saba Mahmood eloquently argues, ethics is less about social norms or values and more about "practices, techniques, and discourses through which a subject transforms herself in order to achieve a particular state of being, happiness, or truth" (2005, 28). The real issue is how to translate filial piety as an abstract moral principle into quotidian practices that engage with a variety of choices that new, material life has provided and a series of constraints that China's political economy and birth control policy have set. For middle-class families, the intergenerational bond is not built simply or primarily upon strategic concerns but upon intense everyday interactions through demonstrating love and practicing care.

Reestablishing Family Values as a Governing Strategy

On July 1, 2013, the newly revised Law on the Protection of the Rights and Interests of the Elderly (*laorenren quanyi baozhang fa*) took effect. Just like its earlier version, the law acknowledges the need to deal with an aging society from a long-term strategic perspective. While it encourages social support for senior citizens, the law reinstates the centrality of the family and the need for filial piety. Individuals and their spouses are obliged to take care of their parents in various ways. The revised law has one new stipulation: those who live apart from their parents should visit or greet the elderly regularly. Although the law does not specify punishment for violations, courts started to receive cases in which parents sued their children and asked for regular visits.

The new stipulation provoked controversy in newspapers, Weibo (the Chinese version of Twitter), and other forms of mass media. Some considered it a good move of the government to provide legal support for the elderly who lack attention from their children. However, many also complained that it was not that they did not want to go home and visit their parents, but pressure from work prevented them from doing so. In addition, it was easy to say, "Go visit your parents," but who was to pay for the trips?

To some extent, the state-orchestrated campaign for the revival of filial piety and other Confucian virtues bears ironic similarities to the attack on filial piety in the "antifeudalism" political movement during the Maoist period: both can be seen as an institutional and ideological reformation to establish and sustain the legitimacy of the nation-state. China's quest for modernity since the early twentieth century and its socialist revolution required turning individuals into subjects of the nation-state (Glosser 2003). Patriarchy and the family system, in which filial piety was both a moral and legal principle, came under heavy attack. Yet, as mentioned before, the socialist transformation had contradictory effects in that it simultaneously weakened patriarchy and reproduced close family ties (Davis and Harrell 1993; Whyte 2005). Immobility intentionally imposed by the state through the household registration system and the centrally planned economy enabled specific practices of filial piety, as observed by Yan (2003), to continue in the socialist period.

The postsocialist state pushed an agenda of individualization, relinquishing its previous promise to take care of its citizens' basic needs in exchange for their loyalty and substituting its socialist ideology with the market logic of choice and survival of the fittest. Market-oriented reforms turned individuals into mobile labor subjected to the global chain of production and consumption. The younger generation gravitated toward the big cities in the east and the south due to the imbalanced distribution of job opportunities. Mobility, rigid work schedules, and the high cost of travel underlie the growing number of seemingly not so filial children. Thus, the postsocialist reforms provided the structural forces to continue the unfinished Maoist task of destroying filial piety.

It is in this context that the state is seeking to revive filial piety, family values, and the fostering of the parent-child relationship, sometimes even at the expense of the conjugal relationship (D. Davis 2014). To a great extent, the reassertion of filial piety, on the ideological level, legitimizes the withdrawal of the state as a social welfare provider by shifting the responsibility of care from the state to the family. On the institutional level, the reassertion of filial piety is an essential part of reestablishing the family as a social institution to deal with a rapidly aging society after decades of strict birth control. On the global level, the refocus on filial piety and family values can be seen as part of the CCP-led government's larger project of establishing the country as a superpower different from countries like the United States. To achieve this goal, the government strives to promote economic development, but it also proactively seeks to produce and export so-called Chinese values—that is, soft power. The government believes these romanticized Chinese values are able to save China and the world (Callahan 2012).

The government thus has adopted a series of actions to promote Chinese culture and traditions, of which filial piety is at the core. The revision of the Law on the Protection of the Rights and Interests of the Elderly is one such effort. Scholars who have advocated the revival of traditional values, such as Dr. Yu Dan, a student of the Analects of Confucius, were invited to reinterpret the Confucian classics for the public via state-owned newspapers and TV. State-sponsored Confucius Institutes have been established in different parts of the world to spread Chinese culture and values.

Filial as middle-class professionals are, however, the relationship between the government agenda and individuals' initiative is not a one-way causal relationship nor a simple case of resistance and submission (Ortner 1995). In general, my middle-class interlocutors considered themselves to be apolitical.

They stressed that dealing with daily life and work took all their time and strength. They were apathetic about the campaigns to revive national culture, which they considered to be merely propaganda. When I talked to Cecilia and other middle-class interlocutors about the abovementioned law on elderly care, they were against the legalization of filial piety. The reason was that a moral issue was involved that could not be clearly defined and therefore was unenforceable or could not be enforced consistently.

However, despite their doubt about the rationality of the law and the government campaign, these urban middle-class professionals never questioned family values on a general level. They strived to be filial children and responsible parents, juggling their own preferences and familial expectations within the material constrains of daily life. They admitted that returning to one's hometown for family visits is costly and psychologically exhausting, because it involved a large amount of driving, gift giving, banquets, and intense interaction with family members and distant relatives. Yet more and more middle-class families drove home for the traditional holidays, although showing off with their car was not their intention. I asked them why they did it if travel was so stressful. Many replied, "The family should stay together."

These middle-class car owners assumed that filial piety was a virtue that everyone, regardless of their occupational background, would cherish. If a person did not act in a filial way, she or he usually had some reasons. They showed understanding and sympathy for people who could not go home regularly to see their parents in the rural hinterland. People such as their domestic helpers (Yan 2008) and factory assembly line workers (Pun 2005) did not have paid vacations. Traveling was time and money consuming, and train tickets were difficult to get during public holidays. Not all parents could retire. Nor did every family have an apartment big enough to accommodate the parents and their grown children. These professionals were aware that their material resources and jobs put them in a privileged position to practice filial piety in ways associated with their car-oriented lifestyle.

Their commitment to family ethics is illustrative of what it means to be a good Chinese and to uphold Chinese cultural values. Members of the Chinese middle class seem to disappoint observers because of their inability to bring about a political transformation due to the fragmented nature of the middle class and its focus on consumption (Chen J. 2013). Yet intriguingly even when they intentionally distance themselves from state propaganda, their commitment echoes the state-orchestrated revival of Confucianism as a way to reshape the image of postsocialist China on the global stage.

Conclusion

For a self-conscious middle-class person, being autonomous is as important as being a responsible family member. Similarly, a car is as much a status symbol and a vehicle for individual freedom as a material medium to negotiate family relationships. Unraveling the ways in which the car-oriented, middle-class lifestyle is embedded in family relationships provides insights into some key issues in the ongoing intellectual debate regarding modernity and governance. Family forms and dynamics are shaped by and are shaping an array of institutional and discursive forces that cannot be reduced to a unilinear narrative of industrialization, urbanization, and the consequential emergence of the nuclear family.

In postsocialist China, the supposedly "modern" sector of the population—the urban middle class—has not simply adopted the nuclear family as the main family form. Instead, the middle-class family has undergone cyclical shrinkage and expansion, in which the nuclear family predominates for only a short time. China's changing political economy has been a powerful force behind individualization; yet paradoxically it has also provided strong incentives to hold the multigenerational family together.

I am not contending that family values are limited only to the middle class. Filial piety as the quintessential family tie may be cherished across all social strata. But how it is practiced in daily life may be class specific. In China's highly volatile and mobile labor market, translating abstract family values into mundane practices under new material conditions faces challenges and must be negotiated. Many young people have left home for better life opportunities, leaving their parents and sometimes their own children back in their natal home. While many work in unwholesome environments and struggle to survive, some with a good education have taken advantage of the opportunities the economic transformation has provided and have become middle-class professionals. State-orchestrated family planning and the emerging class-based parenting culture have created close emotional ties within the family. Mutual care in middle-class families—physically, economically, ethically, and emotionally—is as much an option as an obligation. The family in turn makes feasible, economically and ethically, a middle-class lifestyle increasingly associated with car ownership. Proper conduct of the self in relation to the family is important for urban professionals to think of themselves as properly middle class. At the same time, filial piety as a resilient cultural form has been reimbued with new meanings in the new middle-class material culture, with a focus less on hierarchical authority and more on mutual care and love.

This engagement with persistent cultural forms has further implications for middle-class culture and political legitimacy. From the previous life experiences of the senior generations who expected the state would take care of them to the precarious life under fierce competition without much of a social safety net, from the classical stories of filial piety to the ideology of the self-reliant individual, conflicts and ambiguities abound in familial expectations and obligations. Once Shao Jing, the abovementioned engineer, told me, "If I had a car, I'd have to drive around my parents and my wife's parents and become a driver. I'd rather not have a car." Five years later, he had a big car with plenty of legroom in the back seat for his parents and parents-in-law. Practicing filial piety was a result of state policies and individuals' conscious decisions. Even though the urban middle class does not intend to respond to the state-building agenda of reclaiming Confucianism, it is reinventing traditional family relations and values. In doing so, the middle class is not simply producing an imagined community of the middle class but also producing values and practices of what we consider to be China.

Chapter 3

The Emerging Middle Class and the Car Market

Mobilities and Trajectories

On a sunny Saturday afternoon in October 2006, I had an interview for an internship with Auto-Fan, a Peugeot dealership in Guangzhou. At the time, according to news reports, business analyses, and statistics, China was undergoing a car boom, and citizens were flocking over to dealerships to buy cars. I had been excited by the possibility of working in a dealership for my research on car consumption, but when I finally stood in front of Auto-Fan, I hesitated. The dealership was quiet. A couple of mechanics were working on a car. In the showroom area, salespeople were either chatting or leafing through magazines. No customers that I could see were there to look at cars.

Auto-Fan's owner, Ms. Huang, and vice general manager, Kang, greeted me in Huang's spacious office. Huang was a tall, intelligent-looking woman in either her late forties or early fifties. Kang was in his midforties. After introducing myself, I told them my plan to study car consumption and social changes. Huang perused my résumé quietly for a while and then proceeded to say, "You should work on something more interesting—a topic that can generate actual monetary returns—so that your research can help you get a job in the future." Although I carefully explained that business potentials were not my primary research interest, Kang and Huang insisted that my research question had no real value. Any worthwhile topics, they felt, should have to do with the business of buying and selling cars.

For the rest of the interview, they used the "4S dealership" (*4S dian*) model as an example to show, in a rather intense manner, what questions I should study, such as whether the current 4S model was good for China's auto market. I did not know at the time what 4S—sales, spare parts, service, survey—stood for, and, coupled with their loquacity, I had no chance to inject so much as a word. Half an hour later, I was about to give up my hope for the internship, only to hear Huang suddenly asking, "Since we won't pay you, it's fine for me that you work here as an intern. When would you like to start?"

This somewhat bewildering interview started my internship at Auto-Fan, which lasted from October 2006 to February 2007. Thereafter, I conducted follow-up interviews with some key figures until 2015. Over the course of time, Huang's anxiety and questions raised during my internship interview finally made sense to me: they reflected a series of challenges that small dealerships were confronted with in a fast-growing auto market. The growth of the auto market can easily be seen as a result of China's reforms that have, on the one hand, created a middle class with considerable consumptive power and, on the other hand, animated the force of the market and the entrepreneurial spirit of the individuals through, as Li Zhang and Aihwa Ong (2008) argue, a set of neoliberal techniques of privatization. Yet grand changes often become clear only in retrospect; individual and institutional actors that are experiencing the process of transformation are themselves unclear about where their actions might lead. The grand narrative about the reforms may have missed the lingering effects from the previous era, conflictual practices and ideologies of the present, and ongoing uncertainties that may have given individuals rather different perceptions about the reforms from the grand narrative.

To capture these complexities, contingencies, and dynamics, I recount the transformation of the auto market and the rise of the middle class through the life stories of Auto-Fan's owner and two of the managers. I reconstruct these life stories based primarily on our conversations and through working with them and with other employees, on observations, and also on statistical yearbooks, news reports, laws, and policies. These life stories show the interactions between policies and individual endeavors and the effects of such interactions. With these stories, I highlight two points that not only complement existing literature but are in fact critical to understanding China's post-Mao transformation. First, the old system of the planned economy has played as important a role as the new economic policies in configuring the practices in the auto market and the upward social mobility of the emerging middle class. In this process, new and old elements and practices recombined in nuanced ways to configure individuals' networks, strategies, and struggles. Second, through the trajectories of the rises of the automotive regime and the middle class, we can discern a discrepancy between the grand narrative on the reforms and the individuals' perceptions regarding space for entrepreneurial initiatives. While on the macro level the Reform era seems to be defined by a neoliberal order in the making in the economic domain but with deviations (or Chinese characteristics), the state constantly asserts control in new ways that have often led to the empowerment of big corporations, instead of individuals or small businesses.

From a Trading Company to a Dealership

The owner of Auto-Fan, Huang, came from a medium-sized city in northern China. She went to Beijing to study French in college. Huang belonged to the earliest batch of college students in China after higher education was resumed in the late 1970s. At that time, getting into college was extremely difficult, but once someone was admitted, tuition was free. The state even provided a stipend, which, though meager, was enough to cover basic daily necessities for most students. Upon graduation, they would be assigned by the state to take up posts in various work units in the cities.

In 1985, one of the three earliest auto joint ventures, Guangzhou-Peugeot, was set up in the capital city of Guangdong (more on Guangzhou-Peugeot in the prologue). Because of her language skills, Huang was assigned to the factory of this joint venture to facilitate communication between the French management and their Chinese partner. It was on this post that Huang established good personal connections with Peugeot, French consulate personnel, and local business partners. Peugeot withdrew from Guangzhou-Peugeot in the mid-1990s, but any Guangzhou-Peugeot cars on the road would still need spare parts and maintenance. With her previous connections, Huang and her business partner started a trading company in the late 1990s to import Peugeot spare parts.

Throughout the 1990s, the state remained very cautious about controlling foreign trade, and the domestic market was guarded by such measures as import-export permits, high tariffs, and importation quotas. These measures entailed trading companies to handle the applications for import-export permits and quotas. Domestic producers and consumers relied on these trading companies to access foreign goods, and foreign companies relied on them to get into China. Foreign trade was a very lucrative business.

Huang's spare parts business was very successful, so much so that she and her partner soon expanded their business to include importing whole cars. Selling cars through a trading company was very different from selling through a dealership. In 2000 and 2001, Huang's trading company had only one office, where Huang, her partner, and her assistants—some of whom became managers in Auto-Fan—mainly handled paperwork and obtained and exchanged documents regarding sales, payment, shipping, and customs clearance. There was no showroom, no repair shop, no salespeople, not to mention mechanics. When cars arrived in China, they were stored in garages in a tariff-free zone that the municipal government had set up to encourage foreign trade. Huang's company would not pay the tariff until it had sold a car, gathered the money, and moved the car out of the tariff-free zone. The early 2000s was Huang's heyday. According to several of Huang's long-term employees, Huang had very few competitors in the market for Peugeot cars. Many local car dealers nationwide had to get their Peugeot cars from Huang's trading company, which had offices in several cities.

While her trading business was doing well, Huang, sensing the rising desire for cars in the private sector, decided to try a different business model. Around 2002, Huang and her business partner set up Auto-Land, a Peugeot dealership on the southern fringe of Guangzhou. Auto-Land had a showroom of 1,600 square meters and a garage of 3,000 square meters. Huang was responsible for sales, and her business partner for car maintenance. Auto-Land's burgeoning sales convinced Huang that there was a future for dealerships. She expanded her dealership business in 2003 with a new dealership in the new auto plaza in Tianhe, an up-and-coming district with shopping malls, high-rise office buildings, and middle-class gated complexes. Originally a racecourse, this plaza was now, with the intervention of the municipal government, a space for dealerships, garages, and other auto shops. Huang and her partner initially set up this dealership to sell the first Chinese (domestically) designed and produced coupe, Meirenbao, by the company called Geely. However, according to Manager Wang at Auto-Fan, this coupe was very poorly built, and owners had to come back for repair so frequently that the shop was turned more garage than dealership. Finally Huang went back to Peugeot cars and named the dealership Auto-Fan. Unlike many other Peugeot dealerships during this period, Auto-Land and Auto-Fan sold both domestically produced and imported fully assembled Peugeot cars, as well as imported spare parts, facilitated through Huang's trading company.

While Huang's business was doing well, there were rough currents beneath the surface. In 2001, China joined the WTO. Foreign carmakers were granted more freedom to choose their local partners and set up joint ventures to produce passenger cars. Tariffs were substantially lowered, and import quotas were eliminated. Whereas these changes have reshaped the auto market in general, the policy that directly and immediately influenced Huang's business was the termination of the tariff-free zones. Those zones had made it possible for Huang's trading company to operate without an enormous amount of cash flow even though tariffs on passenger cars were high. But in 2004, new regulations stipulated that tariffs would be due as soon as an imported car arrived at any Chinese port. Since then, trading companies or dealerships have had to find customers who are willing to pay a deposit before a car arrives; otherwise, they themselves will have to pay the tariffs before they sell the car. Because of that, even with substantial reductions in tariffs, Huang and those in a similar business have had to carry a lot more cash to import cars than in earlier days.

Changes also came from the carmakers. In 2002, Peugeot returned to China, a decade after its withdrawal from Guangzhou. This time it chose to partner with DFM, one of China's former "big three" auto manufacturers, located in the city of Wuhan in Hubei Province (more information in the prologue). The production of domestically produced Dongfeng-Peugeot cars and some spare parts in 2004 started to undermine Huang's car importation business.

Meanwhile, starting in 2003, French Peugeot divided the China market into the north and the south sales regions. The north region included Shanghai, the Yangtze River delta, and anywhere north of that and was given to the Southeast Asian firm mentioned previously. Auto-Fan took the south, which covered Guangdong, Fujian, and other southern provinces. Although Beijing was open to both, Auto-Fan had lost access to one of the wealthiest regions—Shanghai and the Yangtze River delta areas. Within a few years, Auto-Fan's sales territory for imported Peugeot cars shrank farther to only the city of Guangzhou. During my internship period, Auto-Fan sold an imported coupe to a buyer who came all the way from neighboring Fujian Province. Before the buyer even reached home in his new car, a local dealership in Fujian complained to Peugeot's sales management company, accusing Auto-Fan of crossing the boundaries into their sales turf. Peugeot's sales management company decided that Auto-Fan should turn in the profit from this transaction as punishment for breaching the rules. Huang and her managers were furious: "If customers come all the way here to buy a car from us, what are we supposed to do? Tell them, 'No, sir. You have to go back to where you are from to buy it'?"

A legal change in the spring of 2005 caused Huang further losses in her power to negotiate with the carmaker. According to the new regulation,[1] a foreign automaker needed a Chinese registered company to take charge of organizing and managing their network of dealerships for both domestically produced and imported cars that bear their brand name. According to government officials, the new regulation made it clear the legal responsibilities of different levels of authorization, which enabled manufacturers to oversee their dealerships and informed customers which agents would be responsible for the cars they purchased.[2] To comply with the new regulation, French Peugeot established a new company and hired many people who were, to use Huang's words, "the same people having dealings with Peugeot in the old days."

The new regulations empowered the manufacturers at the expense of dealerships' ability to negotiate with them. Before the new regulation, Huang could negotiate directly with the French manufacturer on car prices, models, and the targeted volume of sales. In addition, Huang and her assistant managers could choose ports where local policies were favorable for their imports to land in order to reduce cost. However, with the new regulation, the new China-registered company, which was in charge of sales, determined which models and at what prices to supply to all Peugeot dealerships across the country. It also imposed minimum sales targets on individual dealerships and arranged shipments of the imported cars. This change left Huang little room to control importation costs on her end.

With the domestically produced cars, the situation presented a different set of challenges. One key issue was the 4S dealership model that Huang had urged me to study during my job interview. A 4S dealership obtains authorization directly from a car manufacturer to sell cars of a particular brand.[3] This kind of dealership not only sells cars but also provides after-sales services (supplying spare parts, car washing and cleaning, regular maintenance, and repair) and other marketing activities, such as conducting customer surveys and organizing driving tours (see chapter 1). 4S dealerships can sell cars to other dealerships (second-level dealerships), but the latter cannot get cars directly from the automaker. Being on the top of a hierarchy of dealerships, 4S dealerships make money by selling cars to end users and to second-level dealerships and by receiving rebates (a certain percentage of the total price of cars sold) from the automakers in return, if a 4S dealership meets its annual whole-car sales target set by an automaker.

Guangzhou-Honda first introduced this mode of operation to manage its authorized dealerships in 1999 (Yao and Han 2008). Setting up 4S dealerships soon became standard practice for all major brands nationwide, and Dongfeng-Peugeot followed suit and established its own 4S network. A 4S dealership is a product of standardization. An automaker sets a variety of standards for its 4S dealerships, from the size of the dealership to its interior design. Peugeot's dealerships are usually called "blue boxes" because they are distinctly blue both inside and outside. Financial requirements are demanding: the owner not only invests a lot of money to construct and decorate the 4S dealership according to standards but also pays the automaker a deposit. Rumors I heard during fieldwork said that some Japanese automakers asked for millions for deposits. Whether true or not, it was well known that initial investment for a 4S dealership could easily exceed one million RMB in the mid-2000s.

Huang was not convinced that the 4S dealership model would fit the best interests of individual dealerships. On top of the fact that a 4S dealership would have to meet the annual sales amount dictated by an automaker and follow the automaker's general marketing strategies, the idea that a 4S dealership owner had to live according to the whims of the automaker instead of running the business whichever way she pleased made Huang uncomfortable. This may have been one of the reasons that led Huang to sell her shares in Auto-Land to her partner, who converted Auto-Land into a 4S dealership for Dongfeng-Peugeot cars. Auto-Fan, the only dealership Huang owned when I started my internship, was a second-level dealership for Dongfeng-Peugeot cars but a first-level dealership for imported Peugeot. Auto-Land and Auto-Fan continued to collaborate: Auto-Fan got their Dongfeng-Peugeot cars from Auto-Land, and Auto-Land received imported Peugeot cars from Auto-Fan. But they also had conflicts, as they made profits by selling cars to each other. Meanwhile, Huang kept her trading company, the office of which was actually in Auto-Fan. The trading company and the dealership shared a few employees, such as Manager Ning, who was in charge of logistics in both.

As I gradually pieced together the story of Huang and her business, it became clear to me why she seemed bitter and obsessed with the 4S dealership model during my interview. A former employee who was Huang's assistant during her early days of using a trading company to import and sell cars told me that "the car business has been going down since 2000. Selling cars has been difficult from then on." It was a tough game to play against the big transnational corporations that sought to maximize their profits in the growing car market in China on the one hand and the state-affiliated companies and powerful people (*youquan de ren*) who had privileged access to distribution channels, bank loans, and information on the other. He chose to leave Auto-Fan for a different business. The booming car market did not seem a blessing for many who had been in the car business since the early Reform days. This was particularly true with Manager Lu.

From a Cadre to a Salesman

Manager Lu, together with Manager Ning in charge of logistics, led the sales department at Auto-Fan. Roughly ten years younger than Huang, Lu grew up in a province adjacent to Guangdong. Upon his college graduation in the early 1990s, like Huang, Lu was assigned a position in a state-owned commodity company (*wuzi gongsi*) in Guangzhou that specialized in distributing cars. With his college education, Lu was a cadre (*ganbu*, as opposed to *gongren*, "worker") in his work unit right from the beginning.[4]

Until the mid-1990s, passenger cars remained "state-controlled goods" (more in the prologue). Cars were distributed under a quota system through commodity companies, a key bureaucracy that managed the distribution of goods under the centrally planned economy.[5] Car quotas were only given to such institutions as government agencies, state-owned factories, and other organizations, such as hospitals, but not individuals. Those quotas, written on pieces of paper, were called *pitiao* (notes of approval). The government decided to whom to give the quotas, and the commodity companies signed the notes of approval off to specific institutions, who could then claim cars from the automakers. Lu told me that, without a pitiao from a commodity company, the police department would not register a car or issue a license plate.

During the early Reform period, car production was slow. For example, the total number of passenger cars produced nationwide in 1995 was around 325,000, which was less than Guangzhou-Honda's yearly production capacity (360,000) in 2010. Institutions were often willing to pay much more, sometimes double the list prices, to get a car. The car quotas and pitiao became formally tradable, first through the commodity companies in the 1980s and later even directly (but illicitly) between institutions in the 1990s.[6] Brokers lived on trading these quotas and pitiao. According to Lu, one quota could be sold at a price of RMB 50,000 or more,[7] which, in the mid-1990s, amounted to anywhere between a third and nearly a half of the price of a standard-equipped Santana, one of very few cars produced in China in the mid to late 1990s.[8]

Lu's job in a commodity company was to fill pitiao as stated by the government regulations and orders. He sat in the office and signed off thousands of cars without ever seeing any of them. He never had to worry about relationships with the producers and consumers. While the average salary among urban residents was low in the mid- and late 1990s, Lu managed to afford an apartment in a gated complex, one of the earliest private real-estate projects in the Pearl River delta area. His son was born in the private hospital in that complex, which had a reputation for being one of the best-equipped hospitals in the region. His wife stayed at home to take care of their son and the family. Although the gated complex was far away from the city center, Lu commuted with a car that the commodity company assigned him for personal use. During the weekends, he liked to take his binoculars and go on bird-watching road trips.

The mid- and late 1990s witnessed the rise of trading companies and dealerships, such as those owned by Huang, which had become the main channels between the manufacturers and the users. Commodity companies gradually faded away when the market-oriented economy was on its way to replacing the planned economy (Naughton 2007). Some commodity companies managed to transform themselves into corporations in various businesses. But Lu's went bankrupt.[9]

Thanks to networks established during his previous job, Lu became the sales manager leading a team of sales representatives in Auto-Fan. He and his family moved to the city proper in the new Central Business District, where Auto-Fan was located. Although his new home remained in a mid-range gated complex, Lu led quite a different lifestyle. He no longer drove to work or on weekend outings. In the morning, he went to work by bus. In the evening, he often took about thirty minutes to walk home. For lunch, he ordered fast-food delivery from the same street vendors where mechanical workers or sales representatives ordered their lunches, if he did not have to entertain guests. Besides his job at Auto-Fan, he invested or planned to invest in various businesses, such as in tea and antiques.

As a workplace, Auto-Fan was a very different world. Above all, Lu had to deal with various actors. In the past, interested buyers would approach Lu and be willing to wait a long time to get a pitiao for a car. Nowadays, Lu often had to summon all his patience in order to politely handle middle-class car buyers who would carefully compare car prices. If customers did not feel satisfied with the car or the service or simply could not see in the showroom an actual car of the model they wanted, many would simply turn around and walk to the next car dealership.[10] Lu had to learn to talk to the customers, bargain with them, and build rapport with them. At the same time, it was also Lu's job to handle the demanding automakers and other dealerships.

Back in the commodity company, cars sold well regardless of their brands. Now Lu had to sell Peugeot cars, and it was not easy. Unlike the Japanese and German brands, according to everyone at Auto-Fan, Peugeot was not particularly appealing to potential local car buyers. Although the city once hosted a Peugeot factory, local middle-class consumers showed no particular fondness for this brand. Huang and Manager Wang told me that many people had a bad impression of Guangzhou-Peugeot cars because of the dated models that Peugeot introduced during the first joint venture. Some older customers recalled problems with the Guangzhou-Peugeot cars. For example, the heat diffusion system did not work well, failing to prevent engines from getting hot. Drivers had to wait for an overheated car to cool down before starting it up again. Even though Guangzhou-Peugeot was already history and Dongfeng-Peugeot produced cars of different models, Peugeot seemed unable to shake off their previous negative image.

Lu and his team complained that, apart from this legacy, Peugeot did little to help sales. Although U.S. carmakers were latecomers to the China market, the sheer amount of advertisements by the U.S. auto companies completely dwarfed that by Peugeot. Meanwhile, Peugeot's advertisements liked to sell French culture and lifestyle, but Lu and his team described the background music of the Peugeot car commercial, the "Flower Duet" ("Sous le dôme épais"), as "ghosts screaming." They said that the Chinese customers could not care less about the cultural elements in the Peugeot commercial. "They come here for the car, not the culture," a sales representative once told me.

Striving to adapt to the new economy, Lu worked harder than anyone in his sales team, running around to promote car sales and trying to bring income to Auto-Fan. He introduced the "delivered-to-your-doorsteps" service: he or a member of his sales team would deliver the import cars to the customers free of charge. Lu explained to me that such delivery could provide personal service, which would better connect the customer with the dealership. When the customers were in the Pearl River delta area, their delivery service could even save money, because, according to Lu, petrol and tolls cost less than hiring a logistics company.

It was not clear whether these deliveries could reduce costs, but Lu used the delivery trips to explore other opportunities. Once I went with him on a delivery trip. Lu drove a new, imported coupe to Dongguan, an industrial city near Guangzhou, and Auto-Fan's driver-handyman, Ah Fong, came along in Auto-Fan's service car. The coupe was delivered as planned. Afterward the three of us did not go back to Auto-Fan. Instead, Lu told Ah Fong to take us to a luxury car dealership in downtown Dongguan. Lu asked Ah Fong and me to wait inside the car, and he went into the dealership. When he came out, Lu managed to convince a car salesman there to bring us to a factory owner in the area and introduce Lu. It turned out that Lu wanted to try to sell a GPS-enabled antitheft system to the factory owner, who had a fleet of vehicles for private and business uses. The antitheft system was one of many car products that were sold at Auto-Fan with Lu's permission. Other products included TV sets that could be mounted onto the back of a seat plus channel subscriptions. Auto-Fan was promised a certain percentage of the profit or a fixed commission for these products.

Meanwhile, Lu became interested in exploring the rental car market, which was up and coming in the Pearl River delta area. Unlike in the mid-2010s, renting a car in Guangzhou in 2006 was inconvenient and expensive. Rental companies usually offered two types of rental cars: cars only and chauffeured ones. For the regular cars, customers would need to provide their household registration information, resident identity cards, and a huge deposit. Although the chauffeured rentals were deposit-free, customers had to pay for the chauffeur's meals and accommodations on top of the rental and a driver's fee. Lu's plan targeted businessmen who traveled from city to city. According to Lu, these people would have cars where they lived or worked, but when they traveled to other places for business, they would need to rent cars. In his blueprint, Lu wanted to use only Audi cars, hire chauffeurs, and set up pickup spots at major airports throughout the country. Lu prepared a three-year development plan with a budget for twenty or so Audi A6s, and intended to provide service in three cities—Guangzhou, Dongguan, and Zhuhai—in the Pearl River delta.

As Lu strived with various business initiatives, he sometimes talked about his previous job and the commodity company in a nostalgic manner. In recalling his previous work, Lu told me that he liked the big companies' way of doing business: "They could spend millions easily, and people there wouldn't bother to bargain for another ten or twenty thousand off." For Lu, big corporations and the rich people "were straightforward [*shuangkuai*], not calculative [*bu jijiao*]." In contrast, "today people will bargain for half a day just to knock another RMB 1,000 off the price. Poor people watch every cent they spend." Thus, "it is much easier to make money out of the rich than the poor." In our conversations, there was a sense of reluctance in Lu to acknowledge that these calculative middle-class consumers, whom he called the "poor," were the main force that drove car sales.

For most of Lu's endeavors beyond selling Peugeot cars, Huang was lukewarm but accommodating, so long as Lu could bring in cash and add to overall sales. However, many of Lu's endeavors were not successful. During my internship period, Lu's delivery service gradually faded with shrinking profit margins. I never once saw any successful deals for the antitheft GPS system or the TV set. After all, all taxicabs in the city already had TV monitors, so, in Lu's salesman's words, "who would want their private car to feel like a taxicab?" His rental car project never materialized into a real business either. Meanwhile, a few rental companies sprang up, offering simple and convenient access to rental cars with a classified system that was tailored to various levels of consumers.

By the time I returned to Guangzhou in the summer of 2010, Lu had already been demoted from sales manager to salesman. In the summer of 2012, I learned from Manager Wang that Lu left Auto-Fan. After that I lost contact with Lu.

From Gleaning Grains to Operating a Million-Dollar Business

Manager Wang belonged to the same generation as Huang. Wang grew up in a big family in an ethnically mixed area in a southern province. During his primary school years, he and his siblings gleaned stray grains in the field after a harvest to bring extra income to the family. He had wanted to study medicine at college but was assigned to a professional school in Guangzhou to study car mechanics.

Wang's senior year at school was when Guangzhou-Peugeot was founded, and demands had greatly exceeded supply.[11] According to Wang's recollection, even with the quotas, work units still had to pay for a Peugeot car half in U.S. dollars and half in renminbi in the 1980s. At the time of graduation, a bus took Wang and his schoolmates directly to Guangzhou-Peugeot's factory, where they were given their first job. The new company provided dormitories for Wang and other young colleagues, who were all college graduates and were single. They worked together and spent leisure time together. Some became long-term friends and later business partners.

Unlike Huang, whose main work was to facilitate communication within the company, Wang started on the assembly line. According to Wang, Peugeot's cars were better than VW's in terms of speed, stability, and safety. Therefore, both the police and the military favored Peugeot. Granted, neither Peugeot nor Volkswagen brought to China their most advanced technologies. Their cars from the joint ventures had a series of problems. But for

Wang, working at Guangzhou-Peugeot was a unique opportunity to gain some solid knowledge on the technological aspects of cars and spare parts and to build a network in the business world dealing with and fixing cars.

After a period of practical training, Wang and his schoolmates—the few Chinese employees that possessed a higher education—were promoted to management positions. Before logistics became its own profession and its own branch within the business, Wang sometimes had to deliver cars. He told me that he looked at the deliveries as road trips. Once he took more than a week to drive along the coast from Guangzhou to Fujian to deliver a car. The work unit had prepared him, for his way back, a plane ticket, which was surely a privilege linked to certain social status at that time. Because of this experience, Wang showed no interest in Lu's "delivery-to-your-door" service at Auto-Fan. He said that was an old trick Lu had learned from the old days. Wang was also not enthusiastic about the increasingly popular driving tours among the middle-class (see chapter 1), because he "had done that many years ago" when there were not so many cars on the road. In hindsight, these road trips were not merely opportunities for tourism. They also built a wide personal network for Wang, the usefulness of which became visible much later.

In the mid-1990s, Guangzhou-Peugeot collapsed, but Wang and his colleagues received decent compensations, which, together with their social networks, allowed them to stay in the car business. They established a company through which they controlled 4S-level dealerships of QQ cars, the cheapest compact cars made by an emerging Chinese carmaker called Chery. As their business expanded, Huang invited Wang to join Auto-Fan to take charge of the after-sales department that handled auto repairs and maintenance and kept records of Auto-Fan's customers up to date. Wang had known Huang since their common years in Guangzhou-Peugeot.

Yet the friendship between Huang and Wang did not grease the relationship between Wang and other Auto-Fan employees, partly because of Wang's attitude. Wang was very confident in his skills and knowledge about cars. In his opinion, most of the employees in the dealership did not really know much about cars. In addition, Wang told me that he liked to read, and he liked philosophy and poetry. He recalled the happy times when he shared poems and discussed books with other single colleagues in Guangzhou-Peugeot's dormitories. He thought that talking about money all the time, which many other employees did, was simply bad taste. And he did not hide these opinions from his colleagues. The lower-level employees, such as the mechanics, found him arrogant. Others, like Managers Lu and Ning, felt that Wang was pretentious, and there was nothing they could talk to Wang about except work.

Wang's unpopularity was also due to the structural tension that was related to the changes in the auto market. Specifically, it came from the tension between whole-car sales and car maintenance. As mentioned before, due to state policies, selling cars, whether imported or domestically produced ones, had become very cash demanding and was subjected to tremendous control from the automakers. Meanwhile, the increasing competition among automakers had led to dwindling profits per car for the dealerships. This situation favored dealerships that had a stable income and, more importantly, cash supply. In China's context, this often meant dealerships operated by state-owned companies that could secure bank loans.

Auto-Fan was not one of those favored dealerships: it was privately owned and had difficulties accessing bank loans. During my internship, it distributed salaries late to employees. The delays varied from five to ten days. To combat difficulties in cash flow, Auto-Fan needed to sell more cars, especially imported cars. One incident illustrates Auto-Fan's challenge concerning whole-car sales: At the end of 2006, French Peugeot announced to its dealers the arrival of a series of full-sized passenger cars that had not been produced in China yet. The profit margin was higher with imported ones than domestically produced ones. Managers Lu and Ning immediately pressed the sales team to call past and prospective customers—each sales representative had her or his list of customers—to inform them of the new model. Feedback indicated that potential buyers showed interest, but they would like to see the real car before committing to any purchase. Although this sounded like an opportunity for Auto-Fan, Huang and other managers were hesitant to place an order for those new cars because doing so would require a large cash payment up front. While Huang and the managers continued to deliberate, a new 4S Peugeot dealership made an immediate order so as to get the new cars into its showroom as soon as possible. This competitor was operated by a state-owned company, which was transformed from a commodity company in the old days and had sufficient cash flow. Huang eventually made up her mind in February and ordered new cars with money borrowed via her social circle, but the sales representatives said that they had already lost some of the potential customers to the competitor.

Unlike the whole-car sales sector, Wang and his after-sales sector faced far fewer constraints. Auto-Fan had territorial limits in whole-car sales, but its repair, maintenance, and spare parts sales did not. Their customers had to pay before they could get their cars back after repair. Therefore, unlike Lu, who sometimes had to chase after some customers for car payments, Wang did not have to deal with arrears. Inside the dealership, the after-sales sector benefited the most from the growing car sales. Car owners usually do not change cars frequently, but their cars always need maintenance and repair. Customers who bought cars from Auto-Fan often came back for maintenance. Auto-Fan was a Peugeot dealership, so Manager Lu and his team were not supposed to sell cars other than Peugeot. But Wang and his team would fix Peugeot cars as well as cars of other brands. Huang did not mind having the extra income, and the carmaker did not really supervise this part of Auto-Fan's business. Wang and his repair team had brought stable revenue for the dealership.

Meanwhile, the sales department had to use service from the after-sales department. Before every car was given to its customer, the sales representatives would send the car to the mechanics, who would check it, take off the protective film, and wax it. Sometimes accidents and other events happened before delivery, and the sales team needed new spare parts and mechanics to fix the car (see chapter 4). Wang, as the manager of the after-sales department, had the authority to influence and decide the time, price, and quality of the service delivered to his counterparts in the dealership. But Wang did not always prioritize the sales department's requests. Lu was not happy about it, yet Lu needed Wang's cooperation, not the other way around.

Wang knew how his colleagues and his own team of mechanics thought about him. After the Chinese New Year in 2007, Wang left Auto-Fan and went back to his own company to take charge of the repair department. He explained to me that he had to "take care of some business." However, Wang was the head of Auto-Fan's after-sales department again when I visited him in summer 2008. Since 2010 he has been in charge of the sale of imported spare parts for Peugeot cars.

I asked Wang why he would rather be someone's employee than be his own boss. Wang always said that Huang asked him "as an old friend to help her," and he accepted Huang's invitation as "a favor to an old friend." He would sometimes criticize Huang's business decisions and her lack of vision and risk-taking spirit for big business. On other occasions he had thought highly of Huang, saying that she was cosmopolitan, well connected, and entrepreneurial. In the dealership, Huang and Wang were good partners. Huang flew around the world and explored opportunities to negotiate deals, cut importation costs, and open new channels. Wang had an extensive network of car users and dealerships he'd established since his early Guangzhou-Peugeot days. He, with the help of two to three sales people, managed to meet the sales target that the French company set and increased every year.

In 2014, due to the rapid increase of rent, Huang relocated Auto-Fan to a newly designated industrial zone far away from the city center. Many people, including Huang's long-term assistant, Manager Ning, left, but Wang went along with the relocation. Nonetheless, Wang had dealt with cars for decades, and he told me in our conversation in 2015, "The car business is boring." Now big carmakers dominated the game, and room for individuals like Huang was shrinking. He mentioned several times, "The world is big. You need to see beyond this small place." With the money he had accumulated over the years from the car business, Wang was exploring opportunities in the real-estate business in the mid-2010s. His recent initiative was to build a hotel in his hometown. The top floor of the hotel would be a café, decorated with "good taste," "suitable for friends to gather and talk about literature."

Conclusion

With all the challenges Auto-Fan faced, it remained active in the auto market as I finished this manuscript. Huang's life remained hectic, as she traveled around to look for new opportunities for her dealership. Wang's hotel building was under construction. I still have not heard anything about Lu. All three of them manifest the spirit of self-governance, as discussed in existing literature about the rising middle class (Ren 2013; Tomba 2004, 2009; Zhang L. 2010). Meanwhile, factors beyond their control, such as assigned jobs, structural changes, and timing, all made a difference in their life trajectories. Mobilities, both upward and downward, are real life experiences.

The middle class is a heterogeneous entity that can possibly be described but not defined. People described here are different, in many ways, from the middle-class individuals in ethnographies by Osburg (2013), Zhang (2010), and others (for example, Ren 2013; Tomba 2004, 2009; Tsang 2014). Yet with all the diversities and specificities, the three figures here and many of my other interlocutors share some similarities in their life trajectories. These similarities suggest some common patterns of social mobility among a subset of the emerging middle class.

The middle-class individuals of this subset were born mostly between the 1960s and early 1980s. They came from diverse family backgrounds in different parts of the country. They came of age when economic reforms were just launched and the centrally planned economy remained the dominant way of organizing the socioeconomic order. Although income was low in general, the family income gap remained relatively small. Many of my interlocutors were the first generation of college students in their families. No tuition fees and government stipends were available to relieve the families from the burden of paying for college education.[12]

Having a college education had an important benefit: it could provide young people the mobility that was denied by the rigid household registration in the Maoist and early Reform years.[13] College students' household registrations would be transferred from their hometowns to the cities where they had attended college and then to cities where they worked. With such transfers, one's official rural status—as in the case of Wang—could be turned into an urban one. This change, in the past as well as in the present, is generally considered moving up the social ladder.

Up until the early 1990s, the college admission rate was low. Students generally could not choose what to study or where to work after graduating. Yet a college degree would typically guarantee a stable job in the government, a government-affiliated work unit, or a state-owned enterprise. Many of my interlocutors joined the work force between the mid-1980s and the 1990s when a dual-track system of economy (the coexistence of an overall economic plan and the market mechanism) was at work. Whether they stayed with the assigned workplaces or switched to jobs in the private sector later, the education, social networks, wealth, and work experiences they had accumulated thanks to the socialist welfare system and the centrally planned economy have helped them to take advantage of opportunities that the reform practices had brought and to constantly readjust to the often unpredictable changes beyond their control.

Existing literature tends to focus on the new opportunities and practices that the state's agenda to introduce market mechanism has created. But many of my interlocutors pointed out to me the role of the old system in shaping their life courses. In a similar vein, the trajectory of Auto-Fan shows the com-

plexity on the ground. The central government designated the auto industry as one of the few pillar industries to drive economic growth from the
1980s. However, as shown in the prologue, the government went back and
forth regarding what specific action to take to develop the auto industry, and
its attitude toward private car ownership was at best ambiguous and at worst
antagonistic throughout the early Reform era.

The central and the local governments sought after capital and technologies from foreign automakers. Yet, as how to do market economy was new
to individuals and institutional actors, they learned how to negotiate with
foreign capital through working with them on the way. In dealing with foreign capital, domestic entrepreneurs, and a new consumer public, the
government often relies on new regulations learned from global practices
(such as rules stipulated in WTO agreements), as well as old ways of controlling and disciplining market actors. The latter is well exemplified in the
official requirement of one management company under the control of a foreign carmaker and on top of a hierarchy of dealerships mentioned in Huang's
story. This policy follows an administrative model of organizing relationships along the vertical line rather than the contract-and-court model that
emphasizes the equal status of market players typically seen in a market
economy. This policy and related practices can thus be considered as a "rule
of centralized control" instead of "rule of freedom" (Barry, Osborne, and
Rose 1996; Joyce 2003).

The mingling of old and new practices is also illustrated in the case of
bank loans. Banks nowadays provide a series of services, from credit cards
to loans for private use, such as education and housing, which would have
been unimaginable in the Maoist days and even the early Reform era. Yet
Auto-Fan's struggle with cash flow during my internship period was in good
part due to the fact that it is difficult for private businesses to access loans from
the state-owned banks that dominate the banking industry. The state-owned
banks favor SOEs because they believe the government would provide the
ultimate guarantee for loans given to SOEs, a situation that my interlocutors
working in the banking sector readily admit. In other words, the relationship
between the government and SOEs, shaped by and ingrained in the political
economy since the Maoist's years, persists and circumscribes the space for the
spontaneous growth of entrepreneurship in the new era.

Situations presented here through Auto-Fan's trajectory suggest that the
techniques of privatization are historically and politically specific. This echoes

the case of privatization of public properties Osburg (2013) carefully examines. The "transfer of state assets into private hands," Osburg shows, "has in large part followed the dictates of moral economies based on kinship . . . , bureaucratic hierarchies, and ideals of interpersonal morality" (78). Thus, the form of privatization in China does not follow the logic and practices described in the narratives of neoliberalism. My point here is not to deny the existence of elements of neoliberalism in China today as prescribed economic practices, ideology, and/or governing techniques (Eriksen et al. 2015; Ferguson 2010; Ganti 2014). Rather, following Stephen Collier, Ong, and others (Collier 2009; Ong and Collier 2005; Rose 1999), the phenomena of the rising automotive regime and the middle class illustrate that a single or dominant logic, such as that of neoliberalism, cannot account for the complex realities that constitute what is conveniently called the "reforms." Adding to the hybridity illustrated in the existing works on the post-Mao transformation, I argue that more emphasis could be placed on the *experimental* and *contingent* nature of specific policies, rather than any underlying political or economic *logic*. As the government steers the direction of reforms following a hybrid set of rationalities and practices, the processes of reforms have been full of improvisation, uncertainty, and hesitation. There were regular macro and micro adjustments at both the individual and policy levels in the decades of the Reform era.

Such an experimental and contingent nature has left middle-class individuals with perceptions about the Reform era sometimes rather different from the official narrative. In the official narrative, decades of reforms were described as a lineal process. From the centrally planned economy to the dual-track economy to the market-oriented economy, economic practices have moved progressively toward the more liberal, open, and global direction.

But for my interlocutors, the periodization of the post-Mao years is characterized in a different manner. The 1990s and even the early 2000s, as Wang and others mentioned to me on different occasions, were "chaotic" (*hunluan*) and "wild" (*kuangye*) periods: "you didn't know what could be done and what couldn't." They saw a lot of uncertainties but also a lot of opportunities and hope for individual endeavors. For some people, wealth accumulated fast in gray and even illicit areas. Sometimes their endeavors weathered the capricious changes, but sometimes they failed. They were proud of their achievements through hard work, and they did not hesitate to show their achievement through consumer goods, particularly cars.[14]

As time passed, however, people like Huang became less optimistic. Practices in line with global standards have been introduced and enforced through membership in the WTO and the WTO's trade rules. Many informal practices in the past have now been regulated and standardized. If neoliberal policies were about deregulation, people like Huang often felt the opposite: since the 2000s more rules came into being, and their initiatives were more inhibited by various kinds of administrative measurements than in the previous decade. Moreover, they learned from life experience that state policies may change at any time, and they would not know what direction the changes would head toward. If there was anything coherent, Huang and others felt that the government constantly sought to control and maintain the order of the private sector, rather than to liberate its energy. Their efforts have been increasingly overshadowed by powerful players, such as global capitals, state-owned companies, and, last but not least, the government, high-end officials, and their close kin.

Narratives offered by Huang, Lu, Wang, and my other interlocutors are by no means neutral. They speak from a perspective of people with vested interests, whose social and cultural capitals endowed them with structural advantages in specific times. They are not critical of their own positioning. They focus heavily on the present and the near future and do not want to reflect on the past. It is partly because memory has become blurry and partly because they think dwelling on the past is a waste of time, and some happenings should belong only in the past. Nonetheless, the radical, structural transformations of the political economy were made by and absorbed in the mundane efforts of these individuals who strived to thrive, or simply to survive, against the tides of ever-changing state policies and transnational corporations' practices. Their life trajectories and narratives direct our attention to the hybridity and contingent applications of multiple rationalities, practices, ideologies, and structural forces from the socialist past and the post-Mao era that have shaped the transformations, epitomized here by the rise of the automotive regime and the middle class. In highlighting the lasting effects of practices under the planned economy, I do not mean to suggest they are more important than other policies and practices but rather to show the complexity of social and political forces in the configuration of individuals' mobility trajectories. This point will be further elaborated in the next chapter when the middle-class individuals described here encountered the younger generation, who aspired to upward social mobility.

Chapter 4

Car Crash, Class Encounter

Anxiety of Mobility

In an early morning in February 2007, mechanics at Auto-Fan had already begun work as usual before the dealership opened for business. A young salesman, Nanfang, also came in before business hours. He needed to move a brand-new manual Peugeot 206 to the mechanics' work area to get the car ready for delivery—he had to take off the protective film, check its mechanical functions, and wax it. Mr. Zou, the new owner of the car, was scheduled to pick it up later that day. Nanfang went to the garage in the back of the dealership, where Mr. Zou had parked the car the day before after he ran a final test. Soon after Nanfang got inside the car, it suddenly jumped forward and crashed into a glass partition between the parking area and a storage space for spare parts. The hood and the bumper of the car were damaged.

Because the serial numbers of the engine and the frame of the damaged car were already entered into official contract and the receipts of sales tax and fees issued by government agencies, Auto-Fan could not replace the damaged car with a new car without consent from Mr. Zou. This car had no insurance coverage because Mr. Zou had not purchased any, and Auto-Fan's insurance policy did not cover any losses incurred in the garage.

While the mechanics scrambled to repair the car, Mr. Zou and his wife arrived and saw the damage. They cancelled the contract and demanded a full refund from Auto-Fan (including money paid for the car, sales tax, and government fees). The managers had no choice but to heed the Zous' request.

Auto-Fan's owner, Huang, and managers blamed Nanfang for his negligence, an indicator of his lack of *suzhi* (roughly translated as "human quality"). They decided that Nanfang had to bear the cost of repair, and the dealership's sales department should absorb the nonrefundable government fees. In addition, Nanfang and his supervisor Manager Lu were fined. The after-sales department, headed by Manager Wang, billed Nanfang with an amount more than twice that of Nanfang's monthly salary, including charges for new parts and labor costs. The incident and its handling continued to be the topic of intense, emotional discussions in the days to follow. Employees took sides with one of the two camps. The "downstairs" people, including the salespeople, the mechanics, and the janitor, resented the harsh manner in which the "upstairs" people, including the dealership owner, the managers, and their assistants, handled the mishap. Those upstairs in turn complained that the people downstairs had low suzhi and did not know how to do business.

This chapter uses this mishap to get inside the class politics between the "upstairs" people and the "downstairs" people at the dealership and to shed light on the subjective experience of being middle-class in the process of class (re)production. After all, class-specific subjectivity is relational to the conditions of other classes. Scholarship on the service industries has generated valuable insights into class politics through daily interactions in the workplace. Rachel Sherman (2007) and Eileen M. Otis (2012) reveal how social distinction is displayed in encounters between service workers' emotional labor and middle-class customers' enactment of class entitlement in luxury hotels. Similarly, Amy Hanser's (2008) work shows how careful investigation of routine service work at the sales counter, which she calls "relational labor," can contribute to our understanding of how systems of inequality are reproduced. Drawing on this scholarship, my analysis looks into spatial arrangement, work routines and salaries, group dynamics, and language to illustrate how class distinction is made visible, articulated, and solidified through everyday interactions.

I pay particularly attention to the recurring usage of suzhi as a window to unravel the subjective experience of the middle class on social change, mobility, and distinction. Contemporary usages of suzhi can be traced to the state's concern over its population in relation to national development and ensuing campaigns on birth control and education policies. In official usages, suzhi, although "individually embodied," "marks the hierarchical and moral distinction between the high and the low and its improvement is a mission of national importance" (Kipnis 2006, 297). In her study of how suzhi was used against migrant workers, Hairong Yan argues that "suzhi abstracts and reduces the heterogeneity of human beings by coding their value (worth) for Development" (2003, 511). Thus, suzhi "is the quintessential expression of how subjects are set up for the rational choice making that grounds China's capitalist transformation" (Anagnost 2004, 192). Some researchers then relate the suzhi discourse directly to the neoliberal technique that fosters the ethics of being self-responsible individuals so as to allow the state to govern from afar (for example, Lin 2011; Woronov 2016).

By seeing the suzhi discourse as a governing strategy, this scholarship highlights the role of the state but does not pay enough attention to how the term is reappropriated and used in everyday life. In this chapter, I show how suzhi is perceived and in turn informs behaviors among the educated middle class, the main users of the term "suzhi." Based on their daily practices, conversations, and logics of argument within and beyond the dealership, I suggest that the term is full of ambiguity and contradiction, without stable correlation with any specific ethic or logic. The suzhi discourse in China is, to a great extent, similar to the civility discourse in India, which middle-class urbanites deploy to draw a social boundary between themselves and people from the lower classes and other caste backgrounds (Dickey 2012; Donner 2011). In the dealership, what is relatively clear is not the connotation of the term but rather that the usage of "suzhi" correlated with spatial arrangement and class hierarchy at the dealership. In other mundane contexts, the perception of suzhi is closely associated with the belief of education and cultivation, which, as Kipnis (2006, 2007) aptly points out, has its origins in contemporary state policies, as well as in classical teaching in history; and the middle class see education as playing a critical role for achieving their current social status and ways of life. In this sense, the *suzhi* discourse can be seen as a new class terminology, but at the same time, as other scholars have argued (for example, Yan H. 2003), it depoliticizes social inequality. The suzhi discourse provides the rhetorical tool for the Chinese middle class to understand social stratification when class identities have become much more fluid and ambiguous than in the Maoist years. By unpacking the politics of the suzhi discourse, we may catch a glimpse of the subjective experience of being middle-class—full of struggles with upward mobility and anxiety about the future, as they see class boundaries harden and upward social mobility shrink for younger generations at a precarious time.

"Upstairs" and "Downstairs": Spatial Division, Work Routines, and Work Hierarchy

Space is a critical component with which social relations are produced (Lefebvre 1991). It is a tool of action and a field of struggle through which individuals' subjectivity is shaped. Space of socialization and spatial contestation are critical to the production of class identity and boundaries (for example, Caldeira 2000; Low and Smith 2006). The tension between the "upstairs" people and the "downstairs" people at Auto-Fan is the reification of class politics in conjunction with spatial politics in the workplace.

Auto-Fan was located in an up-and-coming part of Guangzhou in the 2000s. It opened from 9:00 a.m. to 9:00 p.m., 7 days a week throughout the year except during the 7-day Chinese New Year holiday. Such a schedule was not unusual among car dealerships. After all, in this city, many supermarkets, shopping centers, and restaurants operated 365 days a year.

The dealership was separated into several functional areas (see the floor plan in figure 5). Each area had its dress code, daily routines, and style of interaction.

On the ground floor, Auto-Fan was composed of two parts separated by a passage wide enough to pass a car through. The part facing the main road—the front—was mostly the showroom, with a small sitting area. A punch clock was mounted near the entrance to the street. The managers had made it clear that no employee should punch someone else's card. If anyone were discovered doing so, both would be punished.

In the showroom, a large-screen TV looped a Peugeot commercial that depicted the scene of Paris with the "Sous le dôme épais" playing in the background. In the summer, this area was well air-conditioned, but it would

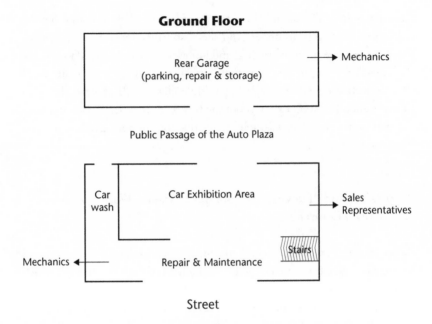

Public Passage of the Auto Plaza

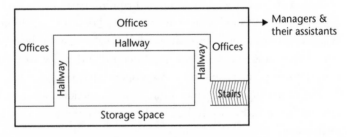

Figure 5. Auto-Fan's floor plan (not proportionate).

usually be rather cold in the winter. This was the sales representatives' area in the dealership.

Auto-Fan had five to seven sales representatives, most of whom were males in their midtwenties. Most of them had graduated from two-year junior colleges, some majoring in automotive marketing. They rarely stayed in a dealership for more than two years. During my five-month internship at Auto-Fan, two representatives left and two arrived. They hopped between dealerships, sometimes just because "other brands always seemed more popular." Because of the frequent hopping, sales representatives from different dealerships were often well connected. Within their circles, information on other brands' marketing moves got exchanged and spread quickly.

The salespeople had one day off per week, but usually it would not be on the weekend or coincide with a public holiday. Because part of their work required them to go to government offices in different parts of the city, they would sometimes take advantage of being out of the office and have lunch or run errands. Salespeople were required to wear their own white shirts and black trousers or skirts. If a jacket was needed, it should also be black.

The salespeople worked from 9:00 a.m. to 6:00 p.m. without clearly defined lunch hours. Most arrived at work early. Some might begin the day by dusting the cars; others might eat breakfast. Their day formally began with the morning briefing session, which I always participated in during my internship. At 9:00 o'clock sharp, everyone in the sales department, including Manager Ning, who was in charge of logistics, would stop whatever they were doing and gather in the showroom area. We stood next to each other in one line, all facing Manager Lu.

The briefing sessions were for relaying such information as incoming models and new prices, as well as any scouting reports on their rivals. Lu would sometimes remind the salespeople to observe the code of conduct; for example, he would sometimes reprimand anyone for snacking during office hours or ask his team to dress properly. After Nanfang's accident, Lu also used the briefings to reiterate the importance of exercising caution. The whole team stood in silence and waited for Lu to finish his speech, which would last no more than five to ten minutes. Afterward, the managers and their assistants would go back to their offices on the mezzanine level. Sales representatives would start their work, waiting to entertain any customers, or leave the dealership to handle any tax or license issues.

A sales representative's salary comprised a basic portion and bonuses. Auto-Fan paid some long-service employees benefits, but usually the salespeople would not have worked enough hours to qualify. In late 2006, the bonus for selling a domestically produced Peugeot was RMB 100, and the bonus for selling an imported Peugeot was substantially higher. However, on average a salesperson sold less than one imported car each month between October 2006 and February 2007.[1] Based on daily conversations among the salespeople and my estimation, their monthly income generally ranged from

RMB 1,800 to RMB 2,500. The salary structure pitted them against each other to compete for customers.[2] Once a sales representative started a conversation with a potential customer, the customer would become hers or his. A customer's profile was tied to a specific salesperson; Mr. Zou, for example, was known to everyone at Auto-Fan as "Nanfang's customer" instead of "Mr. Zou."

That said, the sales representatives were relatively friendly to each other. When there were no customers in the showroom, the sales representatives would joke with each other or chitchat or exchange notes on the best eateries around town or about life and relationships. After work, they sometimes met for dinner and entertainment. They were cooperative (as opposed to being hostile) with each other as work would require. Nowadays customers would typically pay a small service fee and have the sales representative travel around town to get all official documents done on their behalf. The work of a sales representative included paying any taxes and road tolls and sending new cars to the police to be inspected, photographed, and licensed. With collaboration, one salesperson would submit her and her colleagues' cases to one government office, while her colleague would return the favor when handling another government agency's requirements. A good example of their cooperation was that all other salespeople tried hard to help Nanfang after the mishap. Xiaolan, the only female representative at that time, rang the buyer, Mr. Zou, with an attempt to postpone the delivery without mentioning the accident to give the mechanics more time to fix the car. They also discussed various tricks that they had heard from other salespeople who had tried to get insurance companies to cover losses beyond the scope of insurance policies (though none sounded feasible in this case).

Surrounding the showroom area was a car wash connected to the next shop and a service area that faced the street. Opposite the front area and separated by the passage was the rear garage, where, in addition to maintenance and repair work, spare parts were stored and parking spaces were provided. The rear garage had no air conditioning or fanning facilities. When the mechanics, cleaners, and janitors were not working at the front, they would rest in the rear garage as they were not allowed to stay in the showroom.

The twenty or so mechanics were all male. Except the senior mechanic, Master Dai, most were in their early twenties, but several were in their late teens. The majority had finished nine years of compulsory education, and some went to vocational schools and studied car mechanics after the nine years of school.[3] Several described themselves as "bad students" who had dropped out of junior high school. In either case they and their families had thought that fixing cars would be a practical way to make a living. The skills would be useful anywhere in the country, especially with the burgeoning automotive economy. Thanks to their family or hometown connections, many were introduced to jobs in garages and dealerships.

Mechanics received fixed salaries. Depending on skills and experience, the average salaries ranged between RMB 800 and RMB 2,000 in 2006, but Master Dai's pay was comparable to some of the managers. Mechanics sometimes received a bonus when business was good, but unlike the salespeople, who had bonuses written into their contracts, mechanics were not entitled to bonuses. Like the salespeople, young mechanics tended to change jobs frequently and therefore rarely qualified for benefits.

The mechanics wore a uniform given them by Auto-Fan, but the dealership did not provide laundry service. The uniforms were often stained with grease and dirt. Mechanics rotated between two shifts, one from 9:00 a.m. to 6:00 p.m. and the other from noon to 9:00 p.m. They were not supposed to leave the dealership during work hours. Even during lunchtime, they always bought RMB 5–10 lunch boxes from vendors in the auto plaza. Their weekly days off were also rotated. Manager Wang imposed fines on his team members for being late or not obeying the rules, despite the fact that doing so had not led to any particular losses.

Manager Wang also briefed his team of mechanics every morning. The briefings would start at 8:30 a.m. and outlast those led by Lu. Most of the time Wang would use the meeting to reiterate the code of conduct and assign tasks for the day. In addition, Wang organized weekly training sessions in the evening for the young mechanics.

When they ran out of tasks, the young mechanics would stay in the rear garage and, as they would say, "stay away from the ghosts' screaming." (The "voices of the ghosts" referred to the two high-pitched voices in the "Sous le dôme épais" that looped in the showroom.) They would leaf through newspapers, sit idle, crack jokes, and sometimes chase each other for fun. After work, they rarely hung out with each other. They barely cooked in their rented homes in the urban villages.[4] A lot of their free time would be spent gaming at home or at gaming places.

The dealership's front part had a mezzanine level where the managers' and their assistants' offices were (set up against brick walls). The offices were partitioned by glass panels, and each office had its own air-conditioning unit. Beyond the hallway in front of the offices, the managers had a clear view of the floor below, but from the ground floor one could not see into the offices.

Managers did not interact with each other on non-business-related matters. Tension and conflicts among them, due to personalities and business, were well known among the dealership's employees (see chapter 3). However, when necessary, such as in the case of the mishap, they showed a rare solidarity among them.

Managerial personnel worked from 9:00 a.m. to 6:00 p.m. with a two-hour lunch break and had the two-day weekend and all public holidays off. Managers did not wear a uniform. Lu and Ning, because they dealt with customers directly, tended to dress formally, while other managers, such as the vice general manager, Kang, and after-sales manager, Wang, dressed casually except on days when business representatives from the automaker came to visit. Some managers, like Ning, brought their own lunch, while others ordered delivery if no business lunches were scheduled. The owner, Huang, usually would not come to her office before noon. The time when she left the office was also flexible. She dressed in a smart-casual way, or, as Ning and the finance manager, Lan, would call it, "a bit French."

Everyday interactions among the different groups also reinforced spatial boundaries. Salespeople and mechanics routinely walked past each other's territory. Mechanics were not supposed to stay in the showroom unless an issue had necessitated their presence there. While they occasionally exchanged jokes, sales representatives usually would not mingle with mechanics, in the workplace or off work. That said, the line between salespeople and mechanics was more porous and blurrier than that between the managers and the rest. Salespeople might have a higher social status with their clean clothes and desk/paperwork, but an experienced mechanic, such as Master Dai, was more respected and had more job security for the value of his skills. Yet, even though Master Dai was aware that he was paid better than the managerial assistants and even some managers at Auto-Fan, he distrusted the managers and felt comfortable surrounded by people who, like him, had come from other places to make a living with their hands in this city—the mechanics, the janitors, and the salespeople. Despite the differences between them, the sales representatives and mechanics shared a lot of their opinions about the managers, the dealership, the ways they interacted with each other, and their lifestyle in general. As suggested by what happened after the mishap, the mechanics sided with the salespeople.

People from downstairs usually did not go upstairs. The salespeople would sometimes go up to the mezzanine to handle sales issues with the managerial personnel. Mechanics, on the other hand, would not go to the mezzanine except on paydays or on occasions when the managers summoned them, typically for breaking some rule or another. Similarly, the managers and their assistants rarely lingered on the ground floor. Sometimes they spoke loudly from the hallway on the mezzanine with a sales representative or a mechanic.

Spatial arrangement and daily interactions contributed to segregation and solidarity between different groups in the dealership, giving rise to the terms "downstairs" (*louxia de*) and those "upstairs" (*loushang de*). The spatial dimension of everyday class politics—"upstairs" and "downstairs"—further corresponded to the "high" and "low" in the discourse of suzhi, seemingly giving justifications to dividing people between those "upstairs" and "downstairs." Spatial imagination, through physical settings and language, has become an integral part of class politics.

Suzhi: Ambiguities and Contradictions

In its everyday usage, suzhi is often used to explain the existence of a wide range of perceived "improper behaviors" or "misconduct" among the downstairs people. For Auto-Fan's managers, low suzhi referred to behaviors associable with a lack of discipline. For example, some of the low-suzhi behaviors identifiable in the sales representatives included frequently chitchatting with each other, sending personal QQ (an Internet-based messenger service) messages using company computers, snacking during work hours, and not returning to the shop immediately after finishing work outside the dealership. Not proactively informing prospective customers about new car models was also considered low in suzhi. Knowing and fulfilling one's responsibility at work was also important. Thus, Nanfang's negligence in the accident—he should have checked the gear's position—was regarded as an example of low suzhi.

A key aspect of suzhi, as the managers understood it, was continuous self-development. To them, low-suzhi salespeople and mechanics had no motivation or ambition to excel at work or cultivate skills. Such a sales representative would not spend much time learning about every detail of Peugeot cars and how they were superior to other brands nor try to understand consumer mentality or improve their skills so they could sell more cars. A low-suzhi mechanic would rather loaf around in the rear garage than upgrade his skills so he could tackle more car problems.

The managers believed that suzhi made a difference between the people downstairs and those upstairs. High-suzhi people, as they put it, "are always busy, because they are highly motivated. They do not just sit there and wait for opportunities to come to them. They find opportunities." Manager Wang called the owner, Huang, a good example of someone high in suzhi:

> She is a very diligent woman. She flew around the world to look for different kinds of opportunities. She knew where she could get spare parts cheaper than direct from France. She flew to the United States. She went to Paris. She recently discovered Singapore as another source of import. She managed to use her network, which allows her to do business there. She has ambition. She has vision. That is suzhi.

Metaphors related to cars were often used to illustrate the differences between people of different suzhi at Auto-Fan. To use one that Manager Wang told me: People with high suzhi were like a BMW, and people with low suzhi were like a Meirenbao (the first coupe designed and produced by the Chinese carmaker Jili; Auto-Fan used to be a Meirenbao dealership; see chapter 2). According to Wang, a Meirenbao could not even keep a straight line; the design was that unrefined. In contrast, German cars had some of the best industrial designs and engineering.

Yet, if the quality of engineering in a car can be measured through a series of technological standards, suzhi as applied to people is much more ambiguous, and, as Hairong Yan (2003, 2008) points out, suzhi seems to encompass all kinds of contradictions in everyday life. "Low suzhi" behaviors as understood by the managers could be seen among the managers themselves. Punctuality or the lack thereof was one of the key topics in the managers' suzhi discourse, but they were not always punctual themselves. The dealership owner, Huang, for one, came and left as she pleased. On several occasions, I witnessed that an assistant helped punch a manager's card, which was strictly forbidden by the dealership's workplace regulations and code of conduct. During public occasions, such as a morning briefing session, the managers justified this code violation on the grounds that they had more important business to attend to than coming to the dealership to punch a card. But as the casual conversations in the managers' offices suggested, what was called "important business" was no more than an empty excuse for being late. The managers sometimes handled personal matters during office hours, both at and outside the dealership. When they had free time at their office, they browsed the Internet, chatted with others via QQ, gossiped, snacked, and talked about shopping, their children, and other everyday experiences. All of these behaviors, if attributed to the people downstairs, would be associated with a "lack of discipline," a sign of low suzhi.

The managers told the salespeople that one of the self-improvement techniques for sales representatives was to study consumer patterns. However, on other occasions they told me outright that they did not think there were any general car-related consumer patterns. For instance, during my interview, the vice general manager, Kang, lectured me: "Everyone has their own preference. There are no patterns. You can't study them." In our conversation in 2015, Manager Wang expressed a similar opinion: "People's preferences change over time. . . . When a customer walks into the showroom, you don't know what he or she is looking for exactly, so all you can do is to just listen carefully." Seldom did the managers spend time improving their professional skills, even though they constantly told the salespeople and mechanics to improve theirs. "Sous le dôme épais" annoyed the managers as much as it did the mechanics. While the mechanics hid in the garage, the managers and their assistants turned the volume up on pop music from their computers to drown out the "ghosts screaming."

If a lack of vision and of cultural sophistication were features of low suzhi, as the managers often talked about regarding the downstairs people, the latter also saw these features in the dealership owner, Huang, a high-suzhi individual in the eyes of the managers. A case in point involved Huang's decision to make Auto-Fan a second-level dealership that had to buy cars from a first-level dealership instead of directly buying from the manufacturer (for more details, see chapter 3). To be a first-level dealership required an investment of more than one million renminbi, and a first-level dealership had to fulfill an annual sales target set by the manufacturer. Huang did not want to operate within these constraints. But her salespeople criticized this decision, suggesting that this decision showed Huang's lack of vision in long-term developments, inability to forecast gains and losses, and inadequate understanding of market logics. "Market logics stipulate 'no risk, no gain'," said Sam, a young fellow that shared a similar age and life trajectory with Nanfang. For him, Huang's decision showed that Huang could not handle a lot of responsibility or risk. The senior sales representative, Tom, made a detailed comment:

> She [Huang] couldn't see the point [of being a first-level dealership]! If she completed the quota, the manufacturer would give back a certain percentage of the profit from her sales. The more she sold, the more profit would be returned to her from the manufacturer. She could then offer more discounts to the customers. Now we are just a second-level dealership. We don't get any returned profit from the manufacturer. Those first-level dealerships can lower the retail prices, but we can't because our profit margin is not big enough. How can we compete? Also, first-level dealerships would like customers to come to them, not us. All they need to do is to limit the supply of cars they give us.

Auto-Fan's sixty-year-old janitor, Fu, also gave intriguing observations and comments on Huang. Fu used to be a construction worker, moving from place to place to look for work to support his family. As he aged and retired from construction work, he was hired as a janitor when Auto-Fan opened. Every workday Fu came in before everyone else and stayed longer than everyone else. He sometimes helped the mechanics and occasionally washed cars when the after-sales department was short of hands. For the rest of the time, he sat at the exit of the rear garage, reading newspapers, watching people come in and out of the dealership, and listening in on their conversations—as I did as a fieldworker in the dealership. Fu had only a primary-school education, but he was the one who helped me navigate through the tension between the sales and after-sales departments after I had just arrived.

Fu was not impressed by Huang's leadership skills. He gave me two examples. The first example had to do with the hiring of the vice general manager, Kang, who was Huang's close friend. Kang always parked his car—a red Pontiac sports car—in the showroom area at Auto-Fan. Fu noticed that the red Pontiac often attracted more attention than the Peugeot cars in the showroom, but Huang did not stop Kang from using Auto-Fan as his private parking garage. Moreover, as a janitor, Fu found out that Kang used the store for his personal entertainment after work, or to use Fu's words, "had parties after everyone else left." Fu heard from the sales representatives and mechanics that Kang did not know much about marketing and car maintenance but liked to scold employees for not doing their job properly. Rumors also had it that it was under Kang's advice that Huang invested money in futures and commodities, such as cement, which was supposedly "more profitable" than bringing the latest car models to the dealership. To Fu, Huang neither used the right people nor used people right. Fu said, "Friends are important in life, but this is a business."

The second example Fu gave was Huang's belief in fêng shui. Whenever business did not go well, Huang hired a geomancer to move things around in the showroom, from relocating the entrance to rearranging the cars on display and transplanting the Guandi shrine.[5] During my internship period, the showroom was rearranged once, with one entrance to the showroom moved from the center to the side. Fu said, judging from years of experience with different people, that the geomancer was a lunatic. He asked me rhetorically, "She [Huang] is an educated person, but why was she so superstitious?"

Perhaps the best example to illustrate the politics of the suzhi discourse is the difference in views between the people upstairs and those downstairs regarding the car crash mishap. Let me begin with the buyer, Mr. Zou, who in fact played an important role in the mishap. Zou used to be a truck driver before he ran his own business. Zou liked driving and wanted to have a car. His wife rejected the idea of a family car at first but loosened her attitude somewhat after a couple road trips with Zou's friends. When his wife went on a short outing, Zou took the opportunity to examine cars in different dealerships. He had intended to finish a deal before telling his wife, thinking that his wife would accept a done deal. He did not acquire insurance, saying that, as an experienced driver, he did not need insurance. According to Nanfang, Zou had not pulled the hand brake and had left the gearshift in the first gear position after his final test drive, which Zou did not deny at first but denied vehemently later when together with his wife. The accident gave Zou's wife a perfect reason to withdraw from the transaction: as she put it to the salespeople, "Even though it might look like new [after the repair], the image of the damaged car had been sealed in [her] mind and would always be there ever after."

For the managers, what Nanfang said about the hand brake and the gearshift may be true. They also knew that Zou's wife probably just seized this opportunity to cancel a deal that she never really wanted. However, as Manager Lu put it, "You can't blame the customer . . . especially when Nanfang couldn't prove that the customer was at fault." The managers insisted that

Nanfang should have been more careful and checked the hand brake and which gear the car was in before he started the car. Lu thought that Huang was right to impose the fine on Nanfang and him because "she needed to discipline her employees and defend Auto-Fan's reputation. It's not personal. It's only business." Knowing the resentment among the sales representatives and mechanics, the managers thought that the salespeople's suzhi was low and therefore did not understand why Huang had to deal with the mishap the way she did.

Like the managers, the salespeople and the mechanics understood why the Zous could cancel the transaction and Auto-Fan had to fully refund their money. Where they disagreed with the managers was with the punishment. For them, Nanfang was unlucky to get into a unique situation in which the Zous could not agree whether to buy a car. Moreover, the senior mechanic, Master Dai, told me that the accident was not entirely Nanfang's fault. In his experience, drivers of older generations would usually leave the stick in first gear when they parked the vehicle, while young drivers were taught to leave the stick in neutral. Moreover, young drivers were generally more used to the automatic shift system than a manual one. Master Dai's words resonated with those of the young salespeople. For them, if Zou had applied the hand brake or left the shift stick in the neutral position, none of this would have happened.

As for the amount and extent that Nanfang should take responsibility for, some young mechanics told me not all of the spare parts the managers called for were necessary; some damages could be fixed without needing new parts. Master Dai did not specify what could be done to save the car but suggested that the managers could have at least spared Nanfang the cost of labor. Most importantly, there was consensus among the mechanics and the salespeople that it was simply wrong to leave Nanfang with no money to pay rent for that month. The same fine meant very different things to the managers and to Nanfang. For the managers, that amount might be a dinner with a business partner. But for Nanfang, the same amount might be a month's worth of food, and the cost of labor was enough to cover one month's rent for him. For the salespeople, mechanics, and the janitor, the managers and the owner had "no sympathy . . . All they knew was to protect themselves."

In short, the low-suzhi criticism that the managers and the dealership owners put forth can be looked at as following the logic of the market. They were concerned about laws, workplace norms, and the business of the dealership. The salespeople and mechanics clearly understood the rules as well. But their argument can been viewed as following the logic of care: what mattered was not merely what the law said (whether one could prove where responsibility lay) but what was fair in this specific situation. They would like treatment to be based on a sympathetic understanding of their class-specific conditions.

Thus, the significance of the suzhi politics does not lie in the connotations or interpretation of the term. After months of listening to the conversations and observing various practices, I found that people like Fu who belonged "downstairs," the salespeople, and the mechanics were often as sharp as the managers when it came to understanding the business environment and decision making. If we follow the ways in which the middle-class managers used the notion of suzhi, the suzhi of the people "downstairs" was just as good (or as bad) as that of those "upstairs."

The politics of the suzhi discourse, in many ways, is similar to the spatial politics in the dealership, both of which are related to class politics. The case of Auto-Fan is by no means unique. According to my interviews and conversations with other middle-class and lower-class interlocutors over the years, I found a general pattern regarding the suzhi discourse and class encounters. First, the everyday discourse on suzhi had a discursive register. The middle class, particularly those with a higher education, tend to use the term "suzhi" much more often than the lower classes. In the case of Auto-Fan, the managers used the term "suzhi." But the mechanics and the salespeople did not, as I demonstrated in their discussion about Huang, not even when they criticized the managers for behaviors or decisions that according to the managers would be considered showing a lack of suzhi. Second, the logic of suzhi is circular. On the one hand, the perception that some people have high suzhi is, to a great extent, built upon the perception that they have achieved upward social mobility or they have attained a higher social status. On the other hand, the suzhi discourse justifies the upward social mobility that happens to some people but not others. High suzhi thus correlates with high social status, and low suzhi with low social status. Through the everyday language of high and low suzhi, which may be encoded within the spatial arrangement of a workplace, the hierarchy and spatial imagination of social stratification have been reproduced.

The suzhi discourse in everyday life, thus, shall be understood in the context of the mechanism of class (re)production. Moreover, people with higher class status have the unspoken authority to define what counts as low suzhi. Defining and categorizing certain people and behaviors as low suzhi justify their deploying various disciplinary tools, such as the morning briefings, punctuality cards, and fines. These disciplining rules and practices often do little to improve the so-called suzhi of those being disciplined. However, when people like the salespeople and mechanics fail to observe the rules or practices, the breaking of the code of conduct becomes a stamp of low suzhi. In other words, the rules and practices are there to reiterate the lower-class employees' low suzhi, symbolically justifying the managers' higher status in the process.

Yet it would be simplistic to think that the middle class buy into the official discourse of suzhi in which, as Hairong Yan argues (2003), individual's suzhi is bound with national development. Nor do they simply manipulate the suzhi discourse to advance their class interests. Rather, the suzhi discourse provides a rhetorical framework for the middle class to understand their achieved upward social mobility in the past and their anxiety about shrinking mobility and precarious lives in the present and the future.

Anxiety of Mobility, Reproduction of Distinction

For many of my middle-class interlocutors, suzhi is an umbrella term for knowledge, skills, civility, networks, experiences, and other factors that matter in life, and suzhi is about individual survival and success. They may use the term against what they consider as improper ways of being and behaving (such as spitting in the street). They also use the term in reference to themselves and their children (such as one needs to improve or foster one's suzhi). To a good extent, the suzhi discourse manifests an aspect of middle-class subjectivity, an aspect that is linked to the belief and practices of nurture and education.

Undeniably it is difficult to describe what middle-class subjectivity is. Many of my interlocutors were aware of the fragmented, heterogeneous nature of the middle class when they read about the term in the media. As some of them questioned me, "how can one say that a high school teacher or a low-level government employee, who had a monthly salary of less than RMB 10,000, is just as middle-class as a lawyer who made a million a year?" Yet there are moments that suggest a shared subjectivity among the educated middle class. One such moment was when they were tongue-in-cheek about being middle-class. They often jokingly said that "sandwich class" would be a better term for who they were (see also the introduction).

Another moment was when they talked about the value of education. Many interlocutors—schoolteachers, doctors, or lawyers, whatever the case might be—shared a sense of accomplishment for their social upward mobility when they looked at their lives. A key to this upward social mobility is education, particularly higher education. In their eyes, their college education—for some, their advanced degrees—was critical for them to take advantage of the job opportunities in the emerging management and service sector that had been thirsty for educated talents in the 1990s and early 2000s.

My interlocutors recognized that the significance of higher education sometimes may have little to do with the curricula in college. What the middle class had learned during their college years was often not directly related to what they did as professionals. Interlocutors who majored in mathematics might become civil servants, and those who were trained in mechanical engineering could become lawyers.[6] Moreover, in recruitment practices in big corporations, midrange office jobs were usually open to college students regardless of the places they had their household registration. A bachelor's or an advanced degree, in their own words, helped them "pass the threshold" (*kua guo menkan*) into new horizons and professional jobs that were closed to people without such educational qualifications.

Based on their life trajectories and my own observations, higher education provides them with what I call "structural advantages." In addition to the abovementioned advantages my interlocutors identified, another structural advantage is that higher education has helped overcome institutional obstacles, such as those set by the national household registration system. For people like Manager Wang, college education has enabled them to turn their inherited, institutionalized rural status to an urban status and to move from small cities and towns to the provincial capitals and other big cities with full access to social provisions that local residents are entitled to. Another advantage is that, like in many other countries, higher education has brought them alumni networks, which have often been indispensable to their career development and social life.

Education is critical in class distinction not only because of the structural advantages but also the symbolic capital that is sometimes recognized as su-zhi in everyday language. It allows the middle class to distinguish themselves from people who have highly desirable skills, often hold equally well or better paying jobs, but do not have a college certificate or the "right" taste or lifestyle, like the senior mechanic Master Dai. I was probably an illustrative example of this in the dealership. People at Auto-Fan knew well that I did not know much about cars and the everyday business of selling and fixing cars. The managers told me that my research project was futile (see chapter 3). The sales representatives joked about my ignorance of the specificities of car models. The young mechanics laughed at me when I could not name the parts under the hood. However, on various occasions they complimented me, without cynicism, that I was a high-suzhi person for the fact that I had several degrees and studied abroad. Not only the managers but also the mechanics and salespeople recognized the symbolic value of higher education.

That said, the emerging social distinction between the middle class and other classes, as mentioned in the introduction, is not embedded in any institution. It is different from the official class system during the Maoist years and the early Reform era, a system that had everyone's class identity on record and treated different classes with different entitlements. This new distinction is also different from the rural-urban divide, which the household registration system and land ownership have continuously contributed to and maintained to a great extent. Both systems of social distinction—the old class system and the urban-rural divide—provided individuals with a sense of stability, whatever that meant, that the educated professionals do not feel they have. For them, many things in their lives are changing rapidly; mobility is a source of anxiety.

For one thing, downward mobility is real and can happen any time. Manager Lu in Auto-Fan is one example (chapter 3). Because sales records did not fare well, he was first demoted from a managerial position in the sales department to a salesperson position, before finally being driven away. During my internship period, three out of six managers were replaced.

This unnerving feeling about social mobility and job security was expressed from time to time in everyday conversations, which is aptly illustrated in one of my lunch meetings with four lawyers in 2010. All four lawyers were in their mid- or late thirties, and three were car owners. Two were parents, and one was expecting a child. We chatted about cars and gossiped about office politics. Suddenly one young female lawyer sighed: "We are worse than those migrant workers." Two agreed, saying, "Even if those migrant workers can't find jobs in the city, at least they have some land in their hometown. What do we have if we lose our jobs? Nothing!" The soon-to-be-father lawyer followed, "I am the financial pillar of my family. If I have a car accident, my family would not be able to carry on."

Undeniably, the lawyers' comments about migrant workers and their life security was a middle-class fantasy tied to urban real-estate development. According to my observations over the years, with their networks and experience, people like these lawyers usually would not have any difficulty finding new jobs with equally good if not better salaries. With their savings and insurance, taking some time off work would not jeopardize their way of life. In contrast, a work incident like the mishap at Auto-Fan might immediately put people like Nanfang in a dire situation.

Nevertheless, the lawyers' conversation took place within a specific context. The 2008 financial crisis had led to a hiring freeze and mass layoffs in many law firms in the United States. News of this quickly spread to lawyers in China through their alumni circles. They were worried that similar massive layoffs would happen in China as the business world they worked in was closely connected to the global economy. The Chinese government's injection of money to its economy did little to calm them, because, as the lawyers said, "no one knows who would benefit from that money." Recently, a partner who had been bringing in major clients had left the firm; the departure heightened their anxiety and suspicions about the future of the firm.

Their land-as-life-guarantee comment, whether imagined or even stemming from ignorance, reflected the feeling of anxiety among my middle-class interlocutors in the face of the precariousness resulting from the dramatic social transformations in the past several decades. The increasing embeddedness of China's economy in the global economy has led to an awareness that what happens thousands of miles away may have an immediate impact on the lives of the middle-class professionals sitting in their air-conditioned offices. Some of my interlocutors told me that their parents could not understand this kind of volatile work experience because their parents only worked in work units under the centrally planned system in which work life was highly predictable and stable (at least until large-scale layoffs resulted from top-down government decisions). On the other hand, China's reforms have brought down the previous socialist welfare system while a new system is in the process of being built and implemented. Families now have to shoulder senior care, child care, and medical care, which the state used to see as its responsibilities (even though it might not have the full capacity to implement). As the middle generation and the major income earners in the families, many of my interlocutors thought that they lived and worked under much more pressure than their parents at their age.

Meanwhile, according to many of my interlocutors and my own observations, the possibilities of upward mobility have changed dramatically in the past decade. People born in the late 1980s and afterward might have more difficulty in moving upward with one's own effort than those born in the late 1960s to early 1980s. The role of higher education in providing job opportunities seems to have changed. The state has expanded higher education since the late 1990s, allowing for-profit, private colleges to run side by side public universities. The numbers of colleges and of students admitted to colleges have been growing. Paradoxically, a college certificate has also, as the middle class put it, "depreciated" (*bianzhi*). Nowadays a college degree, especially from lesser-known or junior colleges, cannot bring the same kind of structural advantages as in the old days. When talking about work and life's challenges, the lawyer Cecilia (see chapter 2) commented, "When I graduated from law school, I thought the job market was difficult. But retrospectively, I realized none of my classmates were unable to find a job. While our starting salaries were not that high, real-estate prices weren't high either. Look, we all have an apartment now—and cars too. But looking at the younger generation, I always wonder: how can they afford an apartment in this city?"

Such change can be shown by comparing the trajectories of the managers and the owner with those of the salespeople at the dealership. As illustrated in the previous chapter, under the socialist welfare system, Huang, Wang, and Lu were given access to education, from primary school to college, without substantial family investments. Admission to college was highly selective, but they were guaranteed jobs upon graduation. Their education, work experience, and networks built upon their school and work affiliations provided important capital when structural transformations of the economy were on the way. In comparison, Nanfang and other sales representatives came from similar family background to the managers. They managed to be admitted to colleges, even though they would not have made it, given their academic performance, if they had lived in Huang's or Wang's times. When Nanfang and others graduated, there were many more college graduates on the job market. Nanfang and people like him have been struggling to settle down in big cities.

Living with such anxiety about mobility, work, and life, intriguingly, has not weakened many of my middle-class interlocutors' belief in education and suzhi. In fact, it seems to reaffirm their belief that suzhi was important to survive the precariousness. They might joke about suzhi when the government or government-affiliated professional associations (such as the Bar Association) asked them to improve their *yewu suzhi* (professional quality), but the way in which they saw to the suzhi of their children highlighted how serious they are with suzhi. Many middle-class parents invest heavily in cultivating their children's suzhi, and their "educational desire," as Andrew B. Kipnis (2011, 2016) points out, is high. My interlocutors have admitted that, compared to their own parents, they have invested a lot more money and time in their children's future (see also Kuan 2015). They intensely monitor their children's schoolwork. Like many American middle-class parents (Heiman 2015), these Chinese middle-class parents drive their children to attend extracurricular activities and travel with them to see the country and the world from the time their children are young. The goal is not just to go to college but to go to a good college. For them, good schools and colleges mean not only worldwide credibility but also friend circles and alumni networks comprising people of high suzhi. Manager Wang at the dealership sent his daughter to Germany for college education, as he believed that a German university could provide quality education, chances to learn to be independent, and access to job opportunities in the European job market that a Chinese university might not be able to offer.

In short, the suzhi discourse is not a rhetorical tool that the middle class exploit to discriminate against the lower classes. Instead, the suzhi discourse should be understood as part of the process in which class distinction is reproduced socially and symbolically. The term "suzhi" here, with its connection with education and nurture, encapsulates the middle class's understanding about mobility and the eagerness that the middle class strive hard to reproduce the possibility of upward mobility in the next generation.

Conclusion

The emerging automotive regime has become a center of gravity. Not only has it contributed to upward social mobility for educated individuals like Auto-Fan's owner and managers (chapter 3); it has also provided prospects to people like the sales representative Nanfang and the mechanics. Most of the young women and men were born and raised in relatively poor towns and rural areas and had left their families and come to the affluent Pearl River delta for jobs. The car presents opportunities: automobility requires networks of service providers. The car is their shared dream: it is a luxurious item, a symbol of urban lifestyle and upward mobility they desire. These young people hope that one day they can turn from people who serve others and their cars to car owners who are on the receiving end of customer service. Workplaces like the dealership Auto-Fan are where the lives of different groups of people cross paths. They are key sites where class distinctions are negotiated and reproduced through everyday interactions.

Class politics has gradually taken a new form since the beginning of the Reform era. Social differences are highly visible in contemporary urban life. These differences are no longer primary between the rural and the urban or between newcomers (*waidiren*) and local residents (*bendiren*)—the main references of distinction in popular discourses in the 1990s. These differences are manifested in education, employment, salary, social circles, and lifestyle practices. These differences are also experienced and perceived as generational differences in terms of social mobility. Often intertwined with rural-urban divide and other structures of inequality, class differences have been increasingly used as the frame to understand socioeconomic disparity but not necessarily articulated through a language of class and class conflicts, a language that is politically loaded and invokes a Maoist past that many are determined to shed.

At a time when class structure has been reconfigured and new class identities are yet to be consolidated and articulated, the suzhi discourse, in some ways, provides a new terminology to make sense of the transformations. The suzhi discourse has been closely connected to education since it was promoted by the state concerning national development and population. It converges with the belief in the connection between internal quality and nurture that is deeply rooted in literati culture in Chinese history.[7] It speaks to the middle class's lived experience and captures their anxiety about social mobility in precarious times.

The suzhi discourse provides a spatial imagination and understanding of class relationship that is quite different from that with the old class terminology. In the Maoist and early Reform days, the language of class focused on exploitation, opposition, and struggle (thus, often violence). Class categories were described in colorful terms: the red classes and the black classes. The red ones referred to the progressive classes, such as the proletarian and the peasants, and the black the backward classes, such as the capitalists. Class identity, to a large extent, depended on family background and could be inherited.

Unlike the Maoist class language, suzhi is, supposedly, individualized and is not necessarily linked with one's family background. Unlike Maoist class labels that were assigned by the government and were relatively rigid, suzhi can be improved over the course of one's lifetime. Therefore, one could change from being a person of low suzhi to one with high suzhi through cultivation; somewhat resembling the "American dream," the possibility of transformation exists for everyone. In the suzhi discourse, the contrast of class relationship is spatial and hierarchical: low suzhi and lower classes on the one hand and high suzhi and the middle class on the other.[8] Such spatial imagination is often reinforced through spatial arrangement in work relationship: lower-class people working on a lower floor, while the middle class work on an upper floor. This spatial imagination further coincides with a description of upward social mobility—to "move up the social ladder."

Importantly, the use of suzhi by the middle class is not so much about manipulation or enactment as reappropriation of an official discourse to capture their own subjective experience. Thus, unpacking what suzhi means for the educated middle class presents a window for us to understand their perceptions about the past and present, as well as project the future. Paradoxically, despite their occasional cynicism toward the official rhetoric, the middle class's reappropriation of suzhi in their everyday interactions perpetuates the official discourse, which depoliticizes class politics and provides legitimacy to the party-state that is confronted with enlarging social gaps in the new age.

Chapter 5

Bidding for a License Plate

The Importance of Being a Free and Proper Consumer

"RMB 220,000 [roughly $29,062], going for the third time! Sold!" The crisp sound of a gavel banging acknowledged the highest bid of the day for the license plate number 888B8. A congratulatory applause erupted among the bidders and their families and friends. Most journalists sitting in the media section and I paused our note taking and joined in the enthusiastic applause. Behind us, cameramen were busy filming the highest bidders—two middle-aged men in T-shirts and shorts. This was the climax of the fourteenth passenger car license plate auction held in the Xinghai Musical Hall in Guangzhou on July 21, 2007.

Car licensing is a key aspect of the automotive regime in contemporary societies, but social scientists give it hardly any attention. License plates function much like the address of a building and the ID number of an individual. They are a standardized but unique combination of letters and digits inscribed on a metal plate, and they serve as markers for automobiles. Cars are constantly mobile, and the license system makes cars recordable, traceable, and calculable. Car licensing allows the authorities to control and track what would otherwise be uncontrollable individual movements, particularly with the prevalence of such technologies as global positioning systems (GPSs), close-circuit television, and data processing. Licensing creates a digital panopticon—after Foucault (1995)—in which the gaze of the state, be it real or imaginary, can be felt everywhere by car users. To have a car or not may be an option, but to license one's car is an obligation, and by getting a car license, the users, owners, and their families automatically subject themselves to the panoptic surveillance and disciplinary power of the state.

Nevertheless, a license plate is more than a cold sheet of iron with numbers and letters inscribed on it. It can also be the car owner's personal statement. Paying extra money to personalize a license plate is a common practice in many countries. The American Association of Motor Vehicle Administrators conducted a survey in 2007 and found that 9.3 million motor vehicles had personalized "vanity" plates (Lonce 2009).

Unlike in the United States, vanity plates are uncommon in China. The liberalization of the car market has not resulted in the regulation of license plates being liberated. Until the late 2000s in the city of Guangzhou, vanity plates were only available through auctions of license plates with lucky numbers. "Lucky" license plates are a unique form of vanity plates, because car owners can only choose from the limited stock of license numbers designated by the municipal government. They are not personalized plates. However, the competitive bidding, which has led to some license plates costing more than a midsize sedan, makes them undeniably objects of vanity.

What make these license plates cost so much? How are the values of these lucky plates constructed and in particular perceived by the middle class? These are questions for this chapter. I suggest that neither Marx's writing on commodity nor Simmel's theory on value and circulation alone gives us enough to understand the appeal of these lucky plates. Yet seeing these auctions as no more than a contest for status may overlook the complexity of these events in which what is for sale is essentially signs of state power.

To unpack such complexity, we need to peel away the multiple layers of structures that underlie the meaningful construction of the lucky license plates and their auctions. Drawing on others' analysis of auctions, I attend to four institutional and cultural settings. I start with the rules that regulate the issuance of license plate numbers. Institutional constraints on choices make the freedom to choose a licensing number desirable and evaluable, no matter how limited the range of choices is. I then zoom in on the license numbers, showing how the practices of number preference in everyday life are associated with the rising rhetoric on fate and luck. The next section turns to the auctions. It shows how an economic form (auction/market) matters in collapsing the distinction between a state function (licensing) and a commodity. The last part of the analysis before the conclusion examines the views of the middle class as the spectators of the license plates auctions, showing how auctioning lucky license plates embodies the tension between two sets of values regarding consumption, both of which are critical to the middle class's identity making.

The auctioning of lucky license plates thus serves as a prism through which we can see some of the ways through which boundaries are constructed between state and economy, logics, and practices that ordinary people—middle-class professionals in this case—try to make sense of in the precarious lives they lead and of the kind of people they think they are. All of these are important to understand what transformations mean for people who live through them.

Car License Plates: Freedom of Choice as Exception

Observing the case in the United States, Stefan J. Lonce (2009) writes that vanity plates reflect the values of freedom, mobility, and fun, which, according to Cotten Seiler (2008), are embedded in the United States' political ideology of what it means to be its citizens. Such political ideology has an effect on the United States' regulations of vanity plates. Only a small fee is needed to personalize a license plate, without many restrictions on how to choose the letter-number combination.

Such is not the case in China. A very short window was once open for car owners to design their own license plates as they wished. On August 12, 2002, the central government experimented with individualized license plates in four designated cities (Beijing, Tianjin, Hangzhou, and Shenzhen). However, the policy lasted only ten days, without any official explanation (Wang Le. 2002). According to a professor in a newspaper interview (Wang Li 2002), the reasons included that some self-designed license plates were immorally dubious (e.g., SEX-001), some involved trademark infringement (e.g., IBM-001), some were named after an organization and could easily cause confusion (e.g., NBA, FBI), and some touched upon sensitive issues and "could hurt the feelings of people in other countries" (e.g., USA-911).

License plates in China follow a pattern that includes seven symbols: one Chinese character, roman letters, and numbers. Except for high-level government cars or cars of embassies and consulates, the first two symbols identify the place where the car is registered. The first Chinese character represents the province of origin. The Roman letter that follows denotes a city or a town. Usually the letter *A* refers to the capital of a province. The first two symbols are crucial for implementing rules that distinguish locally registered cars from foreign ones.[1] The local government decides the rules for the last five symbols on the license plate, which usually combines numbers and letters, but occasionally the five symbols are all numbers. The current naming system of the license plates tends to have more numbers than letters.

Like many cities in China, Guangzhou has a standardized car registration and licensing procedure. Choosing the license number and mounting the plate takes place in one of the several offices of the traffic police department. When I started my internship in a dealership in fall 2006, the Guangzhou traffic police department had already used a computer program to generate random numbers for car owners to choose. With a click on a palm-sized keypad, tens of numbers then scrolled swiftly over the screen. The numbers moved so quickly that individuals could never tell exactly what the numbers were. The one who was to choose the number clicked again, and a number was displayed (figure 6). During my internship in the dealership, car owners or their representatives could press twice and choose one from the two numbers to be their license plate number. The selection would take less than ten minutes. In 2007 the municipal government increased the number of choices from two to five, and in 2008 from five to ten. Since October 2008, the municipal government has also allowed semi-self-designed license plates within strict rules.[2] It costs less than RMB1,000 to have a car licensed using the standard procedure.

In addition to the standardized licensing procedure, the municipal government launched the lucky number license plate auctions in April 2006. License numbers for auction typically contain three or four of the digits 3, 6, 8, or 9. Another prevalent format of these license numbers was a combination of one single number repeating three or four times, such as 111L1, 388C8, and 8888Q.

Figure 6. A car owner choosing his license plate number in the traffic police department, 2007.
Photo by the author

The municipal government designated the state-owned Guangzhou Enterprises Mergers and Acquisitions Services (GEMAS) to organize and operate the auctions. The auctions were allegedly based on "a folk custom and cultural activity," and their purposes were to satisfy "the needs of high-end car owners for good numbers, while setting up bidding as a way to collect funding for public interests purposes, contributing to building social harmony" (GEMAS 2006). According to the government's statement to the public before each auction, money obtained during the auctions would be used to establish and maintain a public fund for traffic infrastructural building, roadside assistance, and subsidies for traffic accident victims.

The municipal government tested the water by initially offering three hundred passenger car license plate numbers for bidding in the first auction. The number of plates was soon reduced to a hundred fifty, keeping at a hundred for a while, and then further reduced to seventy in recent auctions. The auctions were most frequent in 2006 and 2007, at an almost monthly pace. While there were only twenty-five auctions held between January 2008

Table 6. The first ten top bidding prices in each auction from April 2006 to August 2015 (ranked by price from high to low)*

Rank	Time (Year/Month)	Price (Thousand RMB)	License Plate Number
1	2010/10	1,314	8888Q
2	2011/1	952	9999S
3	2011/12	901	8888V
4	2007/10	747	000F1
5	2012/4	662	9999W
6	2009/12	651	9999K
7	2012/9	609	8888Y
8	2010/4	561	9999M
9	2011/7	454	8888U
10	2015/6	450	K999A

Sources: Reports from major local newspapers, including *Yangcheng Wanbao, Xinkuaibao, Nanfang Dushibao,* and *Xinxi Shibao.*

* There were forty-four auctions in total from April 2006 to August 2015. I could not find in local newspapers price information for the fortieth and forty-second auctions (March and September 2014) and auctions since July 2015. However, based on the style of reporting that pays attention to the spectacular prices, the top bidding prices could not have been close to the top three and were likely to have been outside the top ten.

and October 2015,[3] the highest bids since 2008 tended to be higher than those in earlier auctions (table 6).

The media and car dealers considered July 2007 to be a significant moment for the license plate auction in Guangzhou. Under the previous state policy, the license plates had been assigned primarily to cars, not people.[4] Some owners had a lot of reservations toward bidding, as they knew they would have to part with the expensive license plates when they changed cars. Starting in July 2007, license plate numbers became bound with the car owners, and an old license plate could be mounted to a new car of the same owner.

The first auctions took place in a stadium, and later ones alternated between a grand ballroom in a military-owned hotel, a classical music concert hall, and an exhibition hall usually used for trade fairs. Rules of entry were implemented to ensure exclusivity. Except for journalists, auction participants had to be car owners and present their car registration certificates at the entrance of the venue. Cars waiting to be mounted with auctioned license

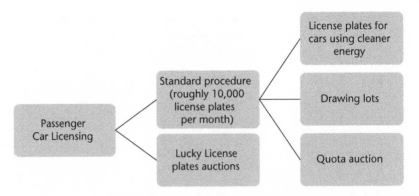

Figure 7. Car licensing procedures in Guangzhou.

numbers were mostly luxury brands, such as Mercedes-Benz, BMW, and Lexus, with an increasing number of Porsches and other high-end sports cars over time.

The lucky license plate auction needs to be distinguished from another form of auction that has taken effect since June 2012. The new auction comes with a new municipal policy that aims to control car growth in the city. Under this policy, a total of 120,000 new license plates would be issued for private cars each year (10,000 per month on average). Quotas first go to hybrid or electric cars. The rest are divided into two categories, half distributed through drawing lots and the other through bidding ("quota auction," see figure 7). A potential car owner could make a bid via a computer connected to the Internet without seeing other bidders. This auction gives owners the right to get a license plate following the standard procedure, while the lucky license plates auction is parallel to the standard procedure that gives the owner a license plate.

Car owners made clear distinctions between the two kinds of auctions: the auction for quota to register one's car was strictly an administrative procedure, a way of controlling car growth in the city. But the lucky license plates auctions were different, partly because, as I will explain later, the auctions were a performance of the market. The lucky license plates auctions were different also because they offered a sense of freedom to choose. In the standard procedure, a computer program decides what number a person could have. Even with the quota auctions, car owners felt that it was rather a strategic choice, instead of choosing what they liked, to increase the possibility of getting a quota so that they could buy and drive a car. In contrast, although car owners still could not compile the content of the license plate they would like, car owners who participated in the auctions could choose, from a given list, the numbers they liked.

In that sense, the lucky license plates auctions embody the saying "freedom has a price," which my middle-class interlocutors would often relate to me. Yet a sense of freedom is not the only source that imbues the license plates with value. The value of the lucky plates also comes from the numbers.

Enchanting License Plates, Lucky Numbers

In his analysis of an art auction, Jean Baudrillard suggests that a painting, by being circulated, would have its symbolic value "resolved into aesthetic function" and sign value (1981, 120). "The essential function of the auction is the institution of a community of the privileged who define themselves as such by agonistic speculation upon a restricted corpus of signs" (117). "'Aesthetic enjoyment' and the values labeled as 'absolute' are all that is left to those who cannot aspire to the privileged potlatch" (121). Domination is produced not because of the economic value that the privileged invest but through their control of the process of signification.

Baudrillard's art auctions have similarities with the license plates auctions described above: neither follows a logic of economic calculation built upon use value, and competitive bidding is a process of building a community of the privileged. Yet in dissecting the process of value transmutation, Baudrillard admits that a painting has a true value—its "genealogical value" being charged with prestige throughout its history (1981, 120). And the aesthetic value of a painting, which is seen as "universal" and maintained by cultural institutions, such as museums, legitimizes the operation of the auction and the art market. If the license plate numbers also have genealogical value, then upon what sociocultural context could such genealogical value be built?

Observers have long noticed a culture of numbers in China. From the number of gates on the city walls to auspicious dates for social events, numbers have played an important role in architecture, city planning, imperial order, and rituals in traditional China. Numbers, such as the number of animals used to decorate a roof or how many vessels are used in a state ceremony, indicate an individual's social and political status. Charles Stafford

(2009, 2010) has keenly examined numeric structure in classical literature, cosmology, and popular religious rituals. In his study on rural Taiwan and mainland China, numbers provide the means for people to make sense of their lives as unique experiences that are distinguished from others' lives. In the Chinese tradition, therefore, the "numbers themselves may be seen as meaningful, creative, even poetic things, and they often figure prominently in accounts of the self" (Stafford 2009, 111).

While the logic of the symbolic significance of numbers may be similar, the configuration of numeric significance in daily life in rural Taiwan may be different from that in mainland China, particularly in the urban areas. During the Maoist era in mainland China, many practices related to numbers were seen as feudalistic and superstitious, associated with the backward China and the ruling elites. In the CCP-led government's efforts to create a new China, these practices were publicly denounced and disappeared, at least in public spaces, particularly in the urban areas. In recent years, special attention to numbers has reemerged. Urban professionals originally from different parts of China told me that until recently such number-luck beliefs did not exist in their hometowns. They believed that such beliefs had come from the southern part of the country, with influence from Hong Kong and Taiwan through mass media, popular culture, and religious exchanges since the Reform era.

In this numeric preference that has reemerged, the number 8 is arguably the most coveted, particularly among business people; 3, 6, and 9 are also popular. Such preference is built upon a phonetic play on sound: all of these numbers have pronunciations similar to a character related to either good fortune (6, 8), longevity (9), or being lively and energetic (3). The numeral 4 is generally avoided because it sounds like "death."[5] Besides these general rules, there are local peculiarities. Take the number 4 for example. Because of the diversity of the Chinese languages, 4 is pronounced like the word for "death" in Cantonese and Mandarin but like the word for "fortune" in some other dialects. The number 4 may be unpopular in Guangzhou, but it is welcomed in some other places.

In some situations, numeric preference is derived from visual similarity between a number and an object, the connection of which is embedded in local knowledge or shared perception among the general public or a specific group of people. An intriguing case is the number 8. While 8 is a favorite in general, it may not be a good sign for government officials. As a reporter following the license plate auction series for a major local newspaper for a while, Kelly told me, "Many government officials came to bid for their own cars. But they don't like 8, because it looks like handcuffs." Kelly's interpretation of the officials' fear of 8 was new to me and to the lower-end and midrange civil servants I later interviewed. But my interlocutors and I instantly caught its connotation because of a popular perception that every Chinese official was guilty of corruption, but the unlucky ones would be singled out in the name of anticorruption to be the scapegoat of internal political struggle.

The fact that the elevators in many high-rise buildings do not have buttons for the fourth, fourteenth, and twenty-fourth floors (those floors do not exist in the buildings) is a manifestation of numeric preference. The prices of cell phone SIM cards also vary according to their numbers (Gerth 2010). The pursuit of lucky license plates is one of the many kinds of practices involving numeric preference. Such pursuit does not only exist inside the auction venues but also in the office of the traffic police, where the standard procedure of car licensing takes place.

Choosing a license number is an important event to new car owners. Most new car owners arrive with family members, sometimes the whole family, to witness the licensing process. It is also common that friends come along to witness the moment when a car officially becomes his or her or the family's car. While waiting for their turn at the police office, many people stand behind a designated line and watch the selection process. Some try hard to get near the monitor so that they can see the numbers. But one does not need to be close to the counter to know whether the number on the screen is good. Whenever a good combination comes up, the whole group applauds and cheers (figure 8).

Some new car owners are more enthusiastic in their pursuit of good numbers than others. During my internship period in the dealership, among all car owners, Mr. Tong was most proactive in getting a good license number. I met Tong at the traffic police office when a salesperson and I were accompanying a customer, a certain Miss Li, to finish the licensing process. A small-time entrepreneur, Tong was there to register his third car, a black Camry. He recognized Miss Li, a manager in a state-owned bank that handled Tong's banking issues. Seeing us there to choose a license plate number as well, Mr. Tong was excited and shared his story.

Mr. Tong liked the number 8. As a veteran of the standard licensing process, Mr. Tong realized that the numbers that the computer system

Figure 8. Car owners and their families and friends watching license plate number selection in the traffic police department, 2007. Photo by the author

generated were only partially random, because certain letters or digits come out in sequence. My colleagues in the dealership confirmed what Mr. Tong said: they alleged that they could tell roughly the issuing date of a new license plate within the past three months by the sequence of the digit-letter combination. After he ordered his new car, Mr. Tong went to the hall first just to observe for several days. At the beginning, most numbers began with 24 or 25. He had waited for two days until the day when the numbers 28 or 29 dominated. To reinforce his luck, Mr. Tong even brought his five-year-old nephew to press the keyboard button for the number selection. An old folk saying alleged that a virgin child's hands (*tongzi shou*) have magic power and could bring luck. Mr. Tong's careful plan paid off: he had only good numbers on the license plate. He was proud of himself for spending little money and getting a good number that could rival the ones from the auction. Mr. Tong did not forget to ask what Miss Li got. Knowing Miss Li got a good number without any preparation, Mr. Tong repeatedly said, "You're so lucky."

In contrast, Miss Li told me initially that she did not care what number she would get. "I deal with numbers all the time at work. They are just numbers." A single woman in her late thirties, Miss Li decided to have a small hatchback, to use her own words, "for fun." She paid the dealership to deal with most of the licensing on her behalf. Only in the final stage did she ask for a half day off work and come to the police office in person to choose a license plate number. She got a bit impatient when we were waiting in a long line. Eventually, she got a license number with 2, 8, and 9, and Mr. Tong told her that it was a really good one, particularly because she had not invested any time or effort. Miss Li was very happy with the license number, particularly after she heard what Mr. Tong had had to do for his. "Luck is on my side," she said. Her good mood made the long wait and other bureaucratic issues, which she originally complained about, seem almost nothing. While I have seen and heard from colleagues in the dealership about other cases in which the new car owners were like Mr. Tong, most of the car owners I have known are like Miss Li, who would wait for luck to come rather than actively pursuing it.

Generally speaking, my middle-class interlocutors did not simply equate such numeric preference to superstition (*mixin*). Rarely did they give me a straightforward answer saying whether they believed in such number-luck practices. "Hard to say" was usually the answer I received. As scholars studying the concept of fate in various Chinese communities suggest (Basu 1991; Harrell 1977, 1987), the relationship between faith and everyday life decisions is by no means straightforward. Such ambiguity has originated, on the one hand, from years of school education that taught them to look at the world scientifically. As my interlocutors told me, there was no evidence to suggest the connection between certain numbers and luck or, for that matter, fate (*ming*). On the other hand, these middle-class professionals felt increasingly the weight of fate on their lives over the years. It was fate that they were not born in extreme poverty, a condition that would give little hope for upward mobility. They were lucky to have grown up in urban areas and to have had decent occupations and earned their upward mobility. But it was also fate that, as they told me, they were not born into rich families, which would have spared them years of hard work, or that they did not get promoted to positions they wanted. They felt fate was against them when they saw a rural resident (generally perceived as "unfortunate") become a millionaire later because rural lands became valuable assets as urban expansion and development took off in the twenty-first century. While, as Harrell (1987) suggests, without denying the significance of individuals' hard work, my middle-class interlocutors increasingly admitted that there was something larger than the self—which they often referred to as "fate"—that shaped their lives and opportunities.

Julie Y. Chu (2010) argues that there is "an economy of blind faith" on the rise in China. Examining ritual practices, particularly ritual offerings, in a rural community in Fujian, where residents took great risks to find new lives overseas, Chu suggests that the economy of blind faith, by creating reciprocal bonds between visible and invisible spheres through ritual offerings, contributes to the production of a sense of security in a highly volatile world. Chu's analysis can be applied to the rise of religious activities in urban areas in recent years, activities that some of my interlocutors have also taken part in. Many of them would not identify themselves as religious, and they believed that fate or fate in relation to certain practices or decisions could only be interpreted retrospectively but not be foreseen. Nevertheless, following religious or common practices regarding luck and fate, in some way, was to show reverence to the forces beyond their control, which, even if they might not do good, would do no harm (*mei huaichu*). The same logic applied to practices of numeric preference (and avoidance) as an expression of the desire for luck and particularly for fortune.

In that sense, such numeric preference practices shall not be reduced to mere "Old World superstitions," as named by an American journalist who observed a license plates auction held in Guangzhou in June 2006.[6] Instead, they are indeed "a folk custom and cultural activity," as GEMAS termed them. If museums are the cultural institutions that sustain the aesthetic value of paintings for the art market, the belief and practice about fate provides a cultural framework through which the auctioning of license plate numbers is made meaningful. Yet the cultural belief and practice, per se, do not determine the market value of the numbers. To understand the economic aspect of the event, we now turn to the mechanism of the auctions.

Lucky License Plates Auctions: A Theater of a Market

A license plate number and the license plate are the material forms of licensing as a governing technique. From the perspective of control and surveillance, each license number is equal in terms of its utility. A license number contains little value in the Marxist sense, as it does not contain much human labor or physical resource. According to Georg Simmel (2004), who emphasizes circulation as the structure for commodity value, a license plate is close to being worthless, because its circulation is highly limited. A license number is meant to establish a specific correspondence between the number and the car for the purpose of management, which thus precludes the owners from exchanging the license numbers freely. A license plate is a onetime trade business for any given car owner, because the owner cannot pass the license number to others.

To understand how the economic value (in terms of money) of a license plate is produced, I suggest that we need to pay attention to the form of interaction—auctions—that collapses the distinction in people's perceptions between an act of the state and an act of consumption. I would not have realized the transforming effect of the auctions had I not seated myself in one and observed the bidding as mentioned at the beginning of this chapter. This auction was held in a classical music concert hall in July 2007. I first saw the government announcement of the auction in local newspapers. I was ignorant of the exclusivity of the event: one had to be a car owner ready to bid, friends or family of such a car owner, or reporters. After pulling a lot of strings, I finally managed to get myself a badge that said I was an intern from a major local newspaper. I sat in the media's section at the second tier on the side facing the stage, a place that gave the reporters a good view of the bidders, their families, and friends seated in the middle of the orchestra. The majority of the bidders were middle-aged. No one seemed to have come alone. Some brought friends. Many came as a family, with young or adolescent children. They were dressed in such low-profile garb that their clothes seemed like ordinary street wear, but the texture of the materials and accessories gave away their real costs. In the seating area behind the stage were staff members processing documents for successful bidders. On the stage, tables and a stand were set up for the staff and auctioneers, all dressed in suits. Staff from the auction company GEMAS sat in the seats behind the stage. A big banner that indicated the occasion was hung on the higher-level seats behind the stage against a large pipe organ (figure 9). I could not help but feel a bit awkward for having an auction in such a nonmarket setting.

The first auctioneer was a young man in his early thirties. Speaking Mandarin with a heavy southern accent, he told the bidders that the average price in the last auction had been RMB 71,000 ($9,379). Although participants could raise their bidding cards to increase the bid at increments of RMB

Figure 9. Auction stage in the concert hall, 2007. Photo by the author

1,000, he encouraged them to call out bids directly to quicken the pace. He said that, given his experience, bidders usually called out the bids when the bidding went beyond RMB 70,000.

The RMB 101,000 ($13,342) bid offered for the fourth plate (for 168B8) was a warm-up. The highest bid came with the fifth plate, 888B8. Unlike many other numbers that had begun with RMB 5,000, bidding for 888B8 commenced at RMB 10,000. The moment after the number and the starting bid were announced, more than ten participants raised their bidding cards, but they were quickly upstaged by a young man who called out, "60,000." Then there was a moment of silence, followed by an eruption of a new wave of bidding. Excited even as an observer, I had sympathy for the young auctioneer, for he could barely keep up with the calling cards being waved in the air. Only when the price had reached RMB 150,000 did the number of bidders shrink. But when the price went up to RMB 189,000, the two remaining competitors were suddenly rejoined by others, and the bidding war reignited. "RMB 220,000 [$29,062], going once! Going twice! Sold, to . . ." The young auctioneer banged the gavel, and we had the highest bid of the day. The journalists and I put our hands together as enthusiastically as the bidders seated at the center of the hall.

Before I went through the auction in person, I found the media's sensationalizing reporting style distasteful. News on the auctions was loaded with phrases such as "sky-high price" (*tianjia*). Even with bids like RMB 440,000, reporters used phrases such as "only" (*zhibuguo*) in a regretful tone after they compared them to the record price. However, as I sat there in the auction, the enthusiasm among the participants was heartfelt and contagious. The journalists and I cheered when the highest bid came; we applauded whenever a number was sold at a high price; we were genuinely disappointed if a good number went without buyers, and we all wanted to see records being set. It was in this moment that I realized those sensational words, the regretful or exhilarative tone in the news articles about the auction, were real reflections of the feelings of being there in the live auction.

The lucky license plate auctions have been spectacular events for the media. The numbers available for bidding are published in all major local newspapers ten days before auction day. Local TV channels broadcast video clips in the evening news, showing car owners enthusiastically bidding. From printed newspapers to online news and forums, one could easily find reports about the most expensive license plate and its price, the total amount of money with all the successful bids, and the average price on the day following the auction, with pictures showing the bidders holding up their calling numbers. Sometimes the make and the model of the car, whose owner battled for the most expensive plate, were disclosed. Although the restrictive rules kept most citizens out of the auction venue, the media brought them back in.

The effect of the auctions in framing the meaning of the transactions can be observed in the ways the middle-class car owners talk about licensing. I talked to different people during the auction and listened to conversations between bidders. It was crystal clear that no one thought of the auction as a charity event as GEMAS had described, and the enthusiasm had no public interest association. Instead, "buying" and "selling" were the terms auction participants used the most to describe this event. Outside the auction venue, my other interlocutors referred to the bidding as "consumption" or "luxury consumption" but called the standard licensing procedure "registering the car" and the payment "an administrative cost," alluding to the latter being a bureaucratic process.

This contrast has little to do with the actual money spent. Not every lucky plate was auctioned off, and a good number of them were sold at their starting bid: RMB 5,000 or RMB 10,000. The average price of a lucky license plate in each auction ranged between RMB 17,000 and RMB 120,000 up until 2015, but in many auctions the average price was between RMB 20,000 and RMB 40,000. This price was high when compared to the expense in the standard licensing procedure before 2012. However, in the abovementioned quota auction, since 2012, Guangzhou car owners who opted to bid for the right to get a license plate had to pay more than RMB 10,000. In Shanghai, where there is also a similar quota auction system, the monthly average biding price has been more than RMB 70,000 for over a decade. Yet rarely have I heard my interlocutors talk about the quota auction as license plate consumption.

On the symbiotic relationship between marketplace and theater, Jean-Christophe Agnew writes eloquently that the "legitimacy of the marketplace as a social institution was inseparable from its theatricality, for the medieval criteria of authority and authenticity required that both attributes be bodied forth: deliberately displayed, performed, and witnessed" (1986, 40). Although his study focuses on medieval times, Agnew's argument remains relevant for the license plate auctions in today's China. Backed by government authority, the auction theatrically stages the act of selling and buying. It engages sellers (government), buyers (wealthy elites), and an audience (the middle class and other media recipients). These major players voluntarily participated in the process of negotiation instead of being coerced into it. The bidding process was confrontational, dramatizing the intense price competition. Its ambience, media hype, and headlines created a concrete sense and a tangible experience of a market, which makes the auction a drastically different experience from registering one's car at the traffic police office through the standard licensing procedure. Arjun Appadurai has noted that auctions "accentuate the commodity dimension of objects" (1986, 15). Here, he seems to suggest that a commodity exists prior to the operation of a market. But if adhering to his argument that the value of something depends on the sociocultural context that it travels through, can the market and commodities be in a more mutually defined process? In the case of the lucky license plate auctions, I thus want to push his point and suggest that the auction is an essential structure and process through which the market is performed. The auction thus creates a liminal time-space in which the boundary between the material form of a governing technique and a commodity becomes blurred, allowing the license plate numbers to be imagined and understood as commodities, objects with market values.

Freedom of Consumption and Proper Consumers

Over the years, I have been asking my interlocutors what they thought about paying so much money for a series of numbers and letters in the lucky license plates auctions. My interlocutors usually described their attitude as "I understand but won't engage" in "this kind of consumption." Their reasoning is twofold. On the one hand, the middle-class car owners felt strongly that consumption should be one's own business. A consumption decision was in the private realm and was subject to an individual's autonomy. They had a consensus that it was an individual's choice and freedom as a consumer to spend the money in whatever ways he or she wished.

A young doctor commented on the lucky license plate auctions in 2007: "What is the problem when someone is willing to sell and someone else is willing to buy? If they believe in those numbers and are willing to pay for them, then so be it." Similar comments surfaced in conversations between interlocutors and me on other topics, such as the reasons to buy a car. Besides all the perceived pragmatic concerns (see chapters 1 and 2), one reason was that buying a car was one's freedom. Lawyer Lu (more in chapter 1) and I had a long conversation when I accompanied him and his wife to shop for their second car in 2010. As we talked about the stereotypes of Chinese consumers abroad—status driven, brand-name sensitive, among other portrayals—Lu said,

> If we spend the money to buy cars we like, the West will blame us for polluting the air. If we don't buy things, the West will blame us for not spending enough to provide stimulus for global economy. But isn't capitalism their own invention? Don't they promote market economy? This is the rule of a market economy: my money, from my own hard work, is mine to decide how it is spent.

When I talked to Lu about the auctions in 2013 and 2014, Lu emphasized that it was the way the market operated. A license plate was a rare resource, because each number could only belong to one person. The government controlled the licensing, and thus it could make profits out of it. The bidders wanted and chose to go to the auctions voluntarily. "This is a mutual consent [*ni qing wo yuan*]. That is what market is," Lu said.

In the same vein, a young banker semijokingly told me when we talked about the million-dollar license plate in 2010, "Didn't the West often say, 'Although I do not agree with what you say, I will defend your freedom of speech?' So, I may not agree with how they spend their money, but I shall defend their right to consume." In a sarcastic but nonetheless serious manner, he added, "It is the only freedom we have."

On the other hand, many of my middle-class interlocutors found it distasteful to pay more money for a license plate than for a car. Although they have the financial ability to bid for a license plate, none of them ever bid for a lucky license number, and they insisted that they would never do it. For them, consumption should be "proper" and "rational."

A rational decision is not solely about price; it also depends on what one could get by paying that price. For them, spending RMB 70,000 to have a Shanghai license plate could be more rational than spending the same amount to bid for a license number with three 6s in one of Guangzhou's lucky license plate auctions. If one had to commute between work in the city center and home at the periurban area every day of the week, a Shanghai license plate would allow him or her to drive in the city, but a nonlocal plate would not. Thus, although a nonlocal license plate would be much cheaper, spending the RMB 70,000 would bring much more convenience for work and life. A Shanghai license plate is undeniably a sign of status, but the high price for it has a practical function. In contrast, an auctioned plate in Guangzhou, while the numbers may sound good, would not grant any driving privilege to its owner.

For my interlocutors, the lucky license plate auction was a game for the new rich. In the August 2009 auction, a car owner paid RMB 159,000 ($23,280) for a plate with 3333 for a QQ, a compact economic car produced by a Chinese car company that usually costs no more than RMB 50,000 ($7,321). The media joked about it as "a pony with an extravagant saddle" (*xiaoma pei haoan*). For my interlocutors, this was a typical nouveau riche way of flaunting wealth. To pay a bit more money to get a number easy to remember or suggestive of good luck was understandable and acceptable. But paying three times the cost of the car for a license plate was "a waste of money," "irrational consumption," and unwise. A lawyer put it cynically:

"Hanging such an expensive license plate on your car is to invite the bad guys to rob or kidnap you. Isn't that stupid?"

While GEMAS claimed that the bidding was a way to collect funding for public interests, my interlocutors considered it a bluff because no one knew where the auction money went and how it was used. Some even claimed that the money went into the pockets of government officials. Their suspicion was not ungrounded. According to journalists, RMB 180,000,000 ($27,272,727) was accumulated in the first thirty-one auctions held between June 2006 and January 2011, but no public fund was ever established to help victims of traffic accidents.[7] My interlocutors also did not believe the bidders were interested in charity or public interest. A college teacher commented on the million-dollar plate in 2010: "Such bad taste! Why can't they spend the money to help children who cannot afford to go to school? Why can't they do something good directly to the society?"

Notably, the middle class were no strangers to some forms of conspicuous consumption. Many of them had the most up-to-date smartphones, trendy suitcases for traveling overseas, brand-name handbags, and other highly recognizable consumer items. They may not agree on whether a Hermès Birkin bag or a Rolex watch matched its price tag, but they agreed that the brands had value, be it their marketing costs or quality guarantee or a fame that had been cultivated through history. In this sense, even with conspicuous consumption, as the middle class understood it, there was more or less a connection between use value and price. But in their eyes, the license plates auctions defy this logic. "They [license numbers] are essentially just numbers," they said, which required no marketing efforts or had no historical value. While they shared the practices of number preference, they also believed that one could not increase one's luck or change one's fate by buying a license plate with lucky numbers.

The nouveau riche, in many ways, is an imagined target. Instead of having a precise definition, the nouveau riche, in the eyes of middle-class professionals, is a synonym for those who have gotten rich in a relatively short time but whose money may have come from dubious operations, which usually involve bribing officials for business opportunities. The middle class consider that, instead of studying hard and working hard like themselves, the nouveau riche achieve their upward mobility from these power-money transactions. To borrow the words of an engineer who commented on the license plate auctions, "Their [the nouveau riche's] money comes easily but goes just as easily. They haven't earned it with hard work. Of course, it does not bother them to throw it around." Lavishing themselves with such things as license plates, in turn, reinforces the middle class's perception of the nouveau riche as people lacking education and cultivation. By invoking "rational choice" and taste, urban professionals distinguish themselves from those with higher economic capital for highly publicized, conspicuous consumption.

In short, by commenting on the lucky license plate auctions, the middle class have articulated two sets of values regarding consumption. They recognized the freedom to consume but also advocated for rational consumption, both of which do not always fit comfortably with each other. These articulations, intriguingly, resonate with the case in Frederick Errington's (1987) study of auctions in a rural community in Montana in which conflicting values of hospitality and of competitiveness were both prominent. When items from a local bankrupt business were put on sale in auctions for others in the community, the auctions, Errington argues, should be seen as a regulating mechanism that simultaneously exemplifies and accommodates these values that maintain social life in the community. In line with his argument, the license plate auctions can also be seen as a structural space through which the two sets of values regarding consumption are both demonstrated and reconciled among the professionals who strive to carve out their middle-class identity.

Conclusion

Licensing is a process in which cars are transformed from a standardized product to a personalized object. The licensing institution, on the one hand, flattens the layers of social relationship between automobiles and individuals into a standardized coding system for the purpose of surveillance and discipline. On the other hand, the uniqueness of each license plate number enables the piece of cold metal to turn into a symbolic and emotional platform, carrying sentiments, perceptions, and ideologies structured by a larger social environment.

In a country such as the United States where political ideology prides itself on individual freedom, licensing leaves plenty of room and charges little for individuals' freedom of expression. This is not the case in China. The governing authority maintains a deep-seated uneasiness and distrust toward the ideas that individuals have the capacity to be responsible decision makers and that individuals' decisions could lead to order instead of chaos. The lucky license plate auctions suggest, in a cynical and metaphorical manner, that freedom is expensive and highly limited. They expose the government's doubt about some fundamental principles associated with liberal or neoliberal governance.

In fact, quite contrary to the neoliberal belief that the government should not interfere with the operation of the market, the lucky plates auctions show clearly how the local government proactively engages in revenue generation in an entrepreneurial manner. Political scientists call it "local state corporatism" (Oi 1992). This is partly a result of the nationwide fiscal reform that requires local governments to be responsible for their own spending. The most salient example of such reform repercussions is in land sales, in which local governments' thirst for revenue is met with real-estate developers' drive for profit (Hsing 2010). In the license plates auctions, what was for sale was essentially signs of state power.

If the rise of the middle class and of the automotive regime in China always leaves observers with the impression that it is all about consumption, it is at least partly because the state and institutional layouts provide highly limited space for alternative imagination, recognition, and practices. The government-orchestrated auctions construct a market space in which a limited group of people can engage in competitive spending. Vanity plates have become truly about "vanity," a state-backed display of new wealth. In this sense, the government legitimizes and further intensifies the manifestation, if not the reproduction, of social stratification.

For the middle class, the auctions and these vanity plates are often familiar yet alien experiences and objects. They are familiar because licensing is an inevitable part of the experience of becoming and being a car owner, and the participants understand or have experience with the joy that comes with lucky numbers in their license plates. They are alien because the spending on vanity plates challenges the participants' and observers' economic rationale in which the commodities should have some use value and spending should not just be a status competition. Rational, calculative consumption behavior becomes a contested ground in which an ethical attempt is made to distinguish them as proper middle class from the unpolished nouveau riche. It should be noted that the middle class and the nouveau riche are not two statistically or sociologically distinguishable groups. After all, much of their social profiles—upward social mobility, economic capital, and occupations—may look rather similar. Hence, the middle-class professionals' efforts to make distinctions in consumption choices should be seen as part of the process of identity making through ethical and aesthetic articulations.

In the process of making such distinctions, middle-class professionals are able to see the enlarging social gaps, poverty, and rampant corruption that accompany the state-choreographed economic reforms. They, or at least some of them, are capable of seeing the structural problems in government operations. Nevertheless, they dare not and are unwilling to think more about these issues. Official suppression and control of dissent is one reason. In addition, as some of them told me, a critique of societal phenomena at large does not explain why each individual ends up in her or his current place, a real-life question that concerns them. In such a context, fate seems a useful rhetorical tool to reconcile the contradictions and live with the realities. But the rhetoric of fate is also, to some degree, contradictory to their beliefs concerning education, self-cultivation, and hard work. But logical coherence is not what they are after. Instead, such competing rhetoric and rationales, and the obscurity they entail, have helped them make sense of their positioning in the society and the happenings around them. Their engagement with the license plates, in a way, embodies these multiple layers of subjective experience: structured opportunities, rational calculation, and careful planning, luck and ethics.

That said, their reluctance to engage in social critique is by no means a guarantee of the limited freedom they enjoy. The central government plans to nationalize and standardize licensing practices throughout the country. In June 2017, the lucky license plates auctions in Guangzhou came to an end.

Chapter 6

PARKING

Contesting Space in Middle-Class Complexes

In May 2007, the developer of City Garden, a middle-class, gated complex in Guangzhou where I resided from July 2006 to July 2007 for fieldwork, hastily sold eighty parking spaces in the complex's underground garage to nonresidents. The number of parking spaces available for temporary or short-term use was greatly reduced as a result, from over a hundred to barely over twenty. Many residents would drive home only to be barred from entering the garage because there were no more parking spaces.

The reduction of parking spaces, unexpected to the residents, caused them to kindle a protest. All of this was not only covered but sensationalized by local news on TV and in the papers. Action broke out just after the morning peak hours on Monday, June 18. Dozens of residents took their cars, including BMWs, Mercedes-Benzes, Toyota Crowns, and other luxury cars, to the road. They lined themselves up to block the driveways into and out of the garage. City Garden's security guards tried to persuade the drivers to put an end to the blockade but to no avail. The demonstration did not end until ten at night, when the police intervened in the name of fire control.

Figure 10. Protest banners in the complex, 2007. Photo by the author

On the following day, more than a hundred red banners appeared outside the windows and balconies of the complex. The larger ones were one meter wide and almost ten meters long. Some balconies and windows had multiple banners. Messages on the banners included "I want to go home! I want to park my car! Give me back my parking space!" "Unite! Take action to protect homeowners' rights and interests," "We homeowners will not accept expensive parking spaces forced upon us," "Harmonious society, inharmonious neighborhood," "Plead with the government to redress injustice."

At first glance, the protest at City Garden is but another example attesting to the emergence of activism in gated communities across Chinese cities. The rise of these gated communities, coupled with the erosion of the work-unit housing system, has transformed urban spatial politics in China. Gated communities allow those in the propertied class to retreat to their private space and offer a way to resist the state's exercise of hegemonic power with layers of gates and self-administration organizations, such as the homeowners committees (Fleischer 2010; Pow 2009; Tomba 2014; Zhang L. 2010).

When a government's proposals to build such things as facilities for handling waste and power substations are seen as a threat to their community, middle-class residents often band together with their neighbors to defend their properties against that threat. Through such community-based activism, they counter and negotiate with powerful actors, such as real-estate developers and the local government. Community-based activism thus encourages a privatized form of urban governance that in fact complements the changing ruling strategies of the state that seeks to govern through self-governing subjects (Tomba 2005; Zhang L. 2010; Zhang and Ong 2008).

Yet careful examination of the dynamic, strategies, and contingencies before and after the protest in the City Garden complex suggests that the spatial politics, initiated by the rising demand of parking spaces among middle-class car owners, is more complicated. This chapter explores parking both as a contingent event and a structural issue that has been shaped by and has been shaping middle-class gated-complex politics and their living environment. This exploration illustrates a sense of both empowerment and vulnerability among the middle class as consumer-citizens. They have felt empowered as state policies to encourage consumption and consumer culture have legitimized their claims on consumer goods, like the car, and consumption spaces, such as parking lots. They have also felt vulnerable because they consider that they would not have legal protection when confronted with powerful stakeholders, such as real-estate developers. As they have stood up and used protests to defend themselves, the base of community support for continuous, collective actions has remained weak. Gatedness does not necessarily contribute to a sense of solidarity among City Garden's residents.

City Garden's protests were unique in that they happened against the backdrop of legal changes and rapidly rising real-estate prices. Nonetheless, the interactions among residents are illustrative of the dynamic in other middle-class gated complexes in the city, if not in other parts of China. As geographers show in their detailed studies of middle-class complexes in Guangzhou, Shanghai, and Beijing (Hazelzet and Wissink 2012; Li, Zhu, and Li 2012; Wang, Li, and Chai 2012; Yip 2012), to assume that a gated complex is a "community" may be misleading, as residents' social networks are based more often on work relationships and other social ties than on shared residency within the same complex boundaries.

The lack of solidarity led to the limited participation of City Garden's residents. Like in other kinds of protests (O'Brien and Li 2006), residents resorted to the state and its authority, by reappropriating official discourses, to secure their claims on parking spaces against real-estate companies. Yet, even with the authority lent by official discourses, the government's strategy of "governing from afar" (Zhang and Ong 2008) did not help the middle class secure their claim. What forced a compromise among all sides, intriguingly, was the unavoidable spatial demand by the automotive regime.

Materials for this chapter draw on my one-year observations about City Garden, regular visits to other middle-class complexes over the past decade, and interviews with judges, government officials, managerial professionals in big real-estate companies, and middle-class gated-complex residents. In this chapter, I first contextualize the protest by delineating the changing national legal regulations, local judiciary practices, and long-term tension between the residents and the property management company in City Garden. I then zoom in on one of the negotiation meetings among the resident representatives, the property management company, and the government-backed street committee, with special attention to the ways in which each party used official rhetoric against one another. In the next section, I turn to internal dynamics among the residents to explore the issue of solidarity that undergirded the protest and other community activities in this complex. After analyzing microdynamics on the complex level, I zoom out to consider parking as a structural issue in the long run and identify trends that have begun to manifest themselves since the protest in City Garden.

Parking in a Gated Complex: Accumulative Tensions

City Garden is conveniently located at the heart of the commercial and business district of Guangzhou. It went for sale in 2003 during the ebb phase of the local real-estate market. Its real-estate developer targeted the upper echelon of the middle class, with City Garden's prime location, public facilities, and architectural design. The complex has roughly 1,200 apartments and studios in five high-rise buildings. These buildings encircle a swimming pool, a basketball court, a fishpond, a children's playground, and plenty of windy walkways and rest areas covered with trees, bushes, and flowers. A clubhouse is in one of the buildings. The encircled area is separated from the outside by a gate with twenty-four-hour security. The lower three floors of three of the buildings (A, D, and E wings) have mostly been rented out to restaurants, housing agents, and other service businesses, the entrances of which all face the main streets. When I lived there, all public facilities and the rentals were entrusted to a property management company called Light Management, which had an office in the A wing. The office took charge of daily affairs.

City Garden has an underground garage with four hundred parking spaces. Two driveways connect the garage to the road without having to pass the guarded gates. When I moved into the complex to do fieldwork in the summer of 2006, roughly eighty parking spaces had been sold to restaurants in the complex, and two hundred or so already belonged to individual apartment owners. The rest were "public" parking spaces. Visitors and those residents that did not have their own parking spots could use the public ones with the payment of an hourly or monthly rental fee.

At the time, residents did not seem to be concerned about buying parking spaces. A housing agent in the A wing put a notice on its glass door that read, "Abundant parking spaces for sale in the complex." It may partly have been because the garage did have enough spaces for those with cars, or it may have been because of rent control in public parking. As a way to accommodate the rapid car growth, the municipal government imposed a standard for parking fees on public parking lots in the early 2000s.[1] An indoor parking space was supposed to charge RMB 400 per month. Public parking spaces in a privately owned gated complex like City Garden were also subject to rent control regulation. According to several residents, to purchase a parking place cost around RMB 50,000 in 2004. The price rose to RMB 150,000 and sometimes up to RMB 200,000 in mid-2007. Under rent control regulation concerning public interests, renting a parking space for ten years was still cheaper than buying it in many gated complexes. Many middle-class homeowners I talked to ended up renting instead of buying their parking spaces throughout the 2000s.

Changes were on the way. Middle-class car owners first felt the changes through the new property law, which was passed in the National People's Congress in March 2007 and would take effect six months later in October. The official announcement said that the more than six-month transition period was for people to familiarize themselves with the new law so that legal changes would not be abrupt. The new law was necessary to deal with many property issues in private housing, such as parking that did not exist under the centrally planned economy. Among many new interventions, the new law stipulates, in a very general manner, that the property right of common areas in a housing complex, including gardens and parking garages, should belong to the collective of the homeowners of the given complex, unless the apartment sale contracts have otherwise agreed.

Previously, real-estate developers had had the unquestionable authority to sell the parking spaces in their real-estate projects as they pleased. With the new property law, developers no longer had self-evident rights over the common spaces in gated complexes. However, this law has not specified how to deal with the property issues of public spaces in gated complexes that were sold before 2007. Up to the mid- or even late 1990s, most apartment sale contracts contained no articles regarding the ownership of parking garages. As early as a couple of years before the passing of the new law, some big developers began to add articles to their standardized contracts, clearly indicating that the property of the garage belonged to the developers. City Garden's sale contracts, however, had no such articles.

Legal consequences of the new law on old complexes like City Garden were unknown at the time of the protest. News reports on local TV channels and online discussion alleged that developers of these complexes with the old sale contracts might not be able to sell any parking spaces anymore, but legal professionals and property companies were much more cautious.

Judge Lei was one of the judges I talked to regarding the new law. Lei chaired hearings of real-estate disputes in the municipal court. He doubted that the new law would really work in the residents' favor. First, the law was ambiguous of what counted as common property and thus left plenty of room for interpretation.[2] Second, Lei pointed out a strong argument in favor of the developer: Since the contracts were signed before the law took effect, it could be argued that the rules governing the contracts should be those that had already been in effect when the contracts were signed. Since there were no legal regulations on this issue, customary practices—which favored the developer—could form the basis of a legal ruling.

Moreover, legal professionals pointed out that a legal ruling had to take into account technical and political concerns. Judge Lei said, "We have to consider the social consequences." In a conflict such as City Garden's case, if the court were to rule in favor of the residents, the municipal court and the lower-level courts in the city would more or less be bound by its decision. As a result, residents in many other complexes with similar claims might initiate lawsuits. The already overloaded courts were unwilling to see the potential rise of cases. Furthermore, as lawyers, judges, and government officials pointed out during our conversations, some major real-estate developers had networks that were *tongtian le* (connected all the way to the sky); that is, their networks connected them to the very top of the state regime. If pressure were to come from the top, Judge Lei admitted, with frustration, there was not much that the local governments and courts could do. As a homeowner who was still paying his loan, Lei accused the law of being "a scam" between the central government and the real-estate crocodiles (*dichan da'e*).

While legal professionals tend to believe that the new law might not be in homebuyers' favor, real-estate companies were not sure toward which direction the law might go. Mr. Guan was an experienced property manager in a big property management company affiliated with one of the biggest real-estate developers in town. Despite his powerful mother company, Guan told me that, according to his company's in-house counsel, the language of the new law was rather vague, and developers and their management companies should wait for the courts to clarify the ownership issues of parking lots and other possibly public areas with judicial interpretation.

I told Guan about the sale of eighty parking spaces in City Garden, and a rumor circulated among the residents that the two individual buyers were the owners of the real-estate developing company. Guan said that he was not surprised. His speculation was that, because City Garden's developer was not one of those real-estate giants, the sale of the parking spaces in the complex was the developer's strategic response to preempt losses with the new law.

Most of City Garden's protesters were aware of the legal risks. Having learned from work and friends, they thought that they would not stand a chance if they were to bring the case to court. "You can't win with a real-estate developer!" a City Garden resident said. "They have money and networks. The court is useless. It's not on the side of us ordinary people." In hindsight, the protest seems to have been the residents' effort to involve the government in dealing with a situation where they could not count on the law or judiciary authorities. (I will come back to this point later.)

However, City Garden's protest was more than a matter of the parking of some cars. Beneath the surface, it revealed the residents' long-term struggle to organize their own governing body—"the homeowners assembly" (*yezhu dahui*) and its executive organ "the homeowners committee" (*yezhu weiyuanhui*). Both the assembly and the committee were new institutions that came with private housing (for more details, see Pow 2009; Tomba 2014). They have the power to make decisions on issues involving public interests in the complex, including how to allocate public facilities and which property management company to hire. Some of City Garden's residents attempted twice to organize the homeowner assembly in 2005 and 2006. Both attempts failed.

In between the attempts, tension built between the residents and Light Management, which had been selected by the developer, not the residents. The practice of the developer choosing the property management company came along with the rise of private housing development in the city in the 1980s and 1990s.[3] Before 2003 there were no explicit guidelines or regulations as to how the developer should choose the management company. Government ordinances issued in 2003 recognized the necessity of such a practice on the condition that the developer should select a proper management company through a bidding process until the formation of the homeowners assembly. The assembly could substitute the developer's choice with its own choice.[4]

However, residents in City Garden had no idea how Light Management had been chosen. Many suspected that the owners of the real-estate development company and of Light Management might be related if not the same people. Such suspicion was not totally ungrounded, because all major developers had their own management companies in charge of their real-estate projects (for example, Mr. Guan's management company and its affiliated real-estate developer).

Such perceived nepotism, in the eyes of residents, was the reason why Light Management failed to do its job properly. Residents complained that Light Management charged a high management fee for poor service: no one replaced broken light bulbs; common areas were not properly cleaned; sport facilities were poorly maintained. In some cases, Light Management rented out privately owned parking spaces before the owners came to claim them. When the owners did come to claim their spaces, Light Management would charge them a management fee calculable from the day of purchase of the space, at the same time refusing to transfer to the owners any rental incomes collected from renting out their space.

To replace Light Management, the residents first had to have their homeowners assembly; thus came the third attempt to form it in 2007. This time, a preparation committee was formed to convene the assembly. In late May, a notice was dropped in each resident's mailbox with the call for a homeowners assembly in early June, aiming at electing members for the committee to change certain practices regarding how public affairs were handled in this complex. By this time the eighty parking spaces had been sold. However, as one of the organizers admitted, it was not their intention to deal with the parking issue when they called for the meeting.

Thus, on a hot summer afternoon, over two hundred apartment owners showed up to the basketball court. Because it was legally required that more than half of the homeowners, who were entitled to vote, be present, there was no quorum, and the preparation committee's effort once again went in vain. Amid heat and high humidity, the gathering became an arena where discontent, frustration, and agony were displayed, reinforced, and aggregated by the continuous accusations of the noncooperative Light Management, which had refused to provide the necessary contact information of all owners in the complex.

Someone brought up the unanticipated disappearance of public parking spaces. Some suspected that the management company was in complicity with the developers to make profits by selling the parking spaces. Others claimed that the management office did not want to give up the income from renting out the parking spaces; therefore, it falsified the transactions without actually having sold the spaces so that it could keep those spaces to charge for rents. The gathering took a sharp turn, with an unplanned outcome. A protest agenda soon came into being: first blocking the driveway and then hanging the banners. All actions were voluntary. Several initiators bore the cost to prepare the banners, the expenses for which hopefully would be covered later by donations from residents in the complex. Some mobilized their network resources in the media to have journalists and TV cameras come witness the protest. Days later, the protest was staged.

In hindsight, the parking-space protests were a contingent action that emerged out of long-term tensions between the residents and the management company, which, in turn, were framed by a rapidly developing market of private housing and the changing legal regulations. As I will show next, ordinary citizens' lack of faith in the legal system manifested itself in the usage of official discourses instead of legal arguments in the negotiations that aimed at settling the dispute.

Negotiating for a Harmonious Community

Soon after the protest, several rounds of negotiation took place between some of the residents, Light Management, and the residents committee (*jumin wei-yuanhui*) that oversaw the blocks where City Garden was located. Residents committees were street-level, official organizations institutionalized in the 1950s in cities (Townsend 1967, 158–165). While these committees are not legal entities that can exercise power or make decisions in their own names in contemporary administrative structure, the residents committees are seen as the joint between the state and communities (Wang J. 2005). As any public protest was a serious issue in China, the residents committee had to be involved in handling the City Garden protest.

One of the negotiation meetings was on a Tuesday morning, one week after the banners showed up in the complex. By this time, most of the banners had already been removed, except three or four still hanging off the building. This meeting was held in the lobby in one of the residential buildings. The lobby was temporarily set up for the meeting. A dozen folding chairs were added opposite to a fixed, wide wooden bench, and two coaches were set facing each other. When I walked in, Mr. Yi, the head of Light Management's office in City Garden, and Mr. Shao, one of the organizers of the protest, were already there. Ten minutes after the scheduled starting time, the party secretary of the residents committee, Comrade Meng, arrived together with a staff member of the residents committee. He asked whether all the protest banners had been taken off. Shao and others assured him that all were off except two or three because they could not find the residents in those apartments. Residents gradually showed up in the lobby. A middle-aged woman brought in a box of bottled water and distributed them to everyone in the lobby. During the negotiation, residents came and went, but the total number of participants remained around twenty.

Without any explicit agreement, the party secretary, Comrade Meng, naturally took charge of the meeting. Meng presented himself as the representative of the government. He cautiously attempted to strike a balance in acknowledging the protest: On the one hand, he showed sympathy to the cause of action—the dissatisfaction and emotions of the residents in the protest. On the other hand, he tried to downplay the effects of protesting by denying that the protests were the reason for the government to get involved;

instead, he came because the government was sincerely working to solve the parking problem for City Garden's residents.

The main theme of Meng's speech was that the government had made an effort to serve the need of both the residents and the management company and to produce a harmonious society. Meng repeatedly mentioned that he and officials from housing, transportation, civil affairs, and other administrative departments had convened on the Friday and Saturday right after the protest. They worked together in order to find a solution to the conundrum. The police department had decided that City Garden could use the large empty area in front of the A wing as a parking lot for its residents. The officials calculated that the empty space—originally planned as space for public transportation—could be divided into two rows, and each row could park twenty cars or so. Meng said, "You had your day off on Saturday, but we were still having meetings! . . . We worked very efficiently and very quickly. . . . We present to you the cake; now the problem is how you should share the cake."

Despite Meng's emphasis on government efforts, Light Management strategically refused the solution proposal without directly saying no to Meng. First, it sent only Mr. Yi, head of the management office at City Garden, as the representative to this meeting. Meng had requested to have a company manager present before the meeting started. Yi made a trip to the management office but came back alone, telling Meng that the manager was not available. Meng made no further requests and proceeded with the meeting. Given his acting capacity, Yi could not make any major decisions regarding the parking facilities at City Garden.

Second, after Meng proposed his resolution, Yi did not give any promise that Light Management would take care of the parking issue in the open area in front of the complex. With a smile on his face, he replied, "That area is not managed by us. How can we manage it? There are also no legal regulations that allow us to charge management fees for taking care of it." Some residents said, "The government would provide the document." Meng also tried to assure Yi, "The government agents have coordinated with each other. The management office is thinking too much into this. The police and the urban management officers [*chengguan*] already knew about this.[5] All you need is to draw out the lots in the empty land and brief it to the police." He instructed that parking charges there should follow the government's public parking rent control (150 RMB per month for outdoor parking). Yi, however, kept silent, making neither counterarguments nor promises of any sort throughout the meeting.

While some residents kept pressing Meng to force Yi to make concrete promises, others were not happy with Meng's solution proposal because parking in front of the A wing was inconvenient for residents in other wings. They tried to have Meng do more with the parking. A middle-aged woman told the audience that in the past she could drive to the garage, stop in front of the elevators leading to her apartment, let her children out, and leave big pieces of luggage there before she parked the car. "Now how am I to manage all the people and suitcases if I have to park outside?" she asked.

Some of the residents brought up other issues with Light Management and asked Meng to intervene. A young man spoke up right after the middle-aged woman. He had bought a parking space in the garage. But he was not home all the time. He turned to Meng. "When I was not here, Light Management rented out my parking space to make money! Can you give a saying to this?" Another resident complained that Light Management charged high management fees but did not do much. Meng waved off all these questions and simply answered, "This is not why I am here today. You have to communicate with Light Management. I am here for the parking issue only."

In the exchanges, all sides used official discourses to articulate their views and to attack the others. The most frequently mentioned one was the "harmonious" (*hexie*) discourse. "A harmonious society" (*hexie shehui*) was the iconic slogan of the previous president Hu Jintao, much like "Mao Zedong's Thoughts" of Chairman Mao, "Deng Xiaoping's Theory" of Chairman Deng Xiaoping, and "the Three Represents" of President Jiang Zemin. The discourse of "a harmonious society" vaguely refers to a society without many conflicts but does not provide any practical guidelines. The "harmonious" discourse is a performative utterance that is standardized and formalized. As Alexei Yurchark (2006) suggests in his provocative study of speech acts in socialist Russia, the standardized form of utterance—the "harmonious" discourse, in this case—helps protect the speaker from political scrutiny.

Yet, as a form of authoritative speech, the "harmonious society" discourse is open to reappropriation. Meng kept emphasizing that the residents and the property management company should coordinate to create a harmonious community. Light Management pointed the finger at the residents, saying that the protest "had a bad impact on the city's landscape [*chengshi jingguan*] and was a nuisance for social stability and harmony." In response to the charges, the residents accused Light Management of creating an "inharmonious" community by selling out most of the parking spaces the residents had been using. The residents' protest and efforts to establish the homeowners committee were to defend their legal rights and interests and to build "a safe, comfortable, and, harmonious community."

Official discourses seemed to have become weapons for challenges and contestation. Meng tried to maintain his authority by resorting to different official rhetoric to make his case. However, every time his argument was countered and his authority undermined by the residents using the same or other but equally authoritative official discourse. In one round of exchange, a senior resident said, "The government's job is to manage [*guanli*]," in order to get Meng to give a decisive saying to the disputes, since Meng kept presenting himself as the government's voice. Meng immediately refuted, "The government is about service [*fuwu*]." The resident answered, "[It is] about management but also service. But the management should be humanized [*renxinghua*]," with which Meng could only agree. Both "humanized management" and "service" were official terms that the government sought to promote as parts of its self-transformation agenda.

One of the official discourses also borrowed from terms from a patriarchal vocabulary. One middle-aged resident addressed Meng and what he represented as "*jiazhang*" when he made a complaint about the parking issue. The term *jiazhang*, or "patriarch," refers to parents or other senior-generation members in one's family and invokes the patriarchic authority. The state has been drawing on the patriarchy model and using the family analogy and the image of a benevolent patriarch as a source to claim legitimacy of its governance. This analogy has been internalized by many people, old and young (see, for example, Fong 2004; Hoffman 2010), to describe and think about their relationship with the nation-state and the government. The official rhetoric lent authority to the voices of the residents and had some binding effect on Meng: he at least had to listen to the complaints.

As the residents fluently used official discourses and terms to pressure Meng to give a definite and clear administrative decision, the limit of Meng and the residents committee's authority was exposed. At one point Meng explicitly told the audience, "We [the residents committee] in fact have no power at all," which was indeed stipulated in administrative laws. The lobby suddenly became quiet. Meng then started to repeat again the abovementioned joint meetings with government officials. A middle-aged woman suddenly threw a water bottle on the ground and said loudly and impatiently, "Stop repeating yourself! Stop the nonsense!" Her comment broke the game of language performance. A moment of silence ensued, and the atmosphere became a bit awkward. Soon Meng left, without further comments. Yi immediately followed, leaving the residents in the lobby.

Mr. Shao tried to calm some residents who directed their dissatisfaction and grievance toward Meng and the residents committee: "We have to do this a step at a time. Didn't he help us with this matter [the parking lot]? We can try again next time." That being said, as most of the participants left and only the core group members remained in the lobby, Shao was frank about his doubt that the residents committee would like to get involved again in another round of negotiations. He was right. At the end of July, when I packed my notes and left, the small square Meng had promised was still not used as a temporary parking lot. Both employees at Light Management's office and residents told me that they had to park their cars in the garage in a complex that was a five-minute walking distance from City Garden.

The negotiation described above shows the undeniable authority but yet limited power of government agencies. The undeniable authority was exemplified in the official discourses, which legitimized claims from different sides, and in the respect for Meng, who was not equipped with any legal power but perceived as a representative of the government. Nonetheless, government agencies had limited power in their dealing with this specific case because they could not intervene in solving the dispute between two nongovernmental agents with specific claims based on civil laws. Moreover, the issue of parking spaces involved a complex set of government agencies and administrative procedures to change the usage of land (more details later).

As the government agencies were not able to solve the parking issue for the residents, the residents were left to deal with it with whatever means they could mobilize. The protests were collective attempts to take the issue in their own hands. However, such collective efforts could not be sustained as there was a lack of solidarity among the residents.

Divided Neighbors, Fragmented Community

When the crowd was about to leave the lobby, a young woman identifying herself as Canadian—a Canadian passport holder in fact—spoke up. "I'll be straightforward. Some people in the preparatory committee [to organize the homeowners convention] seem not so united. Except you, Mr. Shao, I don't see other people working." She concluded, "The last thing the Chinese have is to be united [*tuanjie*]!" The statement of the national character captured the frustration and disappointment among the residents. Yet, to some degree, it also disclosed a structural issue in organizing a self-governing body in a complex like City Garden: the lack of sociality and community solidarity.

City Garden is divided spatially and socially. Four of the five high-rises (the B, C, D, and E wings) comprise large apartments. These apartments were well occupied by two- or three-generation families.[6] Families in these wings tended to be long-term residents. Those who were active in community politics lived in this section.

The A wing is architecturally separated from the other four buildings. The two entrances to A wing face the main street, while the entrances to each of the other four buildings face the encircled garden area with a twenty-four-hour guarded gate. The A wing is a mixed-use building consisting of small-sized studios, medium-sized apartments, and offices. According to the housing agents located on the ground floor of the wing, the majority of the A-wing residents were renters; the owners themselves may or may not reside in City Garden.

Living in a studio in A wing for a year, I met mostly company employees in everyday encounters in the building. My encounters with them in the elevators and hallway often amounted to nothing but silence, as they almost purposefully avoided eye contact with me and instead talked to their colleagues if possible. From time to time, I bumped into Korean or Japanese families. We smiled and nodded at each other, but language barriers prevented further conversations. One of the effects of frequent reshuffling of tenants is that A-wing residents, even neighbors, rarely interacted with each other.

Neither did A-wing residents interact much with residents from other buildings, partly because they used separate entrances. For months I had made efforts to get to know residents in other buildings by spending time and trying to talk to people in the garden area in the complex. But I did not manage to get very far. Even within the guarded area, the more permanent residents seemed to have avoided interaction with a temporary resident like me, even though I was living here legitimately.[7]

A-wing owners and residents were semioutsiders in City Garden. Many of them were indifferent to disputes and tensions in the gated complex. This can be seen in my landlord's reaction to the planned homeowners assembly in June. After I notified him of the date and event, my landlord said, "As a landlord, of course, I hope the complex could get better. If the complex is better, it is easier to attract tenants." Nonetheless, he did not come to the gathering and only learned about the protest on TV.

Active community participants also adopted a utilitarian attitude at best toward the tenants and unit owners in the A wing rather than seeing them as part of the community. Although Mr. Shao had told me that they had left some banners in the lobbies in all the buildings before the protest, I did not see any of them in the A wing. Similarly, there were no notices posted in A wing regarding the negotiation meetings. As a result of such exclusion, only three banners hung outside A wing when the protest was staged. Except me, no A wing residents or owners participated in the negotiation described above.

However, due to the number of units in A wing, it would be difficult to reach the quorum to form the homeowners assembly without votes from the A wing. The preparatory committee finally realized A-wing owners' significance in achieving their goal when it made the fourth attempt to convene the homeowners assembly. In order to mobilize its owners, they acted more proactively than simply dropping a note in the mailboxes like last time. Three days after the meeting with Comrade Meng, the preparatory committee members came to A wing's lobby. Several women approached anyone exiting or entering the elevators, soliciting for homeowners' contact information. Yet they continued to ignore renters, even though renters could act as proxies for the owners.

Internal spatial politics aside, the permanent residents had varied attitudes toward the protest and other community activism. Even though there was a shared understanding that it was important to maintain the real-estate value of the complex, City Garden's residents had different ideas concerning what was good for the complex. Several active participants mentioned that some residents were rather hostile to the protests, blaming the protestors for creating obstacles in getting in and out of the garage. In City Garden's online forum, some users accused the protestors of ruining the harmony in the neighborhood and depreciating the property values in the complex. One user questioned, "Did this [protest] protect our rights? Have they [those planning and participating in the protest] thought about the interests of us homeowners with parking spaces? Who should be responsible for my loss? Simply irresponsible! If [they are] so competent, then sue the government!"

For those who were active in the protest and organizing the homeowners convention, they believed that they were fighting for the good of everyone in the complex, and what they did had brought together individual owners who were originally like "a platter of loose sand" (*yipan sansha*). Some countered the protest opponents in the forum by accusing them of being collaborators sent by the management office and the real-estate developer.

Several residents in the online forum and during the negotiation meetings suggested that the basketball court could be turned into a parking lot. One resident said, "We don't even have spaces to park our cars; what is the use of the basketball court? . . . We need to use what limited resources we have where they are needed the most." His proposal was rejected. Other residents said that the basketball court was a supporting facility for this neighborhood and thus should not be randomly converted into something else.

There was no sustainable structure that facilitated communication among residents who were attached to the complex in different ways. The online forum had very few active users. Before the protest, the contents in the forum were mostly about the availability of the tennis and basketball courts. For its continuous presence in City Garden but being free from the control of the homeowners committee, Light Management would rather see the residents not in alliance with each other than promoting dialogue among all parties involved. More important, except for a few residents, the majority did not seem to share the belief that things could be changed, and community participation was the beginning of changes. All these factors within the boundaries of a gated complex rendered its collective actions fragile.

City Garden is by no means unique. The majority of the complexes where my interlocutors lived did not have their own homeowners committee by 2016. In the very few cases that there were such committees, my interlocutors told me that they had no clue how the committees were founded or what they did.

Parking: Long-Term Challenges

The specific nature of the long-term, structural, and contingent tensions in City Garden should not overshadow the fact that parking is an evolving, persistent issue with a rapidly growing driving population. In Guangzhou, hundreds of new cars have been registered every day in the past decade. The government has been constantly expanding street networks to accommodate the flow of cars. But parking had been systematically ignored in urban planning and real-estate development until recent years.

Generally speaking, the older the part of a city, the fewer the parking spaces are found. In the historic part of Guangzhou, most of the car owners have to park their cars in the streets with busy traffic. Social welfare housing under the work-unit system had no parking design when private ownership of cars was highly restricted. Passenger cars gradually occupied the limited space between the buildings originally designed for pedestrians in these neighborhoods. In the early 1990s market-oriented developers started to build high-rise apartment buildings along with the state-subsidized housing. These commercial high-rises were equipped with elevators, a sign of luxury at that time, but did not have designated parking lots.

When garages gradually became part of the building plans of gated complexes in the late 1990s and early 2000s, the ratio between the number of apartments and parking spaces tended to be high. For instance, one main real-estate developer in the city, which has affiliation with Mr. Guan's property management company, typically set the ratio as 4:1 or 6:1 in its gated complexes. The price for parking spaces in the complexes' garages was not that expensive either, when the car ownership rate was low. Local newspapers in the 1990s had advertisements drawing homeowners into buying parking lots as investments.

In the new millennium, a parking garage is a must in any new gated complex. The price of a parking space has risen quickly, and the price per square meter of a parking spot became more expensive than that of an apartment in the same complex. In City Garden, the apartment–parking space ratio is between 3:1 and 4:1. The unit price of a parking space was similar to that of an apartment in 2004 but has become more expensive since 2007.

The apartment–parking space ratio is indicative of the ranking of a complex. Close to City Garden, another upscale complex went on sale in 2006 and had a 2:1 apartment–parking space ratio. The developer drew lots to decide which owners were entitled to buy parking spaces. Each apartment owner was entitled to be drawn once. The lucky ones with the smaller numbers could choose first. The prices of parking spaces varied depending on their locations in the underground garage: the closer to the elevators, the more expensive. The expensive ones cost close to RMB 300,000 each (for roughly ten square meters) in 2007, while the price of an apartment ranged between RMB 15,000 and RMB 20,000 per square meter.

During 2006 and 2007, many of my interlocutors had already purchased their apartments, with bank loans, in gated complexes. Roughly a third had their own cars, and many had plans to buy one in the near future. But the majority had not purchased a parking space. Some told me that they planned to get one very soon, even though they had not bought a car yet.

Xiaofeng was a twenty-seven-year-old government employee whom I interviewed after the City Garden protest. Having graduated from a good university with a master's degree, he had worked for two years by then. Xiaofeng had recently got married and moved into an apartment in a relatively expensive gated complex, thanks to his parents' help with the down payment. I asked him whether he had a parking space. He said no but that he planned to get one in the garage that was still under construction beneath the second batch of buildings in the same complex. Xiaofeng did not have a car yet. But City Garden's protest, which he got to know through news on TV, raised an alarm for him. Xiaofeng said, "You need to be prepared. I can always rent it out before I get my own car." One year later Xiaofeng bought the parking space. Soon after he had his own car.

The engineer Luo Lei was not so lucky. When Luo Lei bought his apartment in 2010, he did not buy a parking space. He thought that his apartment cost so much, and he did not want to pay more than necessary. Two years later, he bought a car when his wife was pregnant. In my conversation with him in 2014, Luo said that he regretted his decision in 2010. All the parking spaces were sold out. Now he had to pay RMB 1,800 per month to rent a space from a resident also in his complex. Luo said, "It is a rip-off. But what can you do? You have to park the car." Yet, despite the rising rental price, Luo nowadays prayed that the owner of the parking space would not decide to have a car.

The pressure of parking was not only on car owners like Luo Lei and Xiaofeng but also on property management companies. In City Garden in 2007, after the meeting with Comrade Meng, Light Management refused to take responsibility if the empty space outside City Garden was to be used as a parking lot. Light Management had legal grounds: its management could only cover the area of City Garden as outlined in the construction plan approved by the government. Neither the residents committee nor the government departments Meng mentioned had the authority to decide whether a piece of public land could be used for parking. From a cost-benefit point of view, it would also be costly for the management company to take care of an outdoor parking lot outside the gated area, but rental income would be significantly less than indoor parking. Mr. Guan, the experienced manager of another property management company, said in 2007 that he would do the same as Mr. Yi in a similar situation.

Yet, in the 2010s, whenever I passed by City Garden, I would often see the area outside the A wing full of parked cars. Although the basketball court was still there for basketball, the walkways in the gated garden were lined with parked cars. I have not been able to get in touch with Mr. Shao and others since I revisited the complex in 2008 and therefore do not know what has resulted from the protests in the complex. But what happened in City Garden seemed rather common in other gated complexes. In a couple of complexes where my interviewees lived, many residents have to park their cars outside the gates if there are relatively quiet side streets. Residents have to pay property management companies to hire guards to keep an eye on the cars. The legal status of these parking spaces is dubious at best. Yet law enforcement seems to turn a blind eye to the existence of these parking lots, tolerating them as a way to deal with the parking issue.[8]

But what is more common is sidewalks, designed to be car-free, in the gated areas being used as parking spaces because the underground garages can hold no more cars. A gated complex as a car-free, safe area was one of the important considerations for middle-class parents for apartment purchase. They would like their children to have a playground that is shielded from the increasing traffic in the main streets. The car invasion of the safe space concerned many residents, but they felt they could do nothing about it. In our 2014 conversation, the engineer Luo Lei said, "As long as people continue to buy cars, they have to find a place to park them. As a parent, of course I don't want to see all the cars running around in the complex. But as a car owner, I can't object to it [cars taking over walkways]."

In a separate interview, the government employee Xiaofeng also acknowledged the dilemma and added, "You can't count on the real-estate developers to provide enough parking spaces. The more parking spaces they build, the fewer apartments they could sell. But the government should have provided more parking spaces. It could have done better in urban planning to provide more parking lots."

Neither of them thought that the parking issue should be attributed to the profit-driven property management companies or the lack of a homeowners committee in their respective complex. Luo Lei said, "When construction was finished, the available space was then fixed. What can the property management company do? Even if you have a homeowners committee [his complex did not have one], the committee cannot build more parking spaces."

Luo Lei and Xiaofeng spoke for many middle-class car owners that I have talked to over the years. Many of them realized that the continuous growth of cars posed great challenges to urban infrastructures. They did not believe that the market would solve the infrastructural problems. If years of school education in official Marxist interpretation have left any legacy in their perception about the political economy, it may be their skepticism of the capacity of the market. Neither did they believe that the government could solve all the infrastructural problems. Nonetheless, they habitually hoped for the government's intervention as the final remedy when the problems looked insurmountable.

Conclusion

As much as they were sensationalized in newspapers and on local TV, the protests in City Garden seemed to be another ephemeral event in a fast-paced city. Neither did they help reverse the sale of parking spaces or get residents new parking spaces nor offer any long-term impact on political practices in terms of public engagement or activism, as the lack of such evidence suggests. That being said, the staging of the protests and their incapacity to push for changes remain an invaluable window into understanding the complexity of the spatial politics entwined between the rapid rises of the middle class and an automotive regime.

Any automotive regime is undeniably spatially demanding. As we have seen in Chinese cities, infrastructural investment has tilted visibly toward auto-oriented mobility and convenience in recent years. Yet if the fast-growing road networks represent the mobile side of the automotive regime, parking spaces show the immobile side of the regime, which, despite its urgency, has not been given enough attention until recently.

Like housing ownership, car ownership also facilitates a sense of class-based entitlement to urban space, both public and private. Sometimes their demand is frustrated, partly because of the constraints of the existing built environment and partly because of the government's failure in long-term planning. In the case of City Garden, even without the unexpected sale of parking spaces, the number of parking spaces would not have satisfied the residents' demand given how fast car ownership grew. In other words, the dispute about parking seems unavoidable in the long run, but the time of its happening was shaped by legal changes that were supposed to protect the rights of property owners.

The new property law and related regulations, to some degree, did empower the middle class as consumers to make claims on goods and space. However, they did not necessarily make the middle class feel institutionally protected. The middle class could mobilize their social networks and have media exposure to make claims. But the legal regulations and the judiciary-administrative relationship favored powerful actors such as real estate developers and their subsidiary management companies. Distrust and disillusion of the judiciary were obvious among many urban professionals, including lawyers, and government employees.

The new property law seems to empower the middle class with the right to organize their own governing bodies. However, it would be misleading to assume that the Chinese urban middle class would automatically know how to work as a collective and proactively turn the potentiality of self-governance into reality. It is true that people like Mr. Shao would try hard to form their own governing body. However, so far the majority of middle-class homeowners seem to be more passive than active in determining how their everyday life spaces are organized. Despite the dissatisfaction, they have continued to let the property management company, chosen by the real-estate developers, manage their living space. Nor can we simply assume that the middle-class residents had experience in and thus knew how to take collective action. The difficulty in forming their homeowners assembly and committee among City Garden's residents highlights the difficulty in carving out a relatively autonomous, middle-class space.

This situation was further complicated by the ambiguity and tension between privatized governing space and indirect state control. In her study of middle-class gated communities, Zhang (2010) suggests that real-estate developers and property management companies have seized the power and produced an alternative form of urban governance that coexists with forms affiliated with the state. But what happened in City Garden suggests a more complicated picture. Indirect rule required governments and government agencies to withdraw from private disputes. That said, although they had no institutional power to make legally binding decisions, grassroots-level government organizations, such as the residents committees, still had the responsibility to manage local lives. They may rely on property management companies' cooperation on certain issues, but they do not necessarily share the same concerns. As the parking issue in City Garden shows, the residents committee would like to see residents at peace with the management company, but it could not force the management company to do what the latter did not want to.

That said, the inability of the residents committee to force its will should not be read as evidence of a weakened state. As the protests and negotiations show, all sides—residents, the residents committee, and the management company—continuously mobilized the discourses and authority of the state to play against one another. Intriguingly, what eventually challenged the power of real-estate developers and property management companies and forced negotiation and compromises was the unstoppable growth of cars.

Such a power dynamic has led the middle class to feel both empowered and vulnerable as consumer-citizens in the new political economy. As they consider that they do not have a firm power base, the dual sense seems weighted toward the pessimistic side among the middle class in general. Given their educational background and work experience, middle-class individuals have political insights and opinions. Yet they do not want to take a political stance; nor do many of them have the motivation to fight for a collective cause that is beyond their immediate concern. Their actions, as Tomba points out, have been based on locally defined interests and ways of interaction within the complex instead of a "cross-societal middle-class identity" (2005, 950). Their disillusion with the political institution and legal system may have led them to refrain from challenging the state or being a leading force for democratization and instead focus on living a stable and happy individual life and pursuing individual mobility. Nonetheless, this pursuit is paradoxical in nature, just as the parking issue suggests. The parking issue has united them as well as divided them. As they focus on individual mobility and a car-oriented lifestyle, their cars inevitably challenge their ideal home, the safe and quiet space they also would like to have. Yet, whether or not they are conscious of the political implications, their actions suggest a symbiotic relationship between the middle class and the state. The compromise to the long-term shortage of parking space suggests that the state remains an essential force in determining how parking is handled even in privatized spaces.

Epilogue

Politics of Transformation

The automotive regime and the middle class have risen symbiotically in China in the twenty-first century. The car regime and the middle class are very much intertwined on multiple fronts from the labor market to consumption and from sociality to mobility. Such entangled rises embody both the blessings and curses of a consumption-driven economy in the age of globalization. Some of the direct, visible consequences of car growth have widely been reported in newspapers and other forms of media.

A car-oriented lifestyle and mobility, which many Chinese used to see only in American movies and TV dramas in the past, have increasingly become an integral part of the rising middle class's everyday life. The Chinese middle class's desire for cars has revitalized such transnational companies as Volkswagen and General Motors, which have experienced stagnant growth at home. Auto manufacturing has become a pillar industry, and billions of dollars have been invested into roads and highways and other infrastructural constructions, creating millions of job opportunities.

But the extension of road networks has also encroached on agricultural lands and forests and has forever changed the country's landscape. Meanwhile, the number of cars has been growing so fast that any new roads, wide as may be when built, very quickly become insufficient for the volume of traffic. Traffic congestion has been a routine phenomenon in many big cities. Car exhausts have also contributed to the already serious air pollution in the cities. To battle these, many municipal governments began to implement restrictive policies. In Beijing, road space rationing policies, effective since the Olympic Games in 2008, have kept cars with certain last numbers on their license plates off the roads during daytime on certain days of the month. Starting in January 2011, the Chinese capital further limited the number of new license plates issued per month to 20,000. In Guangzhou and Shanghai, the municipal governments restricted the monthly issuance of new license plates and used auctioning as a means to curb car growth. In 2016, the central government formulated new industrial policies, encouraging the development of electric cars to replace fuel engines.

With such a general picture as the background, this book places the middle class at the center of analysis and demonstrates how cars and related forms of mobility have become a critical force in shaping people's sense, imagination, and practices of mobility, freedom, and independence.

The stories of mobility in China are often told through migrant workers and their children (Ling forthcoming; Solinger 1999). Those of middle-class Chinese have been told through gated communities (Pow 2009; Zhang L. 2010), classical music education (Kraus 1989), and child-rearing practices (Kuan 2015). Stories that evolve around cars have been told through such key figures as Henry Ford and his Model T, the safety and environmental impact of cars (Jain 2004; Furness 2010; Kay 1998), and the automotive industry and state policies (Huang Y. 2002; Siegelbaum 2008; Thun 2006). This ethnography weaves these three together. The goal is not to depict a comprehensive picture of either middle-class lifestyle or the automotive regime. Instead, where the car regime and the middle class intersect provides a critical entry into the dynamics of material culture, individual subjectivities, social stratification, and the reproduction of state legitimacy. This dynamic compels a nuanced understanding of social transformations in China in the Reform era.

The Reform era, since the late 1970s, has witnessed processes in which the centralized planned economy has been gradually replaced by a mixed set of organizing and regulating economic activities. To do so, the government introduced special economic zones, privatization of properties, and marketization of labor and goods. Many of these reform practices in China shared a belief and a vision with practices—deregulation, promotion of global trade, privatization, and others—introduced in many other countries since Margaret Thatcher's and Ronald Reagan's governments. The belief is that the market and hence competition are better mechanisms than governments to allocate resources and to stimulate economic growth.

It is in this context that many scholars consider China's reform policies, like those in the United States or Latin America, neoliberal. These neoliberal strategies have introduced the framework of choice and freedom (Hoffman 2010), through which a new self-governing and self-responsible ethic—which Zhang (2010) calls the "post-socialist ethic"—has arisen to give shape to the new subjects that can "govern on their own behalf" (Zhang and Ong 2008, 3). This insight into the formation of new, self-governed subjects resonates well with findings in studies of postsocialist transformations in other countries (see, for example, Dunn 2004; Humphrey 1998).

Although scholars emphasize that neoliberal strategies do not belong to democratic societies (see, for example, Ong 2006), to use the term "neoliberal" in the China context may be in some ways misleading. It is well recognized that, as Polanyi (2001) eloquently shows in his analysis of the rise of a laissez-faire economy, the workings of a market economy require state planning and regulations. Nonetheless, for many neoliberal advocates, such as Friedrich von Hayek (1980), one critical component of their theoretical concerns is individuals' freedom as a safeguard against state power.

This ethical component of neoliberal projects seems absent in the China context. This is more intriguing in the cases of the middle class and the automotive regime, which are supposed to embody freedom and autonomy. In terms of the political economy, the making of the car industry has been the party-state's project to rebuild the national economy and to reshape the job market since the early Reform era. The state has continuously deliberated and exercised control over how the auto market could and should work—down to such specific issues as how many car factories there should be and whether private car ownership should be allowed or encouraged. The introduction of foreign capital was a means for national development, which was then a tool for the party-state to regain political legitimacy. China's entry into the WTO provided means, through adapting to global trade practices and standardizing domestic regulations, for the central government to concentrate power at the expense of local authorities. Despite the state's legitimization of individuals' consumption desire, the state has ingrained distrust of individuals' choices and fear of losing control and order, as shown in the car licensing practices. Control, instead of freedom, has been the keyword in the state project of marketization.

From the middle class's perspective, freedom remains a tricky term to describe their experiences in daily life. While they acknowledge that they have more freedom now than before, such freedom is narrowly defined. For some of the entrepreneurial individuals like the dealership owner Huang, the more China integrates with global trade practices, the less freedom they feel to pursue their initiatives, as the government's new practices—such as limited-access bank loans and industrial policies—favor state-owned or state-affiliated enterprises. As individuals who have achieved upward social mobility, the middle class often feel that they are trapped somewhere along their career paths and have few options to move further up. The car, which has been their dream since young, has made them experience the limit of freedom in physical mobility, as well as in personal life. Even as consumers, they feel a freedom in the form of access to consumer goods, but laws and regulations are not always on their side when they need protection against powerful actors, such as real-estate developers. Such a limited sense of freedom can be seen in their articulations of their experience with cars, in which the term "freedom" is infrequently used.

Even if we focus less on the ethical commitment and more on the politics, the neoliberal thesis may still be problematic in its outline of a clear, causal relationship between state policies and changes on the ground. As Kipnis (2007) eloquently points out in his analysis of the possible origins of the suzhi discourse, the attention given to neoliberalism may overlook the effects of other nonneoliberal institutions, ideas, and practices. This point is well illustrated in the upwardly mobile trajectories of the middle class. It is true that the introduction of the market force and state-orchestrated industrialization has given rise to the new labor structure and occupational hierarchy. This labor market's demand for new talents has shaped the possibility for upward social mobility. As the life trajectories of the middle class portrayed in earlier chapters has shown, equally important are education and personal networks, which bring social and cultural capitals. What has played a critical role in the middle class's educational obtainment and personal networks in early life is not market practices but typical socialist provisions—cheap education (particularly higher education), government-assigned jobs, and the work-unit system. Therefore, the rise of the middle class is a hybrid product of marketization policies and socialist practices regarding work and life.

An awareness of being a self-cultivated, self-responsible individual is indeed evident among the middle class. The ethic of self-cultivation differentiates them from lower-class individuals, whom the middle class would think have little motivation to improve their own suzhi at work. This ethic also differentiates them from an elite with powerful family backgrounds—either superrich or politically well connected, who squander money on license plates.

Yet the ethic of a self-cultivated, self-responsible individual is merely part of the making of the middle-class identity as marketization has unfolded. To use Craig Calhoun's words, "what is important about 'sense of belonging' is not someone's identification of membership in a bounded collectivity, but his modification of his consideration of alternative courses of action on the basis of the communal relations to which he belongs" (1983, 90). These communal relations for the imagined community of the middle class, unlike in the Maoist and early Reform days when class labels were fixed, need to be built, negotiated, and strengthened through specific ways of continuously partaking in the new material world.

Middle-class social solidarity requires continuous engagement and performance of a distinctive lifestyle that is increasingly shaped by the car and driving. In this car-oriented lifestyle, the car is more than a symbol of economic achievement. Family and social relationships are reconstituted through ethical, emotional, and aesthetical engagement with the car and ways of driving. These ethical concerns, emotional expressions, and aesthetic feelings have been identifiably influenced as much by the middle class's early life experience and political culture in the Maoist and early Reform eras as by contemporary consumer culture and popular culture. In other words, these subjective experiences are not merely products of Western values, lifestyle, and globalization but a wide range of symbols, values, styles, and situated understanding of the past and the present. In these processes the public-private divide comprises new, redefined webs of cultural significance and social ethos. It is in the social fields that urban professionals and small-time entrepreneurs gradually develop shared subjectivities that shape their middle-class identity.

In such continuous negotiation of various kinds of social relationship, the middle-class individuals reappropriate state-backed values, political symbols, and official discourses. In doing so, they turn themselves into subjects of new forms of governance and reproduce state authority through everyday practices. The state has sanctioned the emergence of the middle class as a statistical truth, as Hai Ren (2013) suggests, as a way to grasp the new realities. By sanctioning its emergence, the state has also officially reckoned the social stratification created since the Reform era.

The point is, if we take the calculative, self-initiated, and self-governed individual as the central characteristic of the middle-class figure as depicted in the neoliberal thesis, this figure also shifts our attention away from alternative ways of producing social stratification and state legitimacy. As recent critics point out, existing anthropological literature tends to use "neoliberalism" as a handy and convenient term for capitalism or globalization without scrutinizing the contexts, configurations, and embeddedness of "free market."[1] This ethnography on the automotive regime and the middle class in contemporary China offers insights to problematize the contexts, configurations, and embeddedness of transformations that require nuanced analyses of how boundaries between the state and society and between state and market are made and remade.

GLOSSARY

4S dian   4S店; 4S dealership (4S stands for sales, spare parts, service, survey)

bainianhaohe   百年好合; a hundred years of harmony (greetings for newlywed couples)

baochi duixing   保持队形; keep the formation of the fleet

Beijing jipu   北京吉普; Beijing Automotive

bendiren   本地人; local residents

benzhi shang yiyang de   本质上一样的; essentially the same

bi shang buzu, bi xia youyu   比上不足，比下有余; not as good as those on top but better than those at the bottom

bianzhi   贬值; depreciate

chengguan   城管; urban management officers

chengshi jingguan   城市景观; urban landscape

chengshu   成熟; mature

danwei 单位; work units

dichan da'e 地产大鳄; the real-estate crocodiles

dik si (Cantonese) 的士; taxi

diwei 地位; status

diyi qiche zhizaochang 第一汽车制造厂; First Auto Works (FAW)

Dongfeng qiche gongsi 东风汽车公司; Dongfeng Motor Corporation (DFM)

fa (as in "facai") 发(发财); have a good fortune, become rich

fangbian 方便; convenient, convenience

Fenghuang 凤凰; Phoenix (Chinese auto brand; later also bicycle brand)

fuwu 服务; serve, service

ganbu 干部; cadre

gexinghua 个性化; personalized

guanche 官车; officials' cars

guanli 管理; manage, management

guli jiaoche jinru jiating 鼓励轿车进入家庭; letting passenger cars into the family is encouraged

Guangzhou Biaozhi qiche gongsi 广州标致汽车公司; Guangzhou-Peugeot Auto Factory

guochanhua 国产化; localization

guojia zhidao jia 国家指导价; state instructed prices

hexie (hexie shehui) 和谐(和谐社会); harmonious, harmony (harmonious society)

Hongqi 红旗; Red Flag (auto brand)

huache 花车; flower cars (cars used in weddings)

huajiao 花轿; flower sedan chairs (sedan chairs used in weddings)

hunluan 混乱; chaotic

jiaozi 轿子; sedan chairs

jiazhang 家长; patriarch

jieceng 阶层; stratum

jieji 阶级; class

jigou gaige 机构改革; institutional reforms

jijiao (bu jijiao) 计较 (不计较); calculative (not calculative)

jingpen 井喷; blowout

jumin weiyuanhui 居民委员会; residents committee

kua guo menkan 跨过门槛; pass the threshold

kuangye 狂野; wild

lang lai le 狼来了; here comes the wolf

laonianren quanyi baozhang fa 老年人权益保障法; Law on the Protection of the Rights and Interests of the Elderly

loushang de / louxia de 楼上的／楼下的; upstairs/downstairs

mei huaichu 没坏处; do no harm

mixin 迷信; superstition

ming 命; fate

minzu qingxu 民族情绪; nationalistic sentiments

mozhe shitou guohe 摸着石头过河; feel the stones to cross the river

niqingwoyuan 你情我愿; mutual consent

pitiao 批条; notes of approval

putongren 普通人; ordinary people

Qirui 奇瑞; Chery (auto brand)

renxinghua 人性化; humanize

san da san xiao 三大三小; three bigs, three smalls (refers to automakers)

sanxiang jiaoche 三厢轿车; three-box sedan

Shanghai qiche jituan 上海汽车集团; Shanghai Automobile Industry Company (SAIC)

shang you lao, xiao you xiao 上有老, 下有小; the elderly above, and the young ones below

shengchan gongju 生产工具; production tools

shichang huan jishu 市场换技术; market share for technologies

shiji 实际; practicality

shuangkuai　爽快; straightforward

suzhi　素质; quality, human quality

tianjia　天价; sky-high price

Tianjin Xiali　天津夏利; Tianjin Automotive

tie fanwan　铁饭碗; iron rice bowls

tongtian le　通天了; connected all the way to the sky

tongzi shou　童子手; virgin child's hands

tougongjianliao　偷工减料; reduce the labor and material input

tuanjie　团结; unite

waidiren　外地人; newcomers

wenzhong　稳重; composed

wuzi gongsi　物资公司; commodity company

xiaoma pei haoan　小马配豪鞍; a pony with an extravagant saddle

xiaoshun/buxiao　孝顺／不孝; filial piety / not filial

xiao zichan jieji　小资产阶级; petite bourgeois

xindeguo　信得过; credibility

xinteng　心疼; care about

yewu suzhi　业务素质; professional quality

yezhu dahui　业主大会; the homeowners assembly

yezhu weiyuanhui　业主委员会; the homeowners committee

yibanren　一般人; ordinary people

yipan sansha　一盘散沙; a platter of loose sand

you gexing　有个性; a person of character

youquan de ren　有权的人; powerful people

yongjietongxin　永结同心; forever in love

yu lang gong wu　与狼共舞; dances with wolves

zhibuguo　只不过; only, no more than

zhide xinren　值得信任; trustworthy

zhifu guangrong　致富光荣; getting rich is glorious

zhizhu hangye　支柱行业; pillar industry

zhongchan　中产; midpropertied (short for midpropertied strata and midpropertied class)

zhongchan jieceng　中产阶层; midpropertied strata

zhongchan jieji　中产阶级; midpropertied class

zhongjian jieceng　中间阶层; middle strata

ziyou　自由; freedom

Notes

Introduction

1. The Chinese term *zhongjian* can be translated as both "in-betweenness" and "middleness."

2. I use the plural form of "middle class" when I accentuate the fragmentation and heterogeneity of the people involved and the singular form when the term is used generically.

3. I use "automotive regime" and "automobility" interchangeably, with preference to "automotive regime." I agree with Steffen Boehm and his coauthors (2006) that using "automobility" might leave the impression that automobiles are about mobility, when in fact they also bring immobility.

4. Just to name a few studies done in other parts of the world, see Boehm et al. 2006; Jackson 1985; Lutz 2014; McShane 1994; Norton 2008; Sheller and Urry 2000; Winner 1986.

5. For an overview of the changes, see Cheek 2006; Naughton 2007.

6. I use "complex" instead of "community," which is used in most studies on contemporary China. The term "community" implies solidarity that, as chapter 6 will show, may not exist in these gated residential areas.

7. For a study of the middle class in India, see Dickey 2012; Donner 2011; Fuller and Narasimhan 2007, 2008; for Nepal, see Liechty 2003; for the middle class in the eastern

European bloc, see Fehérváry 2013; for Latin America, see O'Dougherty 2002; Freeman 2014; for African countries, see Lentz 2015.

8. Mark Liechty (2003) has detailed the relevance of Weber, Bourdieu, and Thompson in the study of the middle class. See also Heiman 2015; O'Dougherty 2002; Zhang L. 2010.

9. Their native tongues comprised a variety of languages. While roughly half speak Cantonese, the dominant language in the Pearl River delta region, all of them could speak Mandarin.

10. See *Guangzhou Statistical Yearbook* 2014 and *China Statistical Yearbook* 2014.

11. Newer generations may have different lifestyle choices. There are younger couples that live in rental apartments and own cars. However, at the moment, to my knowledge, they usually expect to inherit apartments from their two sets of parents.

12. My use of the term "modernity" draws on critical reflection on what it means to be modern and its configuration in specific contexts. See Mitchell 2000; Latour 1993; Rofel 1999.

13. In these cases, the person either has to travel a lot or has not yet felt settled with one particular job. Local regulations often have bias against nonlocal license plates, while changing license plate is a great hassle under Chinese laws and local regulations. Car ownership for them seemed more a constraint than facilitator of mobility.

14. See http://data.worldbank.org/indicator/IS.VEH.PCAR.P3/countries/1W-US ?display=default (accessed August 21, 2013).

15. For a detailed official division of classes, see Li Chu. 2005, 82; Whyte and Parish 1984. Undeniably, class politics was more convoluted and dynamic in reality than what official narratives may suggest. Class labels were hereditary. But during political mobilizations class identities were fluid and inherently unstable (Wu 2014).

16. For more detailed descriptions of the rural-urban divide in relation to household registration, see Chan, Madsen, and Unger 1992; Cheng and Selden 1994; Naughton 2007.

17. Work units are more than production units. Social welfare was distributed through work units. For a detailed discussion on work units in the urban economy, see Friedman and Lee 2010; Lü and Perry 1997.

18. For the research and following reports, see Li Chu. 2005; Li et al. 2004; Lu 2002; Sun 2004; Zhou 2005. For a more detailed analysis of these studies, see Ren 2013; Tomba 2004.

19. While there are other studies on private housing (Fleischer 2010; Pow 2009; Tomba 2014), Li Zhang's study is among the few that explicitly aim to address the formation of the middle class.

20. Ethnographic data in different chapters indicate gendered ways of seeing and using cars in subject making and family making. However, analysis of the dynamics and complexity of the gender issue deserves further research and separate articles.

Prologue

1. See Guangzhou Qishier Hang Shangbao (Guangzhou Seventy-Two Industries Newspaper), 1945–1946.

2. The initiative to use vegetable oil as engine fuel was intriguing, as it echoed some contemporary initiatives to make cars more environmentally friendly in such places as the United States. Unfortunately, Zhong Xu's article did not mention how successful these vegetable-oil-powered buses were.

3. In 2003, academic journals, major newspapers, and popular websites published a series of papers and articles celebrating the fiftieth anniversary of China's auto industry.

4. Although cars were desirable consumer items in the United States and Europe before the world wars, cars for mass consumption became prominent in the post–World War II period (Flink 1988; Jackson 1985; McShane 1994; Warner 1978; Wollen and Kerr 2002).

5. The Development Research Center of the State Council, the Construction Bank of China, and China Auto Industry Company organized a symposium discussing the strategic development of China's auto industry in 1985. Several committees in the state council held a similar symposium two years later. Since then the goal of developing the auto industry became clear. In 1994 the state council published "Policy agenda of national production for the 1990s" (*jiushi niandai guojia chanye zhengce gangyao*), stating that the development of the auto industry, together with the electronics, energy, and real-estate industries, should be facilitated so that they could become the pillar industries for the national economy. "Auto industry policy (1994)" (*qiche gongye chanye zhengce* 1994), which was the first auto-industry-specific official document, soon came out as a follow-up to the general policies. It restated that the auto industry would be the pillar industry *by* 2010, after two five-year plans. "Auto industry policy (2004)" (*qiche gongye chanye zhengce* 2004), the substitute for the 1994 one, not only repeated the goal but also hoped to realize the goal *before* 2010.

6. Following the guidelines in the 7th Five-Year Plan and the subsequent 1987 Beidaihe conference, an industrial structure called "three bigs, three smalls" (*san da san xiao*) gradually came into being. The three big manufacturers included the FAW, the Dongfeng Motor Corporation (DFM), and Shanghai Automobile Industry Company (SAIC), and the three small, Beijing Automotive, Tianjin Automotive, and Guangzhou-Peugeot Auto Factory. See "1988 state council notice on strictly control passenger cars' production sites" (*guowuyuan guanyu yange kongzhi jiaoche shengchandian de tongzhi*).

7. "Policy agenda of national production for the 1990s" (1994) clearly stated that the auto industry should have only a limited number of factory sites with mass production ability and a market structure with orderly competition. See also "Auto industry policy (1994)" and "1989 state council decision on current industrial policy key points" (*Guowuyuan guanyu dangqian chanye zhengce yaodian de jueding*).

8. See the 7th Five-Year Plan (1986–1990).

9. In July 1987, the state council received two reports, one from the National Science and Technology Committee and the other from the Development Research Center of the State Council. Those reports proposed to shift the emphasis on heavy-duty vehicles to passenger cars. In a state council conference held in Beidaihe in August, the issue of passenger cars was listed in its agenda and discussed.

10. Meanwhile, a number of auto-related technical "know-hows" were transferred from foreign auto companies to different local Chinese manufacturers. The foreign companies involved included Suzuki, Fiat, Daihatsu, Chrysler, and Mercedes-Benz.

Because only vehicles produced in joint ventures had the foreign brand names on the car bodies, know-how transfer was much less known and is barely mentioned in media today. See also Li Yo. 2003a.

11. Zheng Yefu put some of the key articles into an edited volume entitled *Jiaoche da lunzhan* (Auto debates), see Zheng 1996.

12. *Guanyu qiche jiaoyi shichang guanli zanxing guiding* (Temporary regulations on the management of car trading market), by the National Industrial and Commercial Administrative Management Bureau, 1985. See also "Qiche jiaoyi shichang guanli xin guiding" (New regulations on managing the car trading market), *Guangzhou Ribao* (Guangzhou Daily), September 19, 1985.

13. *Diyi jixie gongyebu guanyu yange kongzhi qiche chanpn jiage, jiaqiang jiage guanli de tongzhi* (A notice from the First Mechanic Industrial Bureau on strengthening the price control and management of auto products), 1981; *Guowuyuan bangongting zhuanfa guojia jiwei guanyu jiaqiang xiaojiaoche xiaoshou guanli de qingshi de tongzhi* (A notice on strengthening the management of passenger car sales by the National Plan Committee and forwarded by the General Office of the State Council), 1989.

14. *Guojia jihua weiyuanhui guanyu dui guochan xiaojiaoche shixing guojia zhidao jiage de tongzhi* (A Notice by the National Plan Committee on implementing the state-guiding prices of the domestic-produced passenger cars), 1994.

15. *Guanyu fangkai guochan jiaoche jiage wenti de tongzhi* (A notice on eliminating price control on domestic-produced passenger cars), by the National Development and Plan Committee, 2001.

16. The report was entitled *Guanyu Hainan jinkou he daomai qiche deng wuzi wenti de diaocha baogao* (An investigation report on Hainan's importation and reselling for profits of cars and other goods), issued in 1985. Investigation was jointly carried out by the Guangdong Municipal Government, the Central Commission for Discipline Inspection of the Communist Party of China, the National Audit Office, and other national bureaus.

17. See reports in *Guangzhou Ribao* (Guangzhou Daily), August 1, 1985.

18. Official yearbooks explicitly point out that in the 1990s no other provinces were ever close to Guangdong in terms of car smuggling.

19. Income data is from *Guangzhou Statistical Yearbook*, 1980–2000.

20. That said, some practices have been reinvented to circumvent new regulations. See Goldstein 2014a, 2014b. I have seen similar operations described by Matthew Goldstein but on the China end in my fieldwork.

21. *China Auto Trade Yearbook* 1996–1997, 131; *China Auto Market Yearbook* 1999, 104.

22. *Guangzhou Yearbook* began to list "auto manufacture" as a subcategory under "machine-and-electrical industry" in 1986. Starting from 1996, *Guangzhou Yearbook* has listed the auto industry as an independent title under the industry section.

23. The joint venture was created with equity worth $58.5 million, with 46 percent of the contribution from Guangzhou Automobile Manufacturing, 22 percent from Peugeot, 28 percent from the China International Trust & Investment Corporation, and 4 percent from the Banque Nationale de Pairs (Thun 2006).

24. See *Guangzhou Statistical Yearbook*, 1985–1997.

25. Wang mentioned but did not specify that managerial styles and communication were also problematic inside the enterprise.

26. Eric Thun (2006), a scholar who studies industrialization in China, points out that Guangzhou-Peugeot's failure to develop a network of part suppliers was not because of technology or corporate management. Thun compares Guangzhou-Peugeot with Shanghai-Volkswagen. Shanghai-Volkswagen enjoyed full government support and local production capacity based on its previous state-controlled industrial facilities and military factories. In contrast, many suppliers in Guangzhou were small, private businesses, which neither Guangzhou-Peugeot nor Guangzhou Automobile Manufacturing had full ownership of or control over. The lack of ownership led to inefficient investments and insufficient motivation to support those suppliers from the local government. See also Yao and Han 2008.

27. Aiming at fostering and protecting local industry, localization was required by law to be written into the contract for setting up a joint venture in the early Reform period. For the automotive joint ventures, localization stipulated that a whole passenger car had to include a certain percentage of parts produced in China, and that percentage should increase over the designated period of time.

28. Guangzhou government's negotiation for a new joint venture was first with Opel, a Germany-based General Motor's subsidiary (Yao and Han 2008). But for unspecified reasons, this initiative was dropped.

29. *Guangzhou Statistical Yearbooks*, 1997–1998.

1. Driving Alone Together

1. Chinese media reports and popular discourses have it that carmakers use formaldehyde to do internal decoration, and formaldehyde is said to cause headache, nausea, and more severe health issues, such as cancer.

2. Lin Xiaoshan was a sociologist graduate student who also studied car consumption in Guangzhou when I gave a talk at Sun Yat-sen University about my research in 2007. Lin told me that he encountered very similar situations. His informants used "convenience" almost exclusively to describe why they bought their cars.

3. Some colleges and universities still provide subsidized housing options. Nonetheless, new forms of work-related housing exist (Kipnis 2016). For example, many factories may provide lodging (often in poor conditions) for their low-end employees as supplements to the low salaries (Pun 2005).

4. The significance of alumni networks in China is an understudied topic. For the rural part, see Santos 2008.

5. For specific analysis of the workings and significance of networking, see Osburg's (2013) ethnography of whom he calls the elites in northwest China.

6. The use of sedan chairs is briefly mentioned in Dong 2002, 13.

7. If one of the new couple's families does not live locally, the family often rents a hotel room as the pickup place.

8. This may be a regional practice.

9. This differs from road rage, which usually refers to individuals driving alone. My interlocutors became irritated only when they drove as a team.

10. One escalated confrontation involved a car club composed of Mazda 6 owners and a Hummer driver on August 18, 2007. According to the newspaper report, the Mazda car club had an organized tour from Nanjing to Lianyungang in Jiangsu Province. When they were driving as a car fleet on the highway, one Hummer tried to overtake and cut into the fleet. Some Mazda drivers were irritated because the Hummer ruined the formation of the parade (*duixing*). They soon overtook the Hummer and circled it. Then the Mazda drivers slowed down to almost "crawling," in their own language, on the highway. The Hummer had no way to get out. Because the Mazda cars took up all the lanes to encircle the Hummer, they blocked other cars, and a long line behind them quickly developed. The Mazda 6 drivers finally let the Hummer go after ten minutes or so. See Lü 2009.

11. Most of the taxis are included in the 80 percent because most big taxi companies were state owned (*Zhongguo Qiche Shichang Nianjian* 1995). See also Wu and Fei 2002.

12. Xu, Zhong, and Ying Yu, 2007, "Zhang Xiaoyu: Cheshi Zui Buyong Guojia Caoxin" (Zhang Xiaoyu: the auto market is the last for the state to worry about), *Nanfang Zhoumo*, November 27.

13. These compact cars tend to be of the high-end brands. Their drivers are in general young and tend to be women.

14. One good example is the middle class's concern for food safety. See Klein 2013.

15. This reputation of BMW's is related to several car accidents in which BMW drivers either ran over a victim or verbally and physically assaulted victims. BMW was made into a pun with the initials for *bie mo wo*, which means "do not touch me." See also Notar 2017.

2. Family Cars, Filial Consumer-Citizens

1. Historically, middle-class identity could be reduced neither to an identity based on a profession nor to a particular level of income. A good number of women—who did not have occupations, comparable education, or their own income—were nonetheless perceived as middle class because they belonged to middle-class families as wives, mothers, or daughters.

2. A number of interrelated policy and socioeconomic factors have led to the prevalence of this particular form among urban middle-class families. The enforcement of birth control policies is complicated and not uniform across the urban-rural divide and class lines. Meanwhile, changing childbearing and child-rearing practices and gender politics have led to differentiated family and reproduction choices. For more discussion, see Greenhalgh 2008; Santos and Harrell 2017.

3. All official income statistical data in this chapter come from the *Guangzhou Statistical Yearbooks*, 2004–2017.

4. In the very few cases I heard from interlocutors, people of the younger generation had a car and lived in a rented apartment, but they all expected to inherit apartments—often more than one—from their extended families.

5. Singles do invest in apartments, but usually they are quite beyond the average marriage age.

6. In mass media's and popular culture's representation, the pressure is on the groom and his family to provide housing for the newlyweds. I have found this expectation among parents who look for suitors for their daughters in People's Park in Shanghai (Zhang and Sun 2014). However, expectations may be different from practices. I have not seen convincing research on this pattern in practice. This pattern is also not found among my interlocutors. It may be a regional distinction or a generational difference.

7. For more on status inheritance, see Walder and Hu 2009.

8. Using statistics from Shanghai, Yong Cai and Feng Wang (2014) analyze the institutional forces that underpinned this marriage pattern.

9. Harriet Evans (2010) also observed a similar situation in Beijing between 2000 and 2004.

10. Employing a live-in nanny is more common when ailing senior parents live by themselves. Having a live-in nanny to provide childcare was rare among my interlocutors. Many of them told me that their apartments were not big enough to host a live-in nanny. Moreover, while young parents were receptive to the idea of having a nanny at home, their parents were reluctant.

11. Notably, many young wives would rather pay for a domestic helper than rely on their mother-in-law, but they rarely got their wish.

12. It should be noted that there are intriguing discrepancies between perceived safety and actual practices. On the one hand, China has a high mortality rate from car accidents. On the other hand, many car owners decorate the interior of their cars and drive in ways that are unsafe. For example, children are often left standing instead of sitting in a child seat in the car.

3. The Emerging Middle Class and the Car Market

1. "Qiche pinpai xiaoshou guanli shishi banfa" (Regulations on the Sale and Management of Auto Brands), by the Commerce Department in the State Council, the Development and Reform Committee, and the Industry and Commerce Bureau, 2005.

2. "Shaowubu zhuanjia jiedu 'qiche pinpai xiaoshou guanli shishi banfa'" (Experts from the Commerce Department interpreting the "Regulations on the Sale and Management of Auto Brands"), http://news.xinhuanet.com/auto/2005-04/01/content _2771453.htm. Accessed October 29, 2007.

3. For example, the German automaker VW has two joint ventures with different local companies: FAW-VW based in Changchun in the north and SAIC VW in Shanghai. Both FAW-VW and SAIC VW have their own 4S dealerships, and these dealerships do not buy from or sell cars for the other.

4. The personnel structure in state-owned companies during the socialist and early Reform period was similar to that in the government.

5. "Guanyu qiche jiaoyi shichang guanli zanxing guiding" (Temporary Regulations on the Management of Car Trading Market), by the National Industrial and Commercial Administrative Management Bureau, 1985. Quotas and the rationing system in

China were not very different from those in former socialist countries in Eastern Europe. For China, see Naughton 2007. For the former socialist countries in Eastern Europe, see Verdery 1996, 2003.

6. For more details on cars' trade regulations, see the prologue. But in the mid-1990s many state-owned enterprises had traded directly their car quotas without the involvement of the commodities companies. See "Jinzhi xiaoqiche sixia jiaoyi" (Forbid car trading privately), *Renmin Ribao*, November 12, 1994.

7. I would like to see a copy of any of those notes of approval Lu mentioned or the details of how they were traded or used to get real cars. But Lu always stopped before delving into details.

8. Passenger car production relied heavily on imported spare parts in the early years of the joint ventures. Tariffs for parts were between 50 and 80 percent from 1985 to 1996 and then adjusted to 35 to 60 percent in 1997. The prices of the passenger cars assembled in the joint ventures were determined according to the prices of their imported counterparts (Xie and Xu 1998). Therefore, the price reduction had less to do with the production cost than with tariff adjustments over the years.

9. According to Mr. Lu's account, the commodity company made a severe mistake in investing in a car factory in the city of Zhanjiang in Guangdong. This car factory did assembly work, but the origin of the spare parts it used was highly suspicious. In a series of antismuggling campaigns in the late 1990s, this car factory went bankrupt, causing the commodity company to sink with it.

10. A research report by the consultancy McKinsey points out that Chinese car consumers, most of whom are in the market for the first time, have little loyalty to particular brands (Hoffe, Lane, and Nam 2003).

11. "Guangzhou Biaozhi qingxing qiche gongbuyingqiu" (Demand for Guangzhou Peugeot light vehicles exceeded supply), *Guangzhou Ribao*, November 12, 1986.

12. College education started to charge tuition fees in the mid-1990s, a few years before higher education started to expand exponentially. College students still received living stipends throughout the 1990s. But the total amount had not been adjusted to the rapidly growing living expenses in cities.

13. For details about the household registration system and its impact on mobility, see Cheng and Seldon 1994 and Solinger 1999.

14. LiAnne Yu (2014) terms this kind of status demonstration with an emphasis on hard work as "conspicuous accomplishment."

4. Car Crash, Class Encounter

1. With more and more models being made in joint ventures and car prices continuously dropping in China, salespeople's income did not go up very much despite the rapid growth of sales in general.

2. After I figured out the work dynamics, I decided not to sell any cars myself. Even though I could divide the bonus among the salespeople, it would not be satisfactory. Each would think she or he could have had the whole amount if I were not in the way. After I made my decision clear to the salespeople, I had an easier time hanging out with them in the dealership.

3. For a detailed discussion of vocational school education and students' career choices, see Ling 2015.

4. For urban villages, see Siu 2007 and Bach 2010.

5. Guandi is considered the god of business.

6. One needs a college degree, but not necessarily in law, to pass the national legal practice examination.

7. To some degree, the tradition was not lost even in the Maoist years, as the terms "educate" and "reeducate" had frequently appeared in all sorts of political movements.

8. According to my interviews and observations, political elites are not defined by suzhi but rather by their political lineage and network.

5. Bidding for a License Plate

1. Many cities have their own rules that restrict nonlocally registered cars to access the city or require them to pay tolls per use or per day.

2. Among the seven symbols in any given license plate, the first two are fixed with the provincial character and the city's letter. There are two ways to compose the rest: (1) the letter has to be either in the seventh place, and the rest are numbers; or (2) the third *and* the seventh symbols are letters and the rest numbers. In either case, car owners cannot choose which letter(s) to be used. The fifth and the sixth places cannot be 33, 66, 88, 99, and one cannot use the letters *I* and *O*.

3. The municipal government did not give an explanation regarding the frequency of the auctions.

4. As a salesman involved in various kinds of car-related businesses told me, sometimes a used car could cost more than its practical value because of its good license plate number.

5. I have not found historical documents that suggest popularity of the number 8 in the old days. Instead, studies suggest that 9 may have enjoyed more prestige due to its connection to the imperial ruling (Steinhardt 1998). In Guangzhou, older people recalled that, before the Communist Party took over, there were preferable days and numbers determined by popular religious beliefs and calendars for special occasions, such as opening a business or having a wedding, but no such explicit pursuit for particular numbers in relation to fortune due to their phonetic similarities.

6. Jim Yardley, 2006, "First Comes the Car, Then the $10,000 License Plate," *New York Times*, July 5.

7. In early 2011 all major local newspapers—*Yangcheng Wanbao, Xinkuaibao, Nanfang Dushibao,* and others—reported that different municipal government departments pointed fingers at each other, saying that other departments should be responsible for making enforceable rules to put the fund in actual use.

6. Parking

1. The municipal government abolished this rent control in 2016 in order to control car growth and improve traffic.

2. For instance, according to the new property law, if a garage can be separated from the rest of the complex without affecting the integrity of the living area, the article that stipulates parking areas as common properties does not apply.

3. The development of private housing in Guangzhou started earlier than most cities in China. Private housing advertisements, targeted primarily at overseas Chinese, can be found in local newspapers in the mid- and late 1980s. Having learned from Hong Kong, developers established management models for private housing projects.

4. "Wuye guanli tiaoli" (Regulations on Realty Management) Decree of the State Council of the People's Republic of China No. 379 (effective September 1, 2003).

5. *Chengguan*, the legal management officers, are parapolice with dubious legal status. Yet they had tremendous de facto power to confiscate private properties (usually street peddlers without licenses) and inflict fines. See Swider 2015.

6. Standing behind the glass walls in part of the hallway and elevator halls, one can easily, sometimes almost unavoidably, look into people's homes through their huge windows and balconies.

7. I have lived in or visited other complexes over the past decade for research. It should be noted that different complexes have different dynamics. It seems to me that interaction tends to be less in upscale complexes than middle- to lower-middle-class complexes, where grandparents bring their grandchildren out regularly every day.

8. Robert Weller has an insightful analysis of the "one eye open and one eye closed" ruling strategy (Weller 2014). Despite his focus on religion, the underlying logic and practices are similar here.

Epilogue

1. For a summary of neoliberal literature in the field of anthropology, see Eriksen et al. 2015; Ganti 2014. For a critique of the use of neoliberalism in holistic terms with case studies, see, among many others, Collier 2011; Kipnis 2007.

References

Abercrombie, Nicholas, and John Urry. 1983. *Capital, Labour, and the Middle Classes*. London: G. Allen & Unwin.

Agnew, Jean-Christophe. 1986. *Worlds Apart: The Market and the Theater in Anglo-American Thought, 1550–1750*. Cambridge: Cambridge University Press.

Anagnost, Ann. 1997. *National Past-Times: Narrative, Representation, and Power in Modern China, Body, Commodity, Text*. Durham, NC: Duke University Press.

——. 2004. "The Corporeal Politics of Quality (Suzhi)." *Public Culture* 16 (2): 189–208.

——. 2008. "From 'Class' to 'Social Strata': Grasping the Social Totality in Reform-Era China." *Third World Quarterly* 29 (3): 497–519.

Appadurai, Arjun. 1986. "Introduction: Commodities and the Politics of Value." In *The Social Life of Things: Commodities in Cultural Perspective*, edited by Arjun Appadurai, 3–63. Cambridge: Cambridge University Press.

Bach, Jonathan. 2010. "'They Come in Peasants and Leave Citizens': Urban Villages and the Making of Shenzhen, China." *Cultural Anthropology* 25 (3): 421–458.

Barmé, Geremier R. 2002. "Engines of Revolution: Car Cultures in China." In *Autopia: Car and Culture*, edited by Peter Wollen and Joe Kerr, 177–190. London: Reaktion.

Barry, Andrew, Thomas Osborne, and Nikolas S. Rose, eds. 1996. *Foucault and Political Reason: Liberalism, Neo-liberalism, and Rationalities of Government*. Chicago: University of Chicago Press.

Barthes, Roland. 1972. *Mythologies*. New York: Hill and Wang.

Barton, Dominic, Yougang Chen, and Amy Jin. 2013. "Mapping China's Middle Class." *McKinsey Quarterly*. http://www.mckinsey.com/insights/consumer_and_retail/mapping_chinas_middle_class (June). Accessed October 10, 2013.

Basu, Ellen Oxfeld. 1991. "Profit, Loss, and Fate: The Entrepreneurial Ethic and the Practice of Gambling in an Overseas Chinese Community." *Modern China* 17 (2): 227–59.

Baudrillard, Jean. 1981. *For a Critique of the Political Economy of the Sign*. St. Louis: Telos Press.

Berdahl, Daphne. 1999. *Where the World Ended: Re-unification and Identity in the German Borderland*. Berkeley: University of California Press.

———. 2000. "'Go, Trabi, Go!': Reflections on a Car and Its Symbolization over Time." *Anthropology and Humanism* 25 (2): 131–141.

Bian, Yanjie, Ronald Breiger, Deborah Davis, and Joseph Galaskiewicz. 2005. "Occupation, Class, and Social Networks in Urban China." *Social Forces* 83 (4): 1443–1468.

Boehm, Steffen, Campbell Jones, Chris Land, and Matthew Paterson, eds. 2006. *Against Automobility*. Malden, MA: Blackwell.

Borneman, John. 1992. *Belonging in the Two Berlins: Kin, State, Nation*. Cambridge: Cambridge University Press.

Bourdieu, Pierre. 1984. *Distinction: A Social Critique of the Judgement of Taste*. Cambridge, MA: Harvard University Press.

Boyer, Kate, and Maia Boswell-Penc. 2010. "Breast Pumps: A Feminist technology, or (yet) 'More Work for Mother.'" In *Feminist Technology*, edited by Linda L. Layne, Sharra Louise Vostral, and Kate Boyer, 119–135. Urbana: University of Illinois Press.

Bray, David. 2005. *Social Space and Governance in Urban China: The Danwei System from Origins to Reform*. Stanford, CA: Stanford University Press.

Campanella, Thomas J. 2008. *The Concrete Dragon: China's Urban Revolution and What It Means for the World*. New York: Princeton Architectural Press.

Cai, Yong, and Feng Wang. 2014. "(Re)emergence of Late Marriage in Shanghai: From Collective Synchronization to Individual Choice." In *Wives, Husbands, and Lovers: Marriage and Sexuality in Hong Kong, Taiwan, and Urban China*, edited by Deborah Davis and Sara Friedman, 97–117. Stanford, CA: Stanford University Press.

Caldeira, Teresa. 2000. *City of Walls: Crime, Segregation, and Citizenship in São Paulo*. Berkeley: University of California Press.

Calhoun, Craig. 1983. "Community: Toward a Variable Conceptualization for Comparative Research." In *History and Class: Essential Readings in Theory and Interpretation*, edited by R. S. Neale, 86–110. Oxford: Basil Blackwell.

Callahan, William A. 2012. "Sino-speak: Chinese Exceptionalism and the Politics of History." *Journal of Asian Studies* 71 (1): 33–55.

Chan, Anita, Richard Madsen, and Jonathan Unger. 1992. *Chen Village under Mao and Deng: The Recent History of a Peasant Community in Mao's China*. Berkeley: University of California Press.

Cheek, Timothy. 2006. *Living with Reform: China since 1989*. Halifax, Nova Scotia: Zed Books.

Chen, Haoxiong. 1949. *Qiche* (Automobiles). Shanghai: Zhonghua Shuju.

Chen, Jie. 2013. *A Middle Class without Democracy: Economic Growth and the Prospects for Democratization in China.* New York: Oxford University Press.

Cheng, Tiejun, and Mark Selden. 1994. "The Origins and Social Consequences of China's Hukou System." *China Quarterly* 139:644–668.

Cho, Mun Young. 2013. *The Specter of "the People": Urban Poverty in Northeast China.* Ithaca, NY: Cornell University Press.

Chu, Julie Y. 2010. *Cosmologies of Credit: Transnational Mobility and the Politics of Destination in China.* Durham, NC: Duke University Press.

Cockburn, Cynthia, and Susan Ormrod. 1993. *Gender and Technology in the Making.* London: Sage.

Cohen, Myron L. 1992. "Family Management and Family Division in Contemporary Rural China." *China Quarterly* 130:357–377.

Collier, Stephen J. 2009. "Topologies of Power: Foucault's Analysis of Political Government beyond 'Governmentality.'" *Theory, Culture and Society* 26 (6): 78–108.

——. 2011. *Post-Soviet Social: Neoliberalism, Social Modernity, Biopolitics.* Princeton, NJ: Princeton University Press.

Cowan, Ruth Schwartz. 1976. "The 'Industrial Revolution' in the Home: Household Technology and Social Change in the 20th Century." *Technology and Culture* 17 (1): 1–23.

Das, Veena. 2010. "Engaging the Life of the Other: Love and Everyday Life." In *Ordinary Ethics: Anthropology, Language, and Action*, edited by Michael Lambek, 376–399. New York: Fordham University Press.

Davis, Deborah, ed. 2000a. *The Consumer Revolution in Urban China.* Berkeley: University of California Press.

——. 2000b. "Social Class Transformation in Urban China." *Modern China* 26 (3): 251–275.

——. 2014. "Privatization of Marriage in Post-Socialist China." *Modern China* 40 (6): 551–577.

Davis, Deborah, and Stevan Harrell. 1993. "Introduction: The Impact of Post-Mao Reforms on Family Life." In *Chinese Families in the Post-Mao Era*, edited by Deborah Davis and Stevan Harrell, 1–24. Berkeley: University of California Press.

Davis, Natalie Zemon. 1986. "Boundaries and the Sense of Self in Sixteenth-Century France." In *Reconstructing Individualism: Autonomy, Individuality, and the Self in Western Thought*, edited by Thomas C. Heller and Christine Brooke-Rose, 53–63. Stanford, CA: Stanford University Press.

Dickey, Sara. 2012. "The Pleasures and Anxieties of Being in the Middle: Emerging Middle-Class Identities in Urban South India." *Modern Asian Studies* 46 (3): 559–599.

Dikötter, Frank. 2006. *Exotic Commodities: Modern Objects and Everyday Life in China.* New York: Columbia University Press.

Dong, Zenggang, ed. 2002. *Cong Laoshi Che Ma Zhou Qiao dao Xinshi Jiaotong Gongju* (From old-styled carriage, horses, boats and bridges to new-styled transportation means). Chengdu: Sichuan Renmin Chubanshe.

Donner, Henrike, ed. 2011. *Being Middle-Class in India: A Way of Life.* London: Routledge.

Donner, Henrike, and Gonçalo Santos. 2016. "Love, Marriage, and Intimate Citizenship in Contemporary China and India: An Introduction." *Modern Asian Studies* 50 (special issue 4): 1123–1146.

Dudley, Kathryn M. 1994. *The End of the Line: Lost Jobs, New Lives in Postindustrial America*. Chicago: University of Chicago Press.

Dunn, Elizabeth C. 2004. *Privatizing Poland: Baby Food, Big Business, and the Remaking of Labor*. Ithaca, NY: Cornell University Press.

Economist. 1997. "Car Jams in China." June 21, 64.

——. 2003. "Business: The Great Leap Forward; Cars in China." February 1, 53–56.

Edensor, Tim. 2004. "Automobility and National Identity: Representation, Geography and Driving Practice." *Theory Culture Society* 21 (4–5): 101–120.

Ehrenreich, Barbara. 1989. *Fear of Falling: The Inner Life of the Middle Class*. New York: Pantheon Books.

Elegant, Simon. 2007. "China's Me Generation." *Time*, July 26. http://www.time.com/time/magazine/article/0,9171,1647243-3,00.html. Accessed August 10, 2007.

Eriksen, Thomas Hylland, James Laidlaw, Jonathan Mair, Keir Martin, and Soumhya Venkatesan. 2015. "'The Concept of Neoliberalism Has Become an Obstacle to the Anthropological Understanding of the Twenty-First Century.'" *Journal of the Royal Anthropological Institute* 21 (4): 911–923.

Errington, Frederick. 1987. "The Rock Creek Auction: Contradiction between Competition and Community in Rural Montana." *Ethnology* 26 (4): 297–311.

Evans, Harriet. 2010. "The Gender of Communication: Changing Expectations of Mothers and Daughters in Urban China." *China Quarterly* 204: 980–1000.

Featherstone, Mike. 2004. "Automobilities: An Introduction." *Theory Culture Society* 21 (4–5): 279–284.

Featherstone, Mike, N. J. Thrift, and John Urry, eds. 2005. *Automobilities*. London: Sage.

Fehérváry, Krisztina. 2013. *Politics in Color and Concrete: Socialist Materialities and the Middle Class in Hungary*. Bloomington: Indiana University Press.

Ferguson, James. 2010. "The Uses of Neoliberalism." *Antipode* 41:166–184.

Fleischer, Friederike. 2010. *Suburban Beijing: Housing and Consumption in Contemporary China*. Minneapolis: University of Minnesota Press.

Flink, James J. 1988. *The Automobile Age*. Cambridge, MA: MIT Press.

Flonneau, Mathieu. 2010. "Read Tocqueville, or Drive? A European Perspective on US 'Automobilization.'" *History and Technology* 26 (4): 379–388.

Fong, Vanessa. 2004. "Filial Nationalism among Chinese Teenagers with Global Identities." *American Ethnologist* 31 (4): 631–648.

Foucault, Michel. 1995. *Discipline and Punish: The Birth of the Prison*. New York: Vintage Books.

Freeman, Carla. 2014. *Entrepreneurial Selves: Neoliberal Respectability and the Making of a Caribbean Middle Class*. Durham, NC: Duke University Press.

Frevert, Ute. 1990. *Women in German History: From Bourgeois Emancipation to Sexual Liberation*. Oxford: Berg.

Friedman, E., and C. K. Lee. 2010. "Remaking the World of Chinese Labour: A 30-Year Retrospective." *British Journal of Industrial Relations* 48 (3): 507–533.

Fuller, C. J., and Haripriya Narasimhan. 2007. "Information Technology Professionals and the New-Rich Middle Class in Chennai (Madras)." *Modern Asian Studies* 41 (1): 121–150.

———. 2008. "From Landlords to Software Engineers: Migration and Urbanization among Tamil Brahmans." *Comparative Studies in Society and History* 50 (1): 170–196.

Furness, Zachary M. 2010. *One Less Car: Bicycling and the Politics of Automobility*. Sporting. Philadelphia: Temple University Press.

Ganti, Tejaswini. 2014. "Neoliberalism." *Annual Review of Anthropology* 43 (1): 89–104.

Gaubatz, Piper Rae. 1995. "Urban Transformation in Post-Mao China: Impacts of the Reform Era on China's Urban Form." In *Urban Spaces in Contemporary China: The Potential for Autonomy and Community in Post-Mao China*, edited by Deborah S. Davis, Richard Curt Kraus, Barry Naughton, and Elizabeth J. Perry, 28–60. Washington, DC; Cambridge: Woodrow Wilson Center Press; Cambridge University Press.

GEMAS. 2006. "Sui Shouchang Xiaoqiche Haopai Jingjiahui Chengjiao 883.2 Wan Yuan" (Total transactions of 8,832 million RMB in the first auction of license plate numbers). Guangzhou: Guangzhou Enterprises Merges and Acquisitions Services. http://www.gemas.com.cn/report/show.asp?go=cpjj&id=1033. Accessed July 22, 2007.

Gerth, Karl. 2010. *As China Goes, So Goes the World: How Chinese Consumers Are Transforming Everything*. New York: Hill and Wang.

Giddens, Anthony. 1973. *The Class Structure of the Advanced Societies*. London: Hutchinson.

Gilroy, Paul. 2001. "Driving While Black." In *Car Cultures*, edited by Daniel Miller, 81–104. Oxford: Berg.

Glosser, Susan L. 2003. *Chinese Visions of Family and State, 1915–1953*. Berkeley: University of California Press.

Goldman Sachs. 2003. "Global Automobile: The Chinese Auto Industry." In *Goldman Sachs Global Equity Research*, February 21, http://www2.goldmansachs.com/hkchina /insight/research/pdf/chinese_auto_industry.pdf. Accessed April 27, 2005.

Goldstein, Matthew. 2014a. "U.S. Targets Buyers of China-Bound Luxury Cars." *New York Times*, February 11, 2014. https://dealbook.nytimes.com/2014/02/11/u-s-targets -buyers-of-china-bound-luxury-cars/. Accessed January 23, 2017.

———. 2014b. "U.S. Ordered to Return Assets Held in Crackdown of Luxury Cars Exported to China." *New York Times*, April 3, 2014. https://dealbook.nytimes.com/2014 /04/03/u-s-ordered-to-return-assets-seized-in-crackdown-on-exported-cars/?_r=0. Accessed January 23, 2014.

Goode, William Josiah. 1963. *World Revolution and Family Patterns*. New York: Free Press of Glencoe.

Greenhalgh, Susan. 2008. *Just One Child: Science and Policy in Deng's China*. Berkeley: University of California Press.

Gudis, Catherine. 2010. "Driving Consumption." *History and Technology* 26 (4): 369–378.

Gupta, Akhil. 2012. *Red Tape: Bureaucracy, Structural Violence, and Poverty in India*. Durham, NC: Duke University Press.

Hacking, Ian. 2002. "Inaugural Lecture: Chair of Philosophy and History of Scientific Concepts at the Collège de France, 16 January 2001." *Economy and Society* 31 (1): 1–14.

Hanser, Amy. 2008. *Service Encounters: Class, Gender, and the Market for Social Distinction in Urban China*. Stanford, CA: Stanford University Press.

Hao, Zehua. 2004. "Kongque Weihe Dongnan Fei: Guangzhou Biaozhi Hezi Shibai Yuanyin Tanxi" (Why peacocks flied in opposite directions: the reasons for the failure of the Guangzhou-Peugeot joint-venture). *Qiye Wenhua* (3): 19–22.

Harrell, Stevan. 1977. "Modes of Belief in Chinese Folk Religion." *Journal for the Scientific Study of Religion* 16 (1): 55–65.

——. 1987. "The Concept of Fate in Chinese Folk Ideology." *Modern China* 13 (1): 90–109.

Hausen, Karin. 1981. "Family and Role-Division: The Polarisation of Sexual Stereotypes in the Nineteenth Century—an Aspect of the Dissociation of Work and Family Life." In *The German Family: Essays on the Social History of the Family in Nineteenth- and Twentieth-Century Germany*, edited by Richard J. Evans and W. Robert Lee, 51–83. London; Totowa, NJ: Croom Helm; Barnes & Noble.

Hayek, Friedrich A. von. 1980. *The Road to Serfdom*. Chicago: University of Chicago Press.

Hazelzet, Arjan, and Bart Wissink. 2012. "Neighborhoods, Social Networks, and Trust in Post-Reform China: The Case of Guangzhou." *Urban Geography* 33 (2): 204–220.

Heiman, Rachel. 2015. *Driving after Class: Anxious Times in an American Suburb*. Oakland: University of California Press.

Heiman, Rachel, Carla Freeman, and Mark Liechty, eds. 2012. *The Global Middle Classes: Theorizing through Ethnography*. Santa Fe, NM: SAR Press.

Hoffe, Jason, Kevin Lane, and Victoria Miller Nam. 2003. "Branding Cars in China." *McKinsey Quarterly* 4 (special edition): 14.

Hoffman, Lisa. 2010. *Patriotic Professionalism in Urban China: Fostering Talent*. Philadelphia: Temple University Press.

Hsing, You-tien. 2010. *The Great Urban Transformation: Politics of Land and Property in China*. Oxford: Oxford University Press.

Hsu, Carolyn L. 2007. *Creating Market Socialism: How Ordinary People Are Shaping Class and Status in China*. Durham, NC: Duke University Press.

Hu, Yang, and Jacqueline Scott. 2016. "Family and Gender Values in China: Generational, Geographic, and Gender Differences." *Journal of Family Issues* 37 (9): 1267–1293.

Huang, Philip C. 2011. "The Modern Chinese Family: In Light of Economic and Legal History." *Modern China* 37 (5): 459–497.

Huang, Yasheng. 2002. "Between Two Coordination Failures: Automotive Industrial Policy in China with a Comparison to Korea." *Review of International Political Economy* 9 (3): 538.

Hull, Isabel V. 1996. *Sexuality, State, and Civil Society in Germany, 1700–1815*. Ithaca, NY: Cornell University Press.

Humphrey, Caroline. 1998. *Marx Went Away—but Karl Stayed Behind*. Ann Arbor: University of Michigan Press.

Ikels, Charlotte. 1996. *The Return of the God of Wealth: The Transition to a Market Economy in Urban China*. Stanford, CA: Stanford University Press.

Jackson, Kenneth T. 1985. *Crabgrass Frontier: The Suburbanization of the United States*. New York: Oxford University Press.

Jain, Sarah S. Lochlann. 2002. "Urban Errands: The Means of Mobility." *Journal of Consumer Culture* 2 (3): 385–404.

———. 2004. "Dangerous Instrumentality: The Bystander as Subject in Automobility." *Cultural Anthropology* 19 (1): 61–94.Jankowiak, William R. 1993. *Sex, Death, and Hierarchy in a Chinese City: An Anthropological Account.* New York: Columbia University Press.

Joniak-Lüthi, Agnieszka. 2016. "Roads in China's Borderlands: Interfaces of Spatial Representations, Perceptions, Practices, and Knowledges." *Modern Asian Studies* 50 (1): 118–140.

Joyce, Patrick. 2003. *The Rule of Freedom: Liberalism and the Modern City.* London: Verso.

Kay, Jane Holtz. 1998. *Asphalt Nation: How the Automobile Took over America, and How We Can Take It Back.* Berkeley: University of California Press.

Kipnis, Andrew B. 2006. "Suzhi: A Keyword Approach." *China Quarterly* 186:295–313.

———. 2007. "Neoliberalism Reified: Suzhi Discourse and Tropes of Neoliberalism in the People's Republic of China." *Journal of the Royal Anthropological Institute* 13 (2): 383–400.

———. 2011. *Governing Educational Desire: Culture, Politics, and Schooling in China.* Chicago: University of Chicago Press.

———. 2016. *From Village to City: Social Transformation in a Chinese County Seat.* Oakland: University of California Press.

Klein, Jakob A. 2013. "Everyday Approaches to Food Safety in Kunming." *China Quarterly* 214:376–393.

Koshar, Rudy. 2004. "Cars and Nations: Anglo-German Perspectives on Automobility between the World Wars." *Theory Culture Society* 21 (4–5): 121–144.

Kraus, Richard Curt. 1989. *Pianos and Politics in China: Middle-Class Ambitions and the Struggle over Western Music.* New York: Oxford University Press.

Kuan, Teresa. 2015. *Love's Uncertainty: The Politics and Ethics of Child Rearing in Contemporary China.* Oakland: University of California Press.

Kuper, Adam. 2009. *Incest and Influence: The Private Life of Bourgeois England.* Cambridge, MA: Harvard University Press.

Lambek, Michael, ed. 2010. *Ordinary Ethics: Anthropology, Language, and Action.* New York: Fordham University Press.

Latour, Bruno. 1993. *We Have Never Been Modern.* Cambridge, MA: Harvard University Press.

Lee, Ching Kwan. 2007. *Against the Law: Labor Protests in China's Rustbelt and Sunbelt.* Berkeley: University of California Press.

Lee, Leo Ou-fan. 1999. *Shanghai Modern: The Flowering of a New Urban Culture in China, 1930–1945.* Cambridge, MA: Harvard University Press.

Lefebvre, Henri. 1991. *The Production of Space.* Oxford: Blackwell.

Lei, Bin. 1998. "Guangzhou Biaozhi Weihe Jieti" (Why Guangzhou-Peugeot dissolved). *Zhongguo Touzi yu Jianshe* 6:17–18.

Lentz, Carola. 2015. "Elites or Middle Classes? Lessons from Transnational Research for the Study of Social Stratification in Africa." Arbeitspapiere des Instituts für Ethnologie und Afrikastudien der Johannes Gutenberg-Universität Mainz / Working papers of the Department of Anthropology and African Studies of the Johannes Gutenberg University Mainz, number 161. http://www.ifeas.uni-mainz.de/Dateien /AP_161.pdf.

Li, Cheng, ed. 2010. *China's Emerging Middle Class: Beyond Economic Transformation.* Washington, DC: Brookings Institution Press.

Li, Chunling. 2005. *Duanlie yu Suipian: Dangdai Zhongguo Shehui Jieceng Fenhua Shizheng Fenxi* (Cleavage and fragment: an empirical analysis on the social stratification of the contemporary China). Beijing: Zhongguo Shehui Kexue Wenxian Chubanshe.

Li, Fangchun. 2012. "Mass Democracy, Class Struggle, and Remolding the Party and Government during the Land Reform Movement in North China." *Modern China* 38 (4): 411–445.

Li, Lin, and Jie Huang. 2004. "Biaozhi Shibai de Wenhua Qishi" (The cultural implication from Peugeot's failure). *Qiye Yanjiu* 10:15–16.

Li, Peilin. 2004. "Huashuo Shehui Fengceng" (On social stratification). In *Zhongguo Shehui Fenceng* (Social stratification in China), edited by Peilin Li, Qiang Li, Liping Sun, and Others, 1–15. Beijing: Shehui Kexue Wenxian Chubanshe.

Li, Peilin, Qiang Li, Liping Sun, and Others, eds. 2004. *Zhongguo Shehui Fenceng* (Social stratification in China). Beijing: Shehui Kexue Wenxian Chubanshe.

Li, Qiang. 2004. *Zhuanxing Shiqi: Zhongguo Shehui Fenceng* (An era of transformation: social stratification in China). Shenyang: Liaoning Jiaoyu Chubanshe.

Li, Si-ming, Yushu Zhu, and Limei Li. 2012. "Neighborhood Type, Gatedness, and Residential Experiences in Chinese Cities: A Study of Guangzhou." *Urban Geography* 33 (2): 237–255.

Li, Yongjun. 2003a. "Zhongguo Qiche Gongye 50 nian Huigu (yi)" (Fifty years of China's auto industry development [1]). *Shanghai Qiche* 5:40–43.

———. 2003b. "Zhongguo Qiche Gongye 50 nian Huigu (san)" (Fifty years of China's auto industry development [3]). *Shanghai Qiche* 7:40–44.

Li, Yu. 2008. "Hunyin de Jiaoyu Pipei: Wushi Nian lai de Bianqian" (Trends in educational assortative marriage: 1949–2000). *Zhongguo Renkou Kexue* 3:73–79.

Liechty, Mark. 2003. *Suitably Modern: Making Middle-Class Culture in a New Consumer Society.* Princeton, NJ: Princeton University Press.

Lin, Yi. 2011. "Turning Rurality into Modernity: Suzhi Education in a Suburban Public School of Migrant Children in Xiamen." *China Quarterly* 206:313–330.

Ling, Minhua. 2015. "'Bad Students Go to Vocational Schools!': Education, Social Reproduction and Migrant Youth in Urban China." *China Journal* 73:108–131, 308–309.

———. Forthcoming. *The Inconvenient Generation: Migrant Youth Coming of Age on Shanghai's Edge.* Stanford: Stanford University Press.

Lonce, Stefan J. 2009. "License to Roam: Vanity License Plates and the Stories They Tell." www.LCNS2ROM.com. Accessed March 4, 2010.

Low, Setha M., and Neil Smith. 2006. *The Politics of Public Space.* New York: Routledge.

Lu, Duanfang. 2006. *Remaking Chinese Urban Form: Modernity, Scarcity, and Space, 1949–2005.* London: Routledge.

Lu, Hanchao. 1999. *Beyond the Neon Lights: Everyday Shanghai in the Early Twentieth Century.* Berkeley: University of California Press.

Lu, Xueyi, ed. 2002. *Dangdai Zhongguo Shehui Jieceng Yanjiu Baogao* (A study on social strata in contemporary China). Beijing: Shehui Kexue Wenxian Chubanshe.

Lü, Minghe. 2009. "Ma 6 Dang de Haofang Qingchun" (Mazda 6 gang's bold youth). *Nanfang Zhoumo*, September 20.

Lü, Xiaobo, and Elizabeth J. Perry, eds. 1997. *Danwei: The Changing Chinese Workplace in Historical and Comparative Perspective*. Armonk, NY: M. E. Sharpe.

Lutz, Catherine. 2014. "The U.S. Car Colossus and the Production of Inequality." *American Ethnologist* 41 (2): 232–245.

Lutz, Catherine, and Lila Abu-Lughod, eds. 1990. *Language and the Politics of Emotion*. Cambridge: Cambridge University Press.

Lutz, Catherine, and Anne Lutz Fernandez. 2010. *Carjacked: The Culture of the Automobile and Its Effect on Our Lives*. New York: Palgrave Macmillan.

Ma, Chunhua, Jinqun Shi, Yinhe Li, Zhenyu Wang, and Can Tang. 2011. "Zhongguo Chengshi Jiating Bianqian de Qushi he Zuixin Faxian" (Family change in urban areas of China: main trends and latest findings). *Shehuixue Yanjiu* 2:182–246.

Mahmood, Saba. 2005. *Politics of Piety: The Islamic Revival and the Feminist Subject*. Princeton, NJ: Princeton University Press.

Mangan, J. A., ed. 2005. *A Sport-Loving Society: Victorian and Edwardian Middle Class England at Play*. New York: Routledge.

Mattingly, Cheryl. 2012. "Two Virtue Ethics and the Anthropology of Morality." *Anthropological Theory* 12 (2): 161–184.

McShane, Clay. 1994. *Down the Asphalt Path: The Automobile and the American City*. New York: Columbia University Press.

Miller, Daniel. 2001. *Car Cultures*. Oxford: Berg.

Mitchell, Timothy. ed. 2000. *Questions of Modernity*. Minneapolis: University of Minnesota Press.

Mol, Annemarie. 2008. *The Logic of Care: Health and the Problem of Patient Choice*. London: Routledge.

Naughton, Barry. 2007. *The Chinese Economy: Transitions and Growth*. Cambridge, MA: MIT Press.

Navaro-Yashin, Yael. 2002. *Faces of the State: Secularism and Public Life in Turkey*. Princeton, NJ: Princeton University Press.

Noble, Gregory W. 2006. *The Emergence of the Chinese and Indian Automobiles Industries and Implications for Other Developing Countries*. http://siteresources.worldbank.org /INTCHIINDGLOECO/Resources/Noble-Emergence_of_Ch_Ind_auto_ind— revMay2006.doc. Accessed January 20, 2017.

Norton, Peter D. 2008. *Fighting Traffic: The Dawn of the Motor Age in the American City*. Cambridge, MA: MIT Press.

Notar, Beth E. 2012. "'Coming Out' to 'Hit the Road': Temporal, Spatial and Affective Mobilities of Taxi Drivers and Day Trippers in Kunming, China." *City and Society* 24 (3): 281–301.

———. 2015. "From Flying Pigeons to Fords: China's New Car Culture." In *East Asia in the World: An Introduction*, edited by Anne Prescott, 122–139. New York: Routledge.

———. 2017. "'My Dad Is Li Gang!'; or, Seeing the State: Transgressive Mobility, Collective Visibility, and Playful Corruption in Contemporary Urban China." *Asian Anthropology* 16 (1): 35–53.

Oakes, Tim. forthcoming. "Leisure as Governable Space: Transcultural Leisure and Governmentality in Contemporary China." In *Testing the Margins of Leisure: Case*

Studies on East Asia, edited by R. Wagner, C. Yeh, E. Menegon, and Robert Weller. Heidelberg: Heidelberg University Press.

O'Brien, Kevin, and Lianjiang Li. 2006. *Rightful Resistance in Rural China*. Cambridge: Cambridge University Press.

O'Dougherty, Maureen. 2002. *Consumption Intensified: The Politics of Middle-class Daily Life in Brazil*. Durham, NC: Duke University Press.

Oi, Jean C. 1992. "Fiscal Reform and the Economic Foundations of Local State Corporatism in China." *World Politics* 45 (1): 99–126.

Ong, Aihwa. 2006. *Neoliberalism as Exception: Mutations in Citizenship and Sovereignty*. Durham, NC: Duke University Press.

Ong, Aihwa, and Stephen J. Collier, eds. 2005. *Global Assemblages: Technology, Politics, and Ethics as Anthropological Problems*. Malden, MA: Blackwell Publishing.

Ortner, Sherry B. 1995. "Resistance and the Problem of Ethnographic Refusal." *Comparative Studies in Society and History* 37 (1): 173–193.

——. 2003. *New Jersey Dreaming: Capital, Culture, and the Class of '58*. Durham, NC: Duke University Press.

——. 2006. *Anthropology and Social Theory: Culture, Power, and the Acting Subject*. Durham, NC: Duke University Press.

Osburg, John. 2013. *Anxious Wealth: Money and Morality among China's New Rich*. Stanford, CA: Stanford University Press.

Otis, Eileen M. 2012. *Markets and Bodies: Women, Service Work, and the Making of Inequality in China*. Stanford, CA: Stanford University Press.

Owensby, Brian Philip. 1999. *Intimate Ironies: Modernity and the Making of Middle-Class Lives in Brazil*. Stanford, CA: Stanford University Press.

Packer, Jeremy. 2008. *Mobility without Mayhem: Safety, Cars, and Citizenship*. Durham, NC: Duke University Press.

Polanyi, Karl. 2001. *The Treat Transformation: The Political and Economic Origins of Our Time*. Boston: Beacon Press (first published in 1944).

Pow, Choon-Piew. 2009. *Gated Communities in China: Class, Privilege and the Moral Politics of the Good Life*. London: Routledge.

Pun, Ngai. 2005. *Made in China: Women Factory Workers in A Global Workplace*. Durham; Hong Kong: Duke University Press; Hong Kong University Press.

Ren, Hai. 2013. *The Middle Class in Neoliberal China: Governing Risk, Life-Building, and Themed Spaces*. London: Routledge.

Rofel, Lisa. 1999. *Other Modernities: Gendered Yearnings in China after Socialism*. Berkeley: University of California Press.

Rolandsen, Unn Målfrid H. 2011. *Leisure and Power in Urban China: Everyday Life in a Medium-Size Chinese City*. London: Routledge.

Rose, Nikolas. 1999. *Powers of Freedom: Reframing Political Thought*. Cambridge: Cambridge University Press.

Rowe, Michael. 1999. *Crossing the Border: Encounters between Homeless People and Outreach Workers*. Berkeley: University of California Press.

Santos, Gonçalo D. 2016. "On Intimate Choices and Troubles in Rural South China." *Modern Asian Studies* 50 (4): 1298–1326.

——. Forthcoming. Intimate Modernities: Reassembling Love, Marriage and Family Life in Rural South China, 1970s–2010s. Seattle: University of Washington Press.

Santos, Gonçalo D., and Stevan Harrell, eds. 2017. *Transforming Patriarchy: Chinese Families in the Twenty-First Century.* Seattle: University of Washington Press.

Sato, Ikuya. 1991. *Kamikaze Biker: Parody and Anomy in Affluent Japan.* Chicago: University of Chicago Press.

Seiler, Cotten. 2008. *Republic of Drivers: A Cultural History of Automobility in America.* Chicago: University of Chicago Press.

Shambaugh, David L. 2000. *The Modern Chinese State.* New York: Cambridge University Press.

Sheller, Mimi. 2004. "Automotive Emotions: Feeling the Car." *Theory Culture Society* 21 (4–5): 221–242.

Sheller, Mimi, and John Urry. 2000. "The City and the Car." *International Journal of Urban and Regional Research* 24 (4): 737–757.

Sherman, Rachel. 2007. *Class Acts: Service and Inequality in Luxury Hotels.* Berkeley: University of California Press

Shove, Elizabeth. 2012. "Comfort and Convenience: Temporality and Practice." In *The Oxford Handbook of the History of Consumption,* edited by Frank Trentmann, 289–306. Oxford Handbooks Online: Oxford University Press.

Siegelbaum, Lewis. 2008. *Cars for Comrades: The Life of the Soviet Automobile.* Ithaca, NY: Cornell University Press.

——. ed. 2011. *The Socialist Car: Automobility in the Eastern Bloc.* Ithaca, NY: Cornell University Press.

Simmel, Georg. 2004. *The Philosophy of Money.* London: Routledge.

Siu, Helen F. 1989. "Socialist Peddlers and Princes in a Chinese Market Town." *American Ethnologist* 16 (2): 195–212.

——. 2007. "Grounding Displacement: Uncivil Urban Spaces in Postreform South China." *American Ethnologist* 34 (2): 329–350.

Smart, Josephine, and Alan Smart. 1999. "Personal Relations and Divergent Economies: A Case Study of Hong Kong Investment in South China." In *Theorizing the City: The New Urban Anthropology Reader,* edited by Setha M. Low, 169–200. New Brunswick, NJ: Rutgers University Press.

Solinger, Dorothy J. 1999. *Contesting Citizenship in Urban China: Peasant Migrants, the State, and the Logic of the Market.* Berkeley: University of California Press.

Stafford, Charles. 2009. "Numbers and the Natural History of Imagining the Self in Taiwan and China." *Ethnos* 74 (1): 110–26.

——. 2010. "Some Qualitative Mathematics in China." *Anthropological Theory* 10 (1–2): 81–86.

Steinhardt, Nancy Shatzman. 1998. "Mapping the Chinese City: The Image and the Reality." In *Envisioning the City: Six Studies in Urban Cartography,* edited by David Buisseret, 1–33. Chicago: University of Chicago Press.

Sun, Liping. 2004. *Zhuanxing yu Duanlie: Gaige Yilai Zhongguo Shehui Jiegou de Bianqian* (Transformation and rupture: the transformation of the social structure in China since the reforms). Beijing: Qianghua Daxue Chubanshe.

Sun, Yuchun, Lin Jin, and Dongshui Su. 2000. "Jiaru WTO dui zhongguo qiche chanye de yingxiang" (Influcence of China's entrance into the WTO on its automobile industry). *Fudan Xuebao (shehui kexue ban)* 2:1.

Swider, Sarah. 2015. "Reshaping China's Urban Citizenship: Street Vendors, Chengguan and Struggles over the Right to the City." *Critical Sociology* 41 (4–5): 701–716.

Thornton, Arland. 2001. "The Developmental Paradigm, Reading History Sideways, and Family Change." *Demography* 38 (4): 449–465.

Thun, Eric. 2006. *Changing Lanes in China: Foreign Direct Investment, Local Government, and Auto Sector Development*. Cambridge: Cambridge University Press.

Tomba, Luigi. 2004. "Creating an Urban Middle Class: Social Engineering in Beijing." *China Journal* 51:1–26.

——. 2005. "Residential Space and Collective Interest Formation in Beijing's Housing Disputes." *China Quarterly* 184:934–951.

——. 2009. "Of Quality, Harmony, and Community: Civilization and the Middle Class in Urban China." *Positions* 17 (3): 591–616.

——. 2014. *The Government Next Door: Neighborhood Politics in Urban China*. Ithaca, NY: Cornell University Press.

Townsend, James R. 1967. *Political Participation in Communist China*. Berkeley: University of California Press.

Tsang, Eileen Yuk-Ha. 2014. *The New Middle Class in China: Consumption, Politics and the Market Economy*. Basingstoke, UK: Palgrave Macmillan.

Urry, John. 2004. "The 'System' of Automobility." *Theory Culture Society* 21 (4–5): 25–39.

——. 2007. *Mobilities*. Cambridge: Polity.

Verdery, Katherine. 1991. *National Ideology under Socialism: Identity and Cultural Politics in Ceausescu's Romania*. Berkeley: University of California Press.

——. 1996. *What Was Socialism, and What Comes Next?* Princeton, NJ: Princeton University Press.

——. 2003. *The Vanishing Hectare: Property and Value in Postsocialist Transylvania*. Ithaca, NY: Cornell University Press.

Vogel, Ezra F. 1989. *One Step ahead in China: Guangdong under Reform*. Cambridge, MA: Harvard University Press.

Walder, Andrew G. 1986. *Communist Neo-traditionalism: Work and Authority in Chinese Industry*. Berkeley: University of California Press.

Walder, Andrew G, and Songhua Hu. 2009. "Revolution, Reform, and Status Inheritance: Urban China, 1949–1996." *American Journal of Sociology* 114 (5): 1395–1427.

Wang, Donggen, Fei Li, and Yanwei Chai. 2012. "Activity Spaces and Sociospatial Segregation in Beijing." *Urban Geography* 33 (2): 256–277.

Wang, Jianfeng. 2005. "The Politics of Neighborhood Governance: Understanding China's State-Society Relations through an Examination of the Residents Committee." PhD diss., West Michigan University.

Wang, Jing. 2001. "The State Question in Chinese Popular Cultural Studies." *Inter-Asia Cultural Studies* 2 (1): 35–52.

Wang, Lei. 2002. "Chepai, Ziyou yu Gexinghua" (Auto license plates, freedom and individualization). *Renmin Fayuan Bao*, September 2. http://www.people.com.cn/GB /guandian/29/173/20020902/813254.html. Accessed January 21, 2017.

Wang, Li. 2002. "'Gexinghua' Chepai Jinji Jiaoting" (Individualized auto license plates suddenly came to an end). *Guoji Jinrongbao*, August 23.

Wang, Ning. 2007. "Xiaofei Zhidu, Laodong Ziyuan yu Hefaxing Ziyuan: Weirao Chengzhen Zhigong Xiaofei Shenghuo yu Laodong Dongji de Zhidu Anpai ji Zhuanxing Luoji" (Consumption institutions, incentives to labor, and legitimacy resources: the change of institutional arrangements regarding consumer lives and laborer motivations in urban China). *Shehuixue Yanjiu* 3:74–98.

Wang, Shaoguang. 1995. "The Politics of Private Time: Changing Leisure Patterns in Urban China." In *Urban Spaces in Contemporary China: The Potential for Autonomy and Community in Post-Mao China*, edited by Deborah S. Davis, Richard Curt Kraus, Barry Naughton, and Elizabeth J. Perry, 149–172. Washington, DC; Cambridge: Woodrow Wilson Center Press; Cambridge University Press.

Wang, Wei. 1998. "Peiyu Qiyejia de Xintai: Cong 'Guangzhou Biaozhi' Jieti Tanqi" (Fostering entrepreneurship: on the dissolution of Guangzhou-Peugeot). *Zhongguo Waizi* 7:24–25.

Wang, Xiying, and Daniel Nehring. 2014. "Individualization as an Ambition: Mapping the Dating Landscape in Beijing." *Modern China* 40 (6): 578–604.

Wang, Xuegong. 2005. "Cong Guangzhou Biaozhi Dao Guangzhou Bentian: Lun Hezi Qiye zhong de Kua Wenhua Guangli" (From Guangzhou-Peugeot to Guangzhou-Honda: cross-cultural management in joint ventures). *Shangchang Xiandaihua* 452 (12): 270–271.

Wang, Yuesheng. 2006. "Dangdai Zhongguo Jiating Jiegou Biandong Fenxi" (The changing family structure in contemporary China: an analysis). *Zhongguo Shehui Kexue* 1:96–108.

Warner, Sam Bass. 1978. *Streetcar Suburbs: The Process of Growth in Boston, 1870–1900*. Cambridge, MA: Harvard University Press.

Weller, Robert P. 2014. "The Politics of Increasing Religious Diversity in China." *Daedalus* 143 (2): 135.

Whyte, Martin King, ed. 2003. *China's Revolutions and Intergenerational Relations*. Ann Arbor: Center for Chinese Studies, University of Michigan.

——. 2005. "Continuity and Change in Urban Chinese Family Life." *China Journal* 53:9–33.

——. 2010. "The Paradoxes of Rural-urban Inequality in Contemporary China." In *One Country, Two Societies: Rural-Urban Inequality in Contemporary China*, edited by Martin King Whyte, 1–25. Cambridge, MA: Harvard University Press.

Whyte, Martin King, and William L. Parish. 1984. *Urban Life in Contemporary China*. Chicago: University of Chicago Press.

Winner, Langdon. 1986. "Do Artifacts Have Politics." In *The Whale and the Reactor: A Search for Limits in an Age of High Technology*, 19–39. Chicago: University of Chicago Press.

Wollen, Peter, and Joe Kerr, eds. 2002. *Autopia: Cars and Culture*. London: Reaktion.

Woronov, Terry E. 2016. *Class Work: Vocational Schools and China's Urban Youth*. Stanford, CA: Stanford University Press.

Wu, Kangping, and Chunlu Fei. 2002. *WTO Kuangjia xia Zhonguo Qiche Jingji de Zengzhangji* (The development of China's auto industry under the WTO framework). Beijing: Jingji Kexue Chubanshe.

Wu, Yiching. 2014. *The Cultural Revolution at the Margins: Chinese Socialism in Crisis*. Cambridge, MA: Harvard University Press.

Xie, Wei, and Yanwu Xu. 1998. "Guanshui zhengce yu Zhongguo jiaoche gongye de fazhan" (Tariff policies and the development of China's automobile industry). *Jiaoche gongye* (Automobile industry) 5:21.

Xu, Zhong. 2007. "Lunzi Shang de Jueqi: Zhongguo Jiaoche 50 Nian" (Rising on the wheels: fifty years of China's auto industry). *Nanfang Zhoumo*, November 27.

Yan, Hairong. 2003. "Neoliberal Governmentality and Neohumanism: Organizing Suzhi Value Flow through Labor Recruitment Networks." *Cultural Anthropology* 18 (4): 493–523.

———. 2008. *New Masters, New Servants: Migration, Development, and Women Workers in China*. Durham, NC: Duke University Press.

Yan, Yunxiang. 2003. *Private Life under Socialism: Love, Intimacy, and Family Change in a Chinese Village, 1949–1999*. Stanford, CA: Stanford University Press.

———. 2009. *The Individualization of Chinese Society*. Oxford: Berg.

———. 2011. "The Changing Moral Landscape." In *Deep China: The Moral Life of the Person; What Anthropology and Psychiatry Tell Us about China Today*, edited by Arthur Kleinman, Yunxiang Yan, Jun Jing, Sing Lee, Everett Zhang, Tianshu Pan, Fei Wu, and Jinhua Guo, 36–77. Berkeley: University of California Press.

———. 2013. "The Drive for Success and the Ethics of the Striving Individual." In *Ordinary Ethics in China*, edited by Charles Stafford, 263–291. London: Berg.

Yang, Xiaohua. 1995. *Globalization of the Automobile Industry: The United States, Japan, and the People's Republic of China*. Westport, CT: Praeger.

Yao, Binhua, and Jianqing Han. 2008. *Jianzheng Guangzhou Qiche Shinian* (Witnessing a decade's Guangzhou auto industry). Guangzhou: Guangdong Renmin Chubanshe.

Yip, Ngai Ming. 2012. "Walled Without Gates: Gated Communities in Shanghai." *Urban Geography* 33 (2): 221–236.

Yu, LiAnne. 2014. *Consumption in China: How China's New Consumer Ideology Is Shaping the Nation*. Cambridge: Polity Press.

Yurchak, Alexei. 2006. *Everything Was Forever, Until It Was No More: The Last Soviet Generation*. Princeton, NJ: Princeton University Press.

Zhang, Boshun. 1998. "Jiaru WTO he qiche guanshui" (Joining the WTO and auto tariffs). *Qiche yu peijian* (18), n.p.

Zhang, Jizhou. 1994. "Jinkou qiche fengyun lu" (A survey of imported cars). *Shanghai qiche* 3:60–61.

Zhang, Jun. 2015. "The Rise and Fall of Qilou: Metamorphosis of Forms and Meanings in the Built Environment of Guangzhou." *Traditional Dwellings and Settlements Review* 26 (2): 25–40.

———. 2016. "Taxis, Traffic, and Thoroughfares: The Politics of Transportation Infrastructure in China's Rapid Urbanization in the Reform Era." *City and Society* 28 (3): 411–436.

———. 2017. "Materializing a Form of Urban Governance: When Street Building Intersected with City Building in Republican Canton (Guangzhou), China." *History and Technology* 33 (2): 153–174.

Zhang, Jun, and Peidong Sun. 2014. "'When Are You Going to Get Married?' Parental Matchmaking and Middle-Class Women in Contemporary Urban China." In *Wives, Husbands, and Lovers: Marriage and Sexuality in Hong Kong, Taiwan, and Urban China*, edited by Deborah Davis and Sara Friedman, 118–144. Stanford, CA: Stanford University Press.

Zhang, Li. 2010. *In Search of Paradise: Middle-Class Living in a Chinese Metropolis*. Ithaca, NY: Cornell University Press.

Zhang, Li, and Aihwa Ong, eds. 2008. *Privatizing China: Socialism from Afar*. Ithaca, NY: Cornell University Press.

Zhang, Weiguo. 2009. "'A Married Out Daughter Is Like Spilt Water'?: Women's Increasing Contacts and Enhanced Ties with Their Natal Families in Post-Reform Rural North China." *Modern China* 35 (3): 256–283.

Zheng, Yefu, ed. 1996. *Jiaoche Da Lunzhan* (Auto debates). Beijing: Jingji Kexue Chubanshe.

Zhou, Xiaohong, ed. 2005. *Zhongguo zhongchan jieceng diaocha* (Survey of the Chinese middle class). Beijing: Shehui kexue wenxian chubanshe.

Zunz, Olivier, Leonard J. Schoppa, and Nobuhiro Hiwatari, eds. 2002. *Social Contracts under Stress: The Middle Classes of America, Europe, and Japan at the Turn of the Century*. New York: Russell Sage Foundation.

Index